THREE BY OSBORNE!

LOOK BACK IN ANGER: "Savage drama . . .
Most vivid play of the decade!"
—**The New York Times**

THE ENTERTAINER: "A brilliant and bitter
play, bawdy . . . shocking!"
—**Los Angeles Mirror-News**

EPITAPH FOR GEORGE DILLON: "This may
well be Osborne's best play!"
—**New York Post**

THREE PLAYS
BY
JOHN OSBORNE

Look Back in Anger

The Entertainer

Epitaph for George Dillon

BANTAM BOOKS · TORONTO · NEW YORK · LONDON

RLI: VLM 4 (VLR 3–7)
IL 9+

THREE PLAYS BY JOHN OSBORNE
*A Bantam Book / published by arrangement with
S. G. Phillips, Inc.*
Bantam edition / July 1977

PRINTED IN THE UNITED STATES OF AMERICA

Contents

LOOK BACK
IN
ANGER

for
my father

CAST

In Order of Appearance

JIMMY PORTER

CLIFF LEWIS

ALISON PORTER

HELENA CHARLES

COLONEL REDFERN

CONTENTS

The action throughout takes place in the
Porters' one-room flat in the Midlands.

TIME: The present.

ACT I

Early Evening. April

ACT II

ACT III

The first performance in Great Britain of LOOK BACK IN ANGER was given at the Royal Court Theatre, Sloane Square, London, on 8th May, 1956, by the English Stage Company. It was directed by Tony Richardson, and the décor was by Alan Tagg. The cast was as follows:

JIMMY PORTER	Kenneth Haigh
CLIFF LEWIS	Alan Bates
ALISON PORTER	Mary Ure
HELENA CHARLES	Helena Hughes
COLONEL REDFERN	John Welsh

ACT I

The Porters' one-room flat in a large Midland town. Early evening. April.

The scene is a fairly large attic room, at the top of a large Victorian house. The ceiling slopes down quite sharply from L. to R. Down R. are two small low windows. In front of these is a dark oak dressing table. Most of the furniture is simple, and rather old. Up R. is a double bed, running the length of most of the back wall, the rest of which is taken up with a shelf of books. Down R. below the bed is a heavy chest of drawers, covered with books, neckties and odds and ends, including a large, tattered toy teddy bear and soft, woolly squirrel. Up L. is a door. Below this a small wardrobe. Most of the wall L. is taken up with a high, oblong window. This looks out onto the landing, but light comes through it from a skylight beyond. Below the wardrobe is a gas stove, and, beside this, a wooden food cupboard, on which is a small, portable radio. Down C. is a sturdy dining table and three chairs, and, below this, L. and R., two deep, shabby leather armchairs.

At rise of curtain, JIMMY and CLIFF are seated in the two armchairs R. and L., respectively. All that we can see of either of them is two pairs of legs, sprawled way out beyond the newspapers which hide the rest of them from sight. They are both reading. Beside them, and between them, is a jungle of newspapers and weeklies. When we do eventually see them, we find that JIMMY is a tall, thin young man about twenty-five, wearing a very worn tweed jacket and flannels. Clouds of smoke fill the room from the

7

pipe he is smoking. He is a disconcerting mixture of sincerity and cheerful malice, of tenderness and free-booting cruelty; restless, importunate, full of pride, a combination which alienates the sensitive and insensitive alike. Blistering honesty, or apparent honesty, like his, makes few friends. To many he may seem sensitive to the point of vulgarity. To others, he is simply a loudmouth. To be as vehement as he is is to be almost non-committal. CLIFF is the same age, short, dark, big boned, wearing a pullover and grey, new, but very creased trousers. He is easy and relaxed, almost to lethargy, with the rather sad, natural intelligence of the self-taught. If JIMMY alienates love, CLIFF seems to exact it—demonstrations of it, at least, even from the cautious. He is a soothing, natural counterpoint to JIMMY.

Standing L., below the food cupboard, is ALISON. She is leaning over an ironing board. Beside her is a pile of clothes. Hers is the most elusive personality to catch in the uneasy polyphony of these three people. She is turned in a different key, a key of well-bred malaise that is often drowned in the robust orchestration of the other two. Hanging over the grubby, but expensive, skirt she is wearing is a cherry red shirt of JIMMY's, but she manages somehow to look quite elegant in it. She is roughly the same age as the men. Somehow, their combined physical oddity makes her beauty more striking than it really is. She is tall, slim, dark. The bones of her face are long and delicate. There is a surprising reservation about her eyes, which are so large and deep they should make equivocation impossible. The room is still, smoke filled. The only sound is the occasional thud of ALISON's iron on the board. It is one of those chilly Spring evenings, all cloud and shadows.

Presently, JIMMY throws his paper down.

JIMMY: Why do I do this every Sunday? Even the book reviews seem to be the same as last week's.

Different books—same reviews. Have you finished that one yet?

CLIFF: Not yet.

JIMMY: I've just read three whole columns on the English Novel. Half of it's in French. Do the Sunday papers make *you* feel ignorant?

CLIFF: Not 'arf.

JIMMY: Well, you *are* ignorant. You're just a peasant. (*To Alison.*) What about you? You're not a peasant are you?

ALISON: (*absently*). What's that?

JIMMY: I said do the papers make you feel you're not so brilliant after all?

ALISON: Oh—I haven't read them yet.

JIMMY: I didn't ask you that. I said——

CLIFF: Leave the poor girlie alone. She's busy.

JIMMY: Well, she can talk, can't she? You can talk, can't you? You can express an opinion. Or does the White Woman's Burden make it impossible to think?

ALISON: I'm sorry. I wasn't listening properly.

JIMMY: You bet you weren't listening. Old Porter talks, and everyone turns over and goes to sleep. And Mrs. Porter gets 'em all going with the first yawn.

CLIFF: Leave her alone, I said.

JIMMY: (*shouting*). All right, dear. Go back to sleep. It was only me talking. You know? Talking? Remember? I'm sorry.

CLIFF: Stop yelling. I'm trying to read.

JIMMY: Why do you bother? You can't understand a word of it.

CLIFF: Uh huh.

JIMMY: You're too ignorant.

CLIFF: Yes, and uneducated. Now shut up, will you?

JIMMY: Why don't you get my wife to explain it to you? She's educated. (*To her.*) That's right, isn't it?

CLIFF: (*kicking out at him from behind his paper*). Leave her alone, I said.

JIMMY: Do that again, you Welsh ruffian, and I'll pull your ears off.

He bangs Cliff's paper out of his hands.

CLIFF: (*leaning forward*). Listen—I'm trying to better myself. Let me get on with it, you big, horrible man. Give it me. (*Puts his hand out for paper.*)

ALISON: Oh, give it to him, Jimmy, for heaven's sake! I can't think!

CLIFF: Yes, come on, give me the paper. She can't think.

JIMMY: Can't think! (*Throws the paper back at him.*) She hasn't had a thought for years! Have you?

ALISON: No.

JIMMY: (*Picks up a weekly.*) I'm getting hungry.

ALISON: Oh no, not already!

CLIFF: He's a bloody pig.

JIMMY: I'm not a pig. I just like food—that's all.

CLIFF: Like it! You're like a sexual maniac—only with you it's food. You'll end up in the *News of the World,* boyo, you wait. James Porter, aged twenty-five, was bound over last week after pleading guilty to interfering with a small cabbage and two tins of beans on his way home from the Builder's Arms. The accused said he hadn't been feeling well for some time, and had been having black-outs. He asked for his good record as an air-raid warden, second class, to be taken into account.

JIMMY: (*Grins.*) Oh, yes, yes, yes. I like to eat. I'd like to live too. Do you mind?

CLIFF: Don't see any use in your eating at all. You never get any fatter.

JIMMY: People like me don't get fat. I've tried to tell you before. We just burn everything up. Now shut up while I read. You can make me some more tea.

CLIFF: Good God, you've just had a great potful! I only had one cup.

JIMMY: Like hell! Make some more.

CLIFF: (*to Alison*). Isn't that right? Didn't I only have one cup?

ALISON: (*without looking up*). That's right.

CLIFF: There you are. And she only had one cup too. I saw her. You guzzled the lot.

JIMMY: (*reading his weekly*). Put the kettle on.

CLIFF: Put it on yourself. You've creased up my paper.

JIMMY: I'm the only one who knows how to treat a paper, or anything else, in this house. (*Picks up another paper.*) Girl here wants to know whether her boy friend will lose all respect for her if she gives him what he asks for. Stupid bitch.

CLIFF: Just let me get at her, that's all.

JIMMY: Who buys this damned thing? (*Throws it down.*) Haven't you read the other posh paper yet?

CLIFF: Which?

JIMMY: Well, there are only two posh papers on a Sunday—the one you're reading, and this one. Come on, let me have that one, and you take this.

CLIFF: Oh, all right.

They exchange.

I was only reading the Bishop of Bromley. (*Puts out his hand to Alison.*) How are you, dullin'?

ALISON: All right thank you, dear.

CLIFF: (*grasping her hand*). Why don't you leave all that, and sit down for a bit? You look tired.

ALISON: (*smiling*). I haven't much more to do.

CLIFF: (*kisses her hand, and puts her fingers in his mouth*). She's a beautiful girl, isn't she?

JIMMY: That's what they all tell me.

His eyes meet hers.

CLIFF: It's a lovely, delicious paw you've got. Ummmmm. I'm going to bite it off.

ALISON: Don't! I'll burn his shirt.

JIMMY: Give her her finger back, and don't be so sickening. What's the Bishop of Bromley say?

CLIFF: (*letting go of Alison*). Oh, it says here that he makes a very moving appeal to all Christians to do all they can to assist in the manufacture of the H-Bomb.

JIMMY: Yes, well, that's quite moving, I suppose. (*To Alison.*) Are you moved, my darling?

ALISON: Well, naturally.

JIMMY: There you are: even my wife is moved. I ought to send the Bishop a subscription. Let's see. What else does he say. Dumdidumdidumdidum. Ah yes. He's upset because someone has suggested that he supports the rich against the poor. He says he denies the difference of class distinctions. "This idea has been persistently and wickedly fostered by—the working classes!" Well!

He looks up at both of them for reaction, but Cliff is reading, and Alison is intent on her ironing.

JIMMY: (*to Cliff*). Did you read that bit?

CLIFF: Um?

He has lost them, and he knows it, but he won't leave it.

JIMMY: (*to Alison*). You don't suppose your father could have written it, do you?

ALISON: Written what?

JIMMY: What I just read out, of course.

ALISON: Why should my father have written it?

JIMMY: Sounds rather like Daddy, don't you think?

ALISON: Does it?

JIMMY: Is the Bishop of Bromley his nom de plume, do you think?

CLIFF: Don't take any notice of him. He's being offensive. And it's so easy for him.

JIMMY: (*quickly*). Did you read about the woman who went to the mass meeting of a certain American evangelist at Earls Court? She went forward, to declare herself for love or whatever it is, and, in the rush of converts to get to the front, she broke four ribs and got kicked in the head. She was yelling her head off in agony, but with 50,000 people putting all they'd got into "Onward Christian Soldiers," nobody even knew she was there.

He looks up sharply for a response, but there isn't any.

Sometimes, I wonder if there isn't something wrong
with me. What about that tea?

CLIFF: (*still behind paper*). What tea?

JIMMY: Put the kettle on.

Alison looks up at him.

ALISON: Do you want some more tea?

JIMMY: I don't know. No, I don't think so.

ALISON: Do you want some, Cliff?

JIMMY: No, he doesn't. How much longer will you be
doing that?

ALISON: Won't be long.

JIMMY: God, how I hate Sundays! It's always so depressing, always the same. We never seem to get any
further, do we? Always the same ritual. Reading the
papers, drinking tea, ironing. A few more hours,
and another week gone. Our youth is slipping away.
Do you know that?

CLIFF: (*throws down paper*). What's that?

JIMMY: (*casually*). Oh, nothing, nothing. Damn you,
damn both of you, damn them all.

CLIFF: Let's go to the pictures. (*To Alison.*) What do
you say, lovely?

ALISON: I don't think I'll be able to. Perhaps Jimmy
would like to go. (*To Jimmy.*) Would you like to?

JIMMY: And have my enjoyment ruined by the Sunday
night yobs in the front row? No, thank you. (*Pause.*)
Did you read Priestley's piece this week? Why on
earth I ask, I don't know. I know damned well you
haven't. Why do I spend ninepence on that damned
paper every week? Nobody reads it except me. Nobody can be bothered. No one can raise themselves
out of their delicious sloth. You two will drive me
round the bend soon—I know it, as sure as I'm
sitting here. I know you're going to drive me mad.
Oh heavens, how I long for a little ordinary human
enthusiasm. Just enthusiasm—that's all. I want to
hear a warm, thrilling voice cry out Hallelujah! (*He
bangs his breast theatrically.*) Hallelujah! I'm alive!
I've an idea. Why don't we have a little game? Let's

pretend that we're human beings, and that we're
actually alive. Just for a while. What do you say?
Let's pretend we're human. (*He looks from one to
the other.*) Oh, brother, it's such a long time since I
was with anyone who got enthusiastic about anything.

CLIFF: What did he say?

JIMMY: (*resentful of being dragged away from his
pursuit of Alison*). What did who say?

CLIFF: Mr. Priestley.

JIMMY: What he always says, I suppose. He's like
Daddy—still casting well-fed glances back to the
Edwardian twilight from his comfortable, disenfran-
chised wilderness. What the devil have you done to
those trousers?

CLIFF: Done?

JIMMY: Are they the ones you bought last week-end?
Look at them. Do you see what he's done to those
new trousers?

ALISON: You are naughty, Cliff. They look dreadful.

JIMMY: You spend good money on a new pair of
trousers, and then sprawl about in them like a savage. What do you think you're going to do when
I'm not around to look after you? Well, what are
you going to do? Tell me?

CLIFF: (*grinning*). I don't know. (*To Alison.*) What
am I going to do, lovely?

ALISON: You'd better take them off.

JIMMY: Yes, go on. Take 'em off. And I'll kick your
behind for you.

ALISON: I'll give them a press while I've got the iron
on.

CLIFF: O.K. (*Starts taking them off.*) I'll just empty
the pockets. (*Takes out keys, matches, handker-
chief.*)

JIMMY: Give me those matches, will you?

CLIFF: Oh, you're not going to start up that old pipe
again, are you? It stinks the place out. (*To Alison.*)

Doesn't it smell awful?

Jimmy grabs the matches, and lights up.

ALISON: I don't mind it. I've got used to it.

JIMMY: She's a great one for getting used to things. If she were to die, and wake up in paradise—after the first five minutes, she'd have got used to it.

CLIFF: (*hands her the trousers*). Thank you, lovely. Give me a cigarette, will you?

JIMMY: Don't give him one.

CLIFF: I can't stand the stink of that old pipe any longer. I must have a cigarette.

JIMMY: I thought the doctor said no cigarettes?

CLIFF: Oh, why doesn't he shut up?

JIMMY: All right. They're your ulcers. Go ahead, and have a bellyache, if that's what you want. I give up. I give up. I'm sick of doing things for people. And all for what?

Alison gives Cliff a cigarette. They both light up, and she goes on with her ironing.

Nobody thinks, nobody cares. No beliefs, no convictions and no enthusiasm. Just another Sunday evening.

Cliff sits down again, in his pullover and shorts.

Perhaps there's a concert on. (*Picks up* Radio Times) Ah. (*Nudges Cliff with his foot.*) Make some more tea.

Cliff grunts. He is reading again.

Oh, yes. There's a Vaughan Williams. Well, that's something, anyway. Something strong, something simple, something English. I suppose people like me aren't supposed to be very patriotic. Somebody said —what was it—we get our cooking from Paris (that's a laugh), our politics from Moscow, and our morals from Port Said. Something like that, anyway. Who was it? (*Pause.*) Well, you wouldn't know anyway. I hate to admit it, but I think I can understand how her Daddy must have felt when he came back from India, after all those years away. The old

Edwardian brigade do make their brief little world look pretty tempting. All homemade cakes and croquet, bright ideas, bright uniforms. Always the same picture: high summer, the long days in the sun, slim volumes of verse, crisp linen, the smell of starch. What a romantic picture. Phoney too, of course. It must have rained sometimes. Still, even I regret it somehow, phoney or not. If you've no world of your own, it's rather pleasant to regret the passing of someone else's. I must be getting sentimental. But I must say it's pretty dreary living in the American Age—unless you're an American of course. Perhaps all our children will be Americans. That's a thought isn't it?

He gives Cliff a kick, and shouts at him.

I said that's a thought!

CLIFF: You did?

JIMMY: You sit there like a lump of dough. I thought you were going to make me some tea.

Cliff groans. Jimmy turns to Alison.

Is your friend Webster coming tonight?

ALISON: He might drop in. You know what he is.

JIMMY: Well, I hope he doesn't. I don't think I could take Webster tonight.

ALISON: I thought you said he was the only person who spoke your language.

JIMMY: So he is. Different dialect but same language. I like him. He's got bite, edge, drive——

ALISON: Enthusiasm.

JIMMY: You've got it. When he comes here, I begin to feel exhilarated. He doesn't like me, but he gives me something, which is more than I get from most people. Not since——

ALISON: Yes, we know. Not since you were living with Madeline.

She folds some of the clothes she has already ironed, crosses to the bed with them.

CLIFF: (*behind paper again*). Who's Madeline?

ALISON: Oh, wake up, dear. You've heard about

Madeline enough times. She was his mistress. Remember? When he was fourteen. Or was it thirteen?

JIMMY: Eighteen.

ALISON: He owes just about everything to Madeline.

CLIFF: I get mixed up with all your women. Was she the one all those years older than you?

JIMMY: Ten years.

CLIFF: Proper little Marchbanks, you are!

JIMMY: What time's that concert on? (*Checks paper.*)

CLIFF: (*yawns*).Oh, I feel so sleepy. Don't feel like standing behind that blinking sweet-stall again tomorrow. Why don't you do it on your own, and let me sleep in?

JIMMY: I've got to be at the factory first thing, to get some more stock, so you'll have to put it up on your own. Another five minutes.

Alison has returned to her ironing board. She stands with her arms folded, smoking, staring thoughtfully. She had more animation in her little finger than you two put together.

CLIFF: Who did?

ALISON: Madeline.

JIMMY: Her curiosity about things, and about people was staggering. It wasn't just a naïve nosiness. With her, it was simply the delight of being awake, and watching.

Alison starts to press Cliff's trousers.

CLIFF: (*behind paper*). Perhaps I will make some tea, after all.

JIMMY: (*quietly*). Just to be with her was an adventure. Even to sit on the top of a bus with her was like setting out with Ulysses.

CLIFF: Wouldn't have said Webster was much like Ulysses. He's an ugly little devil.

JIMMY: I'm not talking about Webster, stupid. He's all right though, in his way. A sort of female Emily Brontë. He's the only one of your friends (*to Alison*) who's worth tuppence, anyway. I'm surprised you get on with him.

ALISON: So is he, I think.

JIMMY: (*rising to window R., and looking out*). He's not only got guts, but sensitivity as well. That's about the rarest combination I can think of. None of your other friends have got either.

ALISON: (*very quietly and earnestly*). Jimmy, please—don't go on.

He turns and looks at her. The tired appeal in her voice has pulled him up suddenly. But he soon gathers himself for a new assault. He walks C., behind Cliff, and stands, looking down at his head.

JIMMY: Your friends—there's a shower for you.

CLIFF: (*mumbling*). Dry up. Let her get on with my trousers.

JIMMY: (*musingly*). Don't think I could provoke her. Nothing I could do would provoke her. Not even if I were to drop dead.

CLIFF: Then drop dead.

JIMMY: They're either militant like her Mummy and Daddy. Militant, arrogant and full of malice. Or vague. She's somewhere between the two.

CLIFF: Why don't you listen to that concert of yours? And don't stand behind me. That blooming droning on behind me gives me a funny feeling down the spine.

Jimmy gives his ears a twist and Cliff roars with pain. Jimmy grins back at him.

That hurt, you rotten sadist! (*To Alison.*) I wish you'd kick his head in for him.

JIMMY: (*moving in between them*). Have you ever seen her brother? Brother Nigel? The straight-backed, chinless wonder from Sandhurst? I only met him once myself. He asked me to step outside when I told his mother she was evil minded.

CLIFF: And did you?

JIMMY: Certainly not. He's a big chap. Well, you've never heard so many well-bred commonplaces come from beneath the same bowler hat. The Platitude from Outer Space—that's brother Nigel. He'll end up in the Cabinet one day, make no mistake. But somewhere at the back of that mind is the vague knowledge that he and his pals have been plundering and fooling everybody for generations. (*Going up-stage, and turning.*) Now Nigel is just about as vague as you can get without being actually invisible. And invisible politicians aren't much use to anyone—not even to *his* supporters! And nothing is more vague about Nigel than his knowledge. His knowledge of life and ordinary human beings is so hazy, he really deserves some sort of decoration for it—a medal inscribed "For Vaguery in the Field". But it wouldn't do for him to be troubled by any stabs of conscience, however vague.

(*Moving down again.*) Besides, he's a patriot and an Englishman, and he doesn't like the idea that he may have been selling out his countrymen all these years, so what does he do? The only thing he *can* do—seek sanctuary in his own stupidity. The only way to keep things as much like they always have been as possible, is to make any alternative too much for your poor, tiny brain to grasp. It takes some doing nowadays. It really does. But they knew all about character building at Nigel's school, and he'll make it all right. Don't you worry, he'll make it. And, what's more, he'll do it better than anybody else!

There is no sound, only the plod of Alison's iron. Her eyes are fixed on what she is doing. Cliff stares at the floor. His cheerfulness has deserted him for the moment. Jimmy is rather shakily triumphant. He cannot allow himself to look at either of them to catch their response to his rhetoric, so he moves across to the window, to recover himself, and look out.

It's started to rain. That's all it needs. This room and the rain.

He's been cheated out of his response, but he's got to draw blood somehow.

(*conversationally*). Yes, that's the little woman's

family. You know Mummy and Daddy, of course. And don't let the Marquess of Queensberry manner fool you. They'll kick you in the groin while you're handing your hat to the maid. As for Nigel and Alison—— (*In a reverent, Stuart Hibberd voice.*) Nigel and Alison. They're what they sound like: sycophantic, phlegmatic and pusillanimous.

CLIFF: I'll bet that concert's started by now. Shall I put it on?

JIMMY: I looked up that word the other day. It's one of those words I've never been quite sure of, but always thought I knew.

CLIFF: What was that?

JIMMY: I told you—pusillanimous. Do you know what it means?

Cliff shakes his head.

Neither did I really. All this time, I have been married to this woman, this monument to non-attachment, and suddenly I discover that there is actually a word that sums her up. Not just an adjective in the English language to describe her with—it's her name! Pusillanimous! It sounds like some fleshy Roman matron, doesn't it? The Lady Pusillanimous seen here with her husband Sextus, on their way to the Games.

Cliff looks troubled, and glances uneasily at Alison.

Poor old Sextus! If he were put into a Hollywood film, he's so unimpressive, they'd make some poor British actor play the part. He doesn't know it, but those beefcake Christians will make off with his wife in the wonder of stereophonic sound before the picture's over.

Alison leans against the board, and closes her eyes.

The Lady Pusillanimous has been promised a brighter easier world than old Sextus can ever offer her. Hi, Pusey! What say we get the hell down to the Arena, and maybe feed ourselves to a couple of lions, huh?

ALISON: God help me, if he doesn't stop, I'll go out of my mind in a minute.

JIMMY: Why don't you? That would be something, anyway. (*Crosses to chest of drawers R.*) But I haven't told you what it means yet, have I? (*Picks up dictionary.*) I don't have to tell her—she knows. In fact, if my pronunciation is at fault, she'll probably wait for a suitably public moment to correct it. Here it is. I quote: Pusillanimous. Adjective. Wanting of firmness of mind, of small courage, having a little mind, mean spirited, cowardly, timid of mind. From the Latin pusillus, very little, and animus, the mind. (*Slams the book shut.*) That's my wife! That's *her* isn't it? Behold the Lady Pusillanimous. (*Shouting hoarsely.*) Hi, Pusey! When's your next picture?

Jimmy watches her, waiting for her to break. For no more than a flash, Alison's face seems to contort, and it looks as though she might throw her head back, and scream. But it passes in a moment. She is used to these carefully rehearsed attacks, and it doesn't look as though he will get his triumph tonight. She carries on with her ironing. Jimmy crosses, and switches on the radio. The Vaughan Williams concert has started. He goes back to his chair, leans back in it, and closes his eyes.

ALISON: (*handing Cliff his trousers*). There you are, dear. They're not very good, but they'll do for now.

Cliff gets up and puts them on.

CLIFF: Oh, that's lovely.

ALISON: Now try and look after them. I'll give them a real press later on.

CLIFF: Thank you, you beautiful, darling girl.

He puts his arms round her waist, and kisses her. She smiles, and gives his nose a tug. Jimmy watches from his chair.

ALISON: (*to Cliff*). Let's have a cigarette, shall we?

CLIFF: That's a good idea. Where are they?

ALISON: On the stove. Do you want one, Jimmy?

JIMMY: No thank you, I'm trying to listen. Do you mind?

CLIFF: Sorry, your lordship.

He puts a cigarette in Alison's mouth, and one in his own, and lights up. Cliff sits down, and picks up his paper. Alison goes back to her board. Cliff throws down paper, picks up another, and thumbs through that.

JIMMY: Do you have to make all that racket?

CLIFF: Oh, sorry.

JIMMY: It's quite a simple thing, you know—turning over a page. Anyway, that's my paper.

(*Snatches it away.*)

CLIFF: Oh, don't be so mean!

JIMMY: Price ninepence, obtainable from any newsagent's. Now let me hear the music, for God's sake.

Pause.

(*to Alison*). Are you going to be much longer doing that?

ALISON: Why?

JIMMY: Perhaps you haven't noticed it, but it's interfering with the radio.

ALISON: I'm sorry. I shan't be much longer.

A pause. The iron mingles with the music. Cliff shifts restlessly in his chair, Jimmy watches Alison, his foot beginning to twitch dangerously. Presently, he gets up quickly, crossing below Alison to the radio, and turns it off.

What did you do that for?

JIMMY: I wanted to listen to the concert, that's all.

ALISON: Well, what's stopping you?

JIMMY: Everyone's making such a din—that's what's stopping me.

ALISON: Well, I'm very sorry, but I can't just stop everything because you want to listen to music.

JIMMY: Why not?

ALISON: Really, Jimmy, you're like a child.

JIMMY: Don't try and patronise me. (*Turning to Cliff.*) She's so clumsy. I watch for her to do the same

things every night. The way she jumps on the bed,
as if she were stamping on someone's face, and draws
the curtains back with a great clatter, in that casually
destructive way of hers. It's like someone launching
a battleship. Have you ever noticed how noisy wom-
en are? (*Crosses below chairs to L.C.*) Have you?
The way they kick the floor about, simply walking
over it? Or have you watched them sitting at their
dressing tables, dropping their weapons and banging down their bits of boxes and brushes and lip-
sticks?

He faces her dressing table.

I've watched her doing it night after night. When you
see a woman in front of her bedroom mirror, you
realise what a refined sort of a butcher she is. (*Turns
in.*) Did you ever see some dirty old Arab, sticking
his fingers into some mess of lamb fat and gristle?
Well, she's just like that. Thank God they don't have
many women surgeons! Those primitive hands would
have your guts out in no time. Flip. Out it comes,
like the powder out of its box. Flop! Back it goes,
like the powder puff on the table.

CLIFF: (*grimacing cheerfully*). Ugh! Stop it!

JIMMY: (*moving upstage*). She'd drop your guts like
hair clips and fluff all over the floor. You've got to
be fundamentally insensitive to be as noisy and as
clumsy as that.

He moves C., and leans against the table.

I had a flat underneath a couple of girls once. You
heard every damned thing those bastards did, all day
and night. The most simple, everyday actions were
a sort of assault course on your sensibilities. I used
to plead with them. I even got to screaming the most
ingenious obscenities I could think of, up the stairs
at them. But nothing, nothing, would move them.
With those two, even a simple visit to the lavatory
sounded like a medieval siege. Oh, they beat me in
the end—I had to go. I expect they're still at it. Or
they're probably married by now, and driving some

other poor devils out of their minds. Slamming their
doors, stamping their high heels, banging their irons
and saucepans—the eternal flaming racket of the
female.

Church bells start ringing outside.

JIMMY: Oh, hell! Now the bloody bells have started!

He rushes to the window.

Wrap it up, will you? Stop ringing those bells!
There's somebody going crazy in here! I don't want
to hear them!

ALISON: Stop shouting! (*Recovering immediately.*)
You'll have Miss Drury up here.

JIMMY: I don't give a damn about Miss Drury—that
mild old gentlewoman doesn't fool me, even if she
takes in you two. She's an old robber. She gets more
than enough out of us for this place every week.
Anyway, she's probably in church, (*points to the
window*) swinging on those bloody bells!

Cliff goes to the window, and closes it.

CLIFF: Come on now, be a good boy. I'll take us all
out, and we'll have a drink.

JIMMY: They're not open yet. It's Sunday. Remember?
Anyway, it's raining.

CLIFF: Well, shall we dance?

*He pushes Jimmy round the floor, who is past the
mood for this kind of fooling.*

Do you come here often?

JIMMY: Only in the mating season. All right, all right,
very funny.

He tries to escape, but Cliff holds him like a vise.

Let me go.

CLIFF: Not until you've apologised for being so nasty
to everyone. Do you think bosoms will be in or out,
this year?

JIMMY: Your teeth will be out in a minute, if you
don't let go!

*He makes a great effort to wrench himself free, but
Cliff hangs on. They collapse to the floor C., below*

the table, struggling. Alison carries on with her iron-
ing. This is routine, but she is getting close to break-
ing point, all the same. Cliff manages to break away,
and finds himself in front of the ironing board. Jim-
my springs up. They grapple.

ALISON: Look out, for heaven's sake! Oh, it's more
like a zoo every day!

Jimmy makes a frantic, deliberate effort, and man-
ages to push Cliff on to the ironing board, and into
Alison. The board collapses. Cliff falls against her,
and they end up in a heap on the floor. Alison cries
out in pain. Jimmy looks down at them, dazed and
breathless.

CLIFF: (*picking himself up*). She's hurt. Are you all
right?

ALISON: Well, does it look like it!

CLIFF: She's burnt her arm on the iron.

JIMMY: Darling, I'm sorry.

ALISON: Get out!

JIMMY: I'm sorry, believe me. You think I did it on
pur——

ALISON: (*her head shaking helplessly*). Clear out of
my *sight!*

He stares at her uncertainly. Cliff nods to him, and
he turns and goes out of the door.

CLIFF: Come and sit down.

He leads her to the armchair. R.

You look a bit white. Are you all right?

ALISON: Yes. I'm all right now.

CLIFF: Let's have a look at your arm. (*Examines it.*)
Yes, it's quite red. That's going to be painful. What
should I do with it?

ALISON: Oh, it's nothing much. A bit of soap on it
will do. I never can remember what you do with
burns.

CLIFF: I'll just pop down to the bathroom and get
some. Are you sure you're all right?

ALISON: Yes.

CLIFF: *(crossing to door)*. Won't be a minute.
EXIT.
She leans back in the chair, and looks up at the ceiling. She breathes in deeply, and brings her hands up to her face. She winces as she feels the pain in her arm, and she lets it fall. She runs her hand through her hair.

ALISON: *(in a clenched whisper)*. Oh, God!
Cliff re-enters with a bar of soap.

CLIFF: It's this scented muck. Do you think it'll be all right?

ALISON: That'll do.

CLIFF: Here we are then. Let's have your arm.
He kneels down beside her, and she holds out her arm.
I've put it under the tap. It's quite soft. I'll do it ever so gently.
Very carefully, he rubs the soap over the burn.
All right? *(She nods.)* You're a brave girl.

ALISON: I don't feel very brave. *(Tears harshening her voice.)* I really don't, Cliff. I don't think I can take much more. *(Turns her head away.)* I think I feel rather sick.

CLIFF: All over now. *(Puts the soap down.)* Would you like me to get you something?
She shakes her head. He sits on the arm of the chair, and puts his arm round her. She leans her head back on to him.
Don't upset yourself, lovely.
He massages the back of her neck, and she lets her head fall forward.

ALISON: Where is he?

CLIFF: In my room.

ALISON: What's he doing?

CLIFF: Lying on the bed. Reading, I think. *(Stroking her neck.)* That better?
She leans back, and closes her eyes again.

ALISON: Bless you.
He kisses the top of her head.

CLIFF: I don't think I'd have the courage to live on my own again—in spite of everything. I'm pretty rough, and pretty ordinary really, and I'd seem worse on my own. And you get fond of people too, worse luck.

ALISON: I don't think I want anything more to do with love. Any more. I can't take it on.

CLIFF: You're too young to start giving up. Too young, and too lovely. Perhaps I'd better put a bandage on that—do you think so?

ALISON: There's some on my dressing table.

Cliff crosses to the dressing table R.

I keep looking back, as far as I remember, and I can't think what it was to feel young, really young. Jimmy said the same thing to me the other day. I pretended not to be listening—because I knew that would hurt him, I suppose. And—of course—he got savage, like tonight. But I knew just what he meant. I suppose it would have been so easy to say "Yes, darling, I know just what you mean. I know what you're feeling." (*Shrugs.*) It's those easy things that seem to be so impossible with us.

Cliff stands down R., holding the bandage, his back to her.

CLIFF: I'm wondering how much longer I can go on watching you two tearing the insides out of each other. It looks pretty ugly sometimes.

ALISON: You wouldn't seriously think of leaving us, would you?

CLIFF: I suppose not. (*Crosses to her.*)

ALISON: I think I'm frightened. If only I knew what was going to happen.

CLIFF: (*kneeling on the arm of her chair*). Give it here. (*She holds out her arm.*) Yell out if I hurt you. (*He bandages it for her.*)

ALISON: (*staring at her outstretched arm*). Cliff——

CLIFF: Um? (*Slight pause.*) What is it, lovely?

ALISON: Nothing.

CLIFF: I said: what is it?

ALISON: You see—— (*Hesitates.*) I'm pregnant.

CLIFF: (*after a few moments*). I'll need some scissors.

ALISON: They're over there.

CLIFF: (*crossing to the dressing table*). That is some-thing, isn't it? When did you find this out?

ALISON: Few days ago. It was a bit of a shock.

CLIFF: Yes, I dare say.

ALISON: After three years of married life, I have to get caught out now.

CLIFF: None of us infallible, I suppose. (*Crosses to her.*) Must say I'm surprised though.

ALISON: It's always been out of the question. What with—this place, and no money, and oh—every-thing. He's resented it, I know. What can you do?

CLIFF: You haven't told him yet.

ALISON: Not yet.

CLIFF: What are you going to do?

ALISON: I've no idea.

CLIFF: (*having cut her bandage, he starts tying it*). That too tight?

ALISON: Fine, thank you.

She rises, goes to the ironing board, folds it up, and leans it against the food cupboard R.

CLIFF: Is it . . . Is it . . . ?

ALISON: Too late to avert the situation? (*Places the iron on the rack of the stove.*) I'm not certain yet. Maybe not. If not, there won't be any problem, will there?

CLIFF: And if it is too late?

Her face is turned away from him. She simply shakes her head.

Why don't you tell him now?

She kneels down to pick up the clothes on the floor, and folds them up.

After all, he does love you. You don't need me to tell you that.

ALISON: Can't you see? He'll suspect my motives at once. He never stops telling himself that I know how vulnerable he is. Tonight it might be all right—we'd

make love. But later, we'd both lie awake, watching
for the light to come through that little window, and
dreading it. In the morning, he'd feel hoaxed, as if I
were trying to kill him in the worst way of all. He'd
watch me growing bigger every day, and I wouldn't
dare to look at him.

CLIFF: You may have to face it, lovely.

ALISON: Jimmy's got his own private morality, as you
know. What my mother calls "loose". It is pretty
free, of course, but it's very harsh too. You know,
it's funny, but we never slept together before we
were married.

CLIFF: It certainly is—knowing him!

ALISON: We knew each other such a short time, everything moved at such a pace, we didn't have much
opportunity. And, afterwards, he actually taunted
me with my virginity. He was quite angry about it,
as if I had deceived him in some strange way. He
seemed to think an untouched woman would defile
him.

CLIFF: I've never heard you talking like this about
him. He'd be quite pleased.

ALISON: Yes, he would.
She gets up, the clothes folded over her arm.
Do you think he's right?

CLIFF: What about?

ALISON: Oh—everything.

CLIFF: Well, I suppose he and I think the same about
a lot of things, because we're alike in some ways.
We both come from working people, if you like.
Oh I know some of his mother's relatives are pretty
posh, but he hates them as much as he hates yours.
Don't quite know why. Anyway, he gets on with me
because I'm common. (*Grins.*) Common as dirt,
that's me.
*She puts her hand on his head, and strokes it thought-
fully.*

ALISON: You think I should tell him about the baby?
He gets up, and puts his arm round her.

CLIFF: It'll be all right—you see. Tell him.

He kisses her. Enter Jimmy. He looks at them curiously, but without surprise. They are both aware of him, but make no sign of it. He crosses to the armchair L., and sits down next to them. He picks up a paper, and starts looking at it. Cliff glances at him, Alison's head against his cheek.

There you are, you old devil, you! Where have you been?

JIMMY: You know damn well where I've been. (*Without looking at her.*) How's your arm?

ALISON: Oh, it's all right. It wasn't much.

CLIFF: She's beautiful, isn't she?

JIMMY: You seem to think so.

Cliff and Alison still have their arms round one another.

CLIFF: Why the hell she married you, I'll never know.

JIMMY: You think she'd have been better off with you?

CLIFF: I'm not her type. Am I, dullin'?

ALISON: I'm not sure what my type is.

JIMMY: Why don't you both get into bed, and have done with it.

ALISON: You know, I think he really means that.

JIMMY: I do. I can't concentrate with you two standing there like that.

CLIFF: He's just an old Puritan at heart.

JIMMY: Perhaps I am, at that. Anyway, you both look pretty silly slobbering over each other.

CLIFF: I think she's beautiful. And so do you, only you're too much of a pig to say so.

JIMMY: You're just a sexy little Welshman, and you know it! Mummy and Daddy turn pale, and face the east every time they remember she's married to me. But if they saw all this going on, they'd collapse. Wonder what they would do, incidentally. Send for the police I expect. (*Genuinely friendly.*) Have you got a cigarette?

ALISON: (*disengaging*). I'll have a look.

She goes to her handbag on the table C.

JIMMY: (*pointing at Cliff*). He gets more like a little mouse every day, doesn't he?
He is trying to re-establish himself.
He really does look like one. Look at those ears, and that face, and the little short legs.

ALISON: (*looking through her bag*). That's because he *is* a mouse.

CLIFF: Eek! Eek! I'm a mouse.

JIMMY: A randy little mouse.

CLIFF: (*dancing round the table, and squeaking*). I'm a mouse, I'm a mouse, I'm a randy little mouse. That's a mourris dance.

JIMMY: A what?

CLIFF: A *Mourris Dance*. That's a Morris Dance strictly for mice.

JIMMY: You stink. You really do. Do you know that?

CLIFF: Not as bad as you, you horrible old bear.
(*Goes over to him, and grabs his foot.*)
You're a stinking old bear, you hear me?

JIMMY: Let go of my foot, you whimsy little half-wit. You're making my stomach heave. I'm resting! If you don't let go, I'll cut off your nasty, great, slimy tail!
Cliff gives him a tug, and Jimmy falls to the floor. Alison watches them, relieved and suddenly full of affection.

ALISON: I've run out of cigarettes.
Cliff is dragging Jimmy along the floor by his feet.

JIMMY: (*yelling*). Go out and get me some cigarettes, and stop playing the fool!

CLIFF: O.K.
He lets go of Jimmy's legs suddenly, who yells again as his head bangs on the floor.

ALISON: Here's half a crown. (*Giving it him.*) The shop on the corner will be open.

CLIFF: Right you are. (*Kisses her on the forehead quickly.*)
Don't forget. (*Crosses upstage to door.*)

JIMMY: Now get to hell out of here!

CLIFF: (*at door*). Hey, shorty!

JIMMY: What do you want?

CLIFF: Make a nice pot of tea.

JIMMY: (*getting up*). I'll kill you first.

CLIFF: (*grinning*). That's my boy!

EXIT.

Jimmy is now beside Alison, who is still looking through her handbag. She becomes aware of his nearness, and, after a few moments, closes it. He takes hold of her bandaged arm.

JIMMY: How's it feeling?

ALISON: Fine. It wasn't anything.

JIMMY: All this fooling about can get a bit dangerous.

He sits on the edge of the table, holding her hand.

I'm sorry.

ALISON: I know.

JIMMY: I mean it.

ALISON: There's no need.

JIMMY: I did it on purpose.

ALISON: Yes.

JIMMY: There's hardly a moment when I'm not—watching and wanting you. I've got to hit out somehow. Nearly four years of being in the same room with you, night and day, and I still can't stop my sweat breaking out when I see you doing—something as ordinary as leaning over an ironing board.

She strokes his head, not sure of herself yet. (sighing). Trouble is—Trouble is you get used to people. Even their trivialities become indispensable to you. Indispensable, and a little mysterious.

He slides his head forward, against her, trying to catch his thoughts.

I think . . . I must have a lot of—old stock. . . . Nobody wants it. . . .

He puts his face against her belly. She goes on stroking his head, still on guard a little. Then he lifts his head, and they kiss passionately.

What are we going to do tonight?

ALISON: What would you like to do? Drink?

JIMMY: I know what I want now.

She takes his head in her hands and kisses him.

ALISON: Well, you'll have to wait till the proper time.

JIMMY: There's no such thing.

ALISON: Cliff will be back in a minute.

JIMMY: What did he mean by "don't forget"?

ALISON: Something I've been meaning to tell you.

JIMMY: (*kissing her again*). You're fond of him, aren't you?

ALISON: Yes, I am.

JIMMY: He's the only friend I seem to have left now. People go away. You never see them again. I can remember lots of names—men and women. When I was at school—Watson, Roberts, Davies. Jenny, Madeline, Hugh . . . (*Pause.*) And there's Hugh's mum, of course. I'd almost forgotten her. She's been a good friend to us, if you like. She's even letting me buy the sweet-stall off her in my own time. She only bought it for us, anyway. She's so fond of you. I can never understand why you're so—distant with her.

ALISON: (*alarmed at this threat of a different mood*). Jimmy—please no!

JIMMY: (*staring at her anxious face*). You're very beautiful. A beautiful, great-eyed squirrel.

She nods brightly, relieved.

Hoarding, nut-munching squirrel. (*She mimes this delightedly.*) With highly polished, gleaming fur, and an ostrich feather of a tail.

ALISON: Wheeeeeeeeee!

JIMMY: How I envy you.

He stands, her arms around his neck.

ALISON: Well, you're a jolly super bear, too. A really soooooooooooooooooper, marvellous bear.

JIMMY: Bears and squirrels *are* marvellous.

ALISON: Marvellous *and* beautiful.

She jumps up and down excitedly, making little "paw gestures".

Oooooooooh! Oooooooooh!

JIMMY: What the hell's that?

ALISON: That's a dance squirrels do when they're happy.

They embrace again.

JIMMY: What makes you think you're happy?

ALISON: Everything just seems all right suddenly. That's all. Jimmy——

JIMMY: Yes?

ALISON: You know I told you I'd something to tell you?

JIMMY: Well?

Cliff appears in the doorway.

CLIFF: Didn't get any further than the front door. Miss Drury hadn't gone to church after all. I couldn't get away from her. (*To Alison.*) Someone on the phone for you.

ALISON: On the phone? Who on earth is it?

CLIFF: Helena something.

Jimmy and Alison look at each other quickly.

JIMMY: (*to Cliff*). Helena Charles?

CLIFF: That's it.

ALISON: Thank you, Cliff. (*Moves upstage.*) I won't be a minute.

EXIT.

CLIFF: You will. Old Miss Drury will keep you down there forever. She doesn't think we keep this place clean enough. (*Comes and sits in the armchair down R.*)

Thought you were going to make me some tea, you rotter.

Jimmy makes no reply.

What's the matter, boyo?

JIMMY: (*slowly*). That bitch.

CLIFF: Who?

JIMMY: (*to himself*). Helena Charles.

CLIFF: Who is this Helena?

JIMMY: One of her old friends. And one of my natural enemies. You're sitting on my chair.

CLIFF: Where are we going for a drink?

JIMMY: I don't know.

CLIFF: Well, you were all for it earlier on.

JIMMY: What does she want? What would make her
ring up? It can't be for anything pleasant. Oh well,
we shall soon know. (*He settles on the table.*) Few
minutes ago things didn't seem so bad either. I've just
about had enough of this "expense of spirit" lark, as
far as women are concerned. Honestly, it's enough
to make you become a scoutmaster or something
isn't it? Sometimes I almost envy old Gide and the
Greek Chorus boys. Oh, I'm not saying that it mustn't
be hell for them a lot of the time. But, at least, they
do seem to have a cause—not a particularly good
one, it's true. But plenty of them do seem to have a
revolutionary fire about them, which is more than
you can say for the rest of us. Like Webster, for
instance. He doesn't like me—they hardly ever do.
*He is talking for the sake of it, only half listening
to what he is saying.*
I dare say he suspects me because I refuse to treat
him either as a clown or as a tragic hero. He's like a
man with a strawberry mark—he keeps thrusting it
in your face because he can't believe it doesn't interest or horrify you particularly. (*Picks up Alison's
handbag thoughtfully, and starts looking through it.*)
As if I give a damn which way he likes his meat
served up. I've got my own strawberry mark—only
it's in a different place. No, as far as the Michael-
angelo Brigade's concerned, I must be a sort of
right-wing deviationist. If the Revolution ever comes,
I'll be the first to be put up against the wall, with all
the other poor old liberals.

CLIFF: (*indicating Alison's handbag*). Wouldn't you
say that that was her private property?

JIMMY: You're quite right. But do you know something? Living night and day with another human
being has made me predatory and suspicious. I know
that the only way of finding out exactly what's going
on is to catch them when they don't know you're
looking. When she goes out, I go through everything
—trunks, cases, drawers, bookcase, everything. Why?

To see if there is something of me somewhere, a reference to me. I want to know if I'm being betrayed.

CLIFF: You look for trouble, don't you?

JIMMY: Only because I'm pretty certain of finding it. (*Brings out a letter from the handbag.*) Look at that! Oh, I'm such a fool. This is happening every five minutes of the day. She gets letters. (*He holds it up.*) Letters from her mother, letters in which I'm not mentioned at all because my name is a dirty word. And what does she do?

Enter Alison. He turns to look at her.

She writes long letters back to Mummy, and never mentions me at all, because I'm just a dirty word to her too.

He throws the letter down at her feet.

Well, what did your friend want?

ALISON: She's at the station. She's—coming over.

JIMMY: I see. She said "Can I come over?" And you said "My husband, Jimmy—if you'll forgive me using such a dirty word, will be delighted to see you. He'll kick your face in!"

He stands up, unable to sustain his anger, poised on the table.

ALISON: (*quietly*). She's playing with the company at the Hippodrome this week, and she's got no digs. She can't find anywhere to stay——

JIMMY: That I don't believe!

ALISON: So I said she could come here until she fixes something else. Miss Drury's got a spare room downstairs.

JIMMY: Why not have her in here? Did you tell her to bring her armour? Because she's going to need it!

ALISON: (*vehemently*). Oh why don't you shut up, please!

JIMMY: Oh, my dear wife, you've got so much to learn. I only hope you learn it one day. If only something—something would happen to you, and wake you out of your beauty sleep! (*Coming in close to her.*) If you could could have a child, and it would die. Let it grow, let a recognisable human face emerge from that little mass of indiarubber and wrinkles. (*She retreats away from him.*) Please—if only I could watch you face that. I wonder if you might even become a recognisable human being yourself. But I doubt it.

She moves away, stunned, and leans on the gas stove down L. He stands rather helplessly on his own.

Do you know I have never known the great pleasure of lovemaking when I didn't desire it myself. Oh, it's not that she hasn't her own kind of passion. She has the passion of a python. She just devours me whole every time, as if I were some over-large rabbit. That's me. That bulge around her navel—if you're wondering what it is—it's me. Me, buried alive down there, and going mad, smothered in that peaceful looking coil. Not a sound, not a flicker from her—she doesn't even rumble a little. You'd think that this indigestible mess would stir up some kind of tremor in those distended, overfed tripes—but not her!

Crosses up to the door.

She'll go on sleeping and devouring until there's nothing left of me.

EXIT.

Alison's head goes back as if she were about to make some sound. But her mouth remains open and trembling, as Cliff looks on.

CURTAIN

END OF ACT I

ACT II

SCENE ONE

Two weeks later. Evening.

ALISON is standing over the gas stove, pouring water from the kettle into a large teapot. She is only wearing a slip, and her feet are bare. In the room across the hall, JIMMY is playing on his jazz trumpet, in intermittent bursts. ALISON takes the pot to the table C., which is laid for four people. The Sunday paper jungle around the two armchairs is as luxuriant as ever. It is late afternoon, the end of a hot day. She wipes her forehead. She crosses to the dressing table R., takes out a pair of stockings from one of the drawers, and sits down on the small chair beside it to put them on. While she is doing this, the door opens and HELENA enters. She is the same age as ALISON, medium height, carefully and expensively dressed. Now and again, when she allows her rather judicial expression of alertness to soften, she is very attractive. Her sense of matriarchal authority makes most men who meet her anxious, not only to please but impress, as if she were the gracious representative of visiting royalty. In this case, the royalty of that middle-class womanhood, which is so eminently secure in its divine rights, that it can afford to tolerate the parliament, and reasonably free assembly of its menfolk. Even from other young women, like ALISON, she receives her due of respect and admiration. In JIMMY, as one would expect, she arouses all the rabble-rousing instincts of his spirit. And she is not accustomed to having to defend herself against cat-calls. However, her sense of modestly exalted responsibility enables her to behave with an impressive

show of strength and dignity, although the strain of
this is beginning to tell on her a little. She is carrying
a large salad colander.

ALISON: Did you manage all right?

HELENA: Of course. I've prepared most of the meals in
the last week, you know.

ALISON: Yes, you have. It's been wonderful having
someone to help. Another woman, I mean.

HELENA: (crossing down L.). I'm enjoying it. Although
I don't think I shall ever get used to having to go
down to the bathroom every time I want some water
for something.

ALISON: It is primitive, isn't it?

HELENA: Yes. It is rather.

She starts tearing up green salad on to four plates,
which she takes from the food cupboard.

Looking after one man is really enough, but two is
rather an undertaking.

ALISON: Oh, Cliff looks after himself, more or less. In
fact, he helps me quite a lot.

HELENA: Can't say I'd noticed it.

ALISON: You've been doing it instead, I suppose.

HELENA: I see.

ALISON: You've settled in so easily somehow.

HELENA: Why shouldn't I?

ALISON: It's not exactly what you're used to, is it?

HELENA: And are you used to it?

ALISON: Everything seems very different here now—
with you here.

HELENA: Does it?

ALISON: Yes. I was on my own before——

HELENA: Now you've got me. So you're not sorry you
asked me to stay?

ALISON: Of course not. Did you tell him his tea was
ready?

HELENA: I banged on the door of Cliff's room, and
yelled. He didn't answer, but he must have heard. I
don't know where Cliff is.

ALISON: (*leaning back in her chair*). I thought I'd feel cooler after a bath, but I feel hot again already. God, I wish he'd lose that damned trumpet.

HELENA: I imagine that's for my benefit.

ALISON: Miss Drury will ask us to go soon, I know it. Thank goodness she isn't in. Listen to him.

HELENA: Does he drink?

ALISON: Drink? (*Rather startled.*) He's not an alcoholic, if that's what you mean.

They both pause, listening to the trumpet.

He'll have the rest of the street banging on the door next.

HELENA: (*pondering*). It's almost as if he wanted to kill someone with it. And me in particular. I've never seen such hatred in someone's eyes before. It's slightly horrifying. Horrifying (*crossing to food cupboard for tomatoes, beetroot and cucumber*) and oddly exciting.

Alison faces her dressing mirror, and brushes her hair.

ALISON: He had his own jazz band once. That was when he was still a student, before I knew him. I rather think he'd like to start another, and give up the stall altogether.

HELENA: Is Cliff in love with you?

ALISON: (*stops brushing for a moment*). No ... I don't think so.

HELENA: And what about you? You look as though I've asked you a rather peculiar question. The way things are, you might as well be frank with me. I only want to help. After all, your behaviour together is a little strange—by most people's standards, to say the least.

ALISON: You mean you've seen us embracing each other?

HELENA: Well, it doesn't seem to go on as much as it did, I admit. Perhaps he finds my presence inhibiting —even if Jimmy's isn't.

ALISON: We're simply fond of each other—there's no more to it than that.

HELENA: Darling, really! It can't be as simple as that.

ALISON: You mean there must be something physical too? I suppose there is, but it's not exactly a consuming passion with either of us. It's just a relaxed, cheerful sort of thing, like being warm in bed. You're too comfortable to bother about moving for the sake of some other pleasure.

HELENA: I find it difficult to believe anyone's that lazy!

ALISON: I think *we* are.

HELENA: And what about Jimmy? After all, he is your husband. Do you mean to say he actually approves of it?

ALISON: It isn't easy to explain. It's what he would call a question of allegiances, and he expects you to be pretty literal about them. Not only about himself and all the things he believes in, his present and his future, but his past as well. All the people he admires and loves, and has loved. The friends he used to know, people I've never even known—and probably wouldn't have liked. His father, who died years ago. Even the other women he's loved. Do you understand?

HELENA: Do you?

ALISON: I've tried to. But I still can't bring myself to feel the way he does about things. I can't believe that he's right somehow.

HELENA: Well, that's something, anyway.

ALISON: If things have worked out with Cliff, it's because he's kind and lovable, and I've grown genuinely fond of him. But it's been a fluke. It's worked because Cliff is such a nice person anyway. With Hugh, it was quite different.

HELENA: Hugh?

ALISON: Hugh Tanner. He and Jimmy were friends almost from childhood. Mrs. Tanner is his mother——

HELENA: Oh yes—the one who started him off in the sweet business.

ALISON: That's right. Well, after Jimmy and I were married, we'd no money—about eight pounds ten in actual fact—and no home. He didn't even have a job. He'd only left the university about a year. (*Smiles.*) No—left. I don't think one "comes down" from Jimmy's university. According to him, it's not even red brick, but white tile. Anyway, we went off to live in Hugh's flat. It was over a warehouse in Poplar.

HELENA: Yes. I remember seeing the postmark on your letters.

ALISON: Well, that was where I found myself on my wedding night. Hugh and I disliked each other on sight, and Jimmy knew it. He was so proud of us both, so pathetically anxious that we should take to each other. Like a child showing off his toys. We had a little wedding celebration, and the three of us tried to get tight on some cheap port they'd brought in. Hugh got more and more subtly insulting—he'd a rare talent for that. Jimmy got steadily depressed, and I just sat there, listening to their talk, looking and feeling very stupid. For the first time in my life, I was cut off from the kind of people I'd always known, my family, my friends, everybody. And I'd burnt my boats. After all those weeks of brawling with Mummy and Daddy about Jimmy, I knew I couldn't appeal to them without looking foolish and cheap. It was just before the General Election, I remember, and Nigel was busy getting himself into Parliament. He didn't have time for anyone but his constituents. Oh, he'd have been sweet and kind, I know.

HELENA: (*moving in C.*). Darling, why didn't you come to me?

ALISON: You were away on tour in some play, I think.

HELENA: So I was.

ALISON: Those next few months at the flat in Poplar were a nightmare. I suppose I must be soft and squeamish, and snobbish, but I felt as though I'd been dropped in a jungle. I couldn't believe that two people, two educated people could be so savage, and so—so uncompromising. Mummy has always said

that Jimmy is utterly ruthless, but she hasn't met
Hugh. He takes the first prize for ruthlessness—from
all comers. Together, they were frightening. They
both came to regard me as a sort of hostage from
those sections of society they had declared war on.

HELENA: How were you living all this time?

ALISON: I had a tiny bit coming in from a few shares
I had left, but it hardly kept us. Mummy had made
me sign everything else over to her, in trust, when
she knew I was really going to marry Jimmy.

HELENA: Just as well, I imagine.

ALISON: They soon thought of a way out of that. A
brilliant campaign. They started inviting themselves
—through me—to people's houses, friends of Nigel's
and mine, friends of Daddy's, oh everyone: The
Arksdens, the Tarnatts, the Wains——

HELENA: Not the Wains?

ALISON: Just about everyone I'd ever known. Your
people must have been among the few we missed out.
It was just enemy territory to them, and, as I say,
they used me as a hostage. We'd set out from head-
quarters in Poplar, and carry out our raids on the
enemy in W.1, S.W.1., S.W.3. and W.8. In my name,
we'd gatecrash everywhere—cocktails, week-ends,
even a couple of houseparties. I used to hope that
one day, somebody would have the guts to slam the
door in our faces, but they didn't. They were too
well-bred, and probably sorry for me as well. Hugh
and Jimmy despised them for it. So we went on
plundering them, wolfing their food and drinks, and
smoking their cigars like ruffians. Oh, they enjoyed
themselves.

HELENA: Apparently.

ALISON: Hugh fairly revelled in the role of the barbarian invader. Sometimes I thought he might even
dress the part—you know, furs, spiked helmet,
sword. He even got a fiver out of Old Man Wain
once. Blackmail, of course. People would have signed
almost anything to get rid of us. He told him that

we were about to be turned out of our flat for not paying the rent. At least it was true.

HELENA: I don't understand you. You must have been crazy.

ALISON: Afraid more than anything.

HELENA: But letting them do it! Letting them get away with it! You managed to stop them stealing the silver, I suppose?

ALISON: Oh, they knew their guerrilla warfare better than that. Hugh tried to seduce some fresh-faced young girl at the Arksdens' once, but that was the only time we were more or less turned out.

HELENA: It's almost unbelievable. I don't understand your part in it all. Why? That's what I don't see. Why did you——

ALISON: Marry him? There must be about six different answers. When the family came back from India, everything seemed, I don't know—unsettled? Anyway, Daddy seemed remote and rather irritable. And Mummy—well, you know Mummy. I didn't have much to worry about. I didn't know I was born as Jimmy says. I met him at a party. I remember it so clearly. I was almost twenty-one. The men there all looked as though they distrusted him, and as for the women, they were all intent on showing their contempt for this rather odd creature, but no one seemed quite sure how to do it. He'd come to the party on a bicycle, he told me, and there was oil all over his dinner jacket. It had been such a lovely day, and he'd been in the sun. Everything about him seemed to burn, his face, the edges of his hair glistened and seemed to spring off his head, and his eyes were so blue and full of the sun. He looked so young and frail, in spite of the tired line of his mouth. I knew I was taking on more than I was ever likely to be capable of bearing, but there never seemed to be any choice. Well, the howl of outrage and astonishment went up from the family, and that did it. Whether or no he was in love with me, that did it. He made up his mind to marry me. They did just about everything they could think of to stop us.

HELENA: Yes, it wasn't a very pleasant business. But you can see their point.

ALISON: Jimmy went into battle with his axe swinging round his head—frail, and so full of fire. I had never seen anything like it. The old story of the knight in shining armour—except that his armour didn't really shine very much.

HELENA: And what about Hugh?

ALISON: Things got steadily worse between us. He and Jimmy even went to some of Nigel's political meetings. They took bunches of their Poplar cronies with them, and broke them up for him.

HELENA: He's really a savage, isn't he?

ALISON: Well, Hugh was writing some novel or other, and he made up his mind he must go abroad—to China, or some God-forsaken place. He said that England was finished for us anyway. All the old gang was back—Dame Alison's Mob, as he used to call it. The only real hope was to get out, and try somewhere else. He wanted us to go with him, but Jimmy refused to go. There was a terrible, bitter row over it. Jimmy accused Hugh of giving up, and he thought it was wrong of him to go off forever, and leave his mother all on her own. He was upset by the whole idea. They quarrelled for days over it. I almost wished they'd both go, and leave me behind. Anyway, they broke up. A few months later we came up here, and Hugh went off to find the New Millennium on his own. Sometimes, I think Hugh's mother blames me for it all. Jimmy too, in a way, although he's never said so. He never mentions it. But whenever that woman looks at me, I can feel her thinking "If it hadn't been for you, everything would have been all right. We'd have all been happy." Not that I dislike her—I don't. She's very sweet, in fact. Jimmy seems to adore her principally because she's been poor almost all her life, and she's frankly ignorant. I'm quite aware how snobbish that sounds, but it happens to be the truth.

HELENA: Alison, listen to me. You've got to make up your mind what you're going to do. You're going to have a baby, and you have a new responsibility. Before, it was different—there was only yourself at stake. But you can't go on living in this way any longer. (*To her.*)

ALISON: I'm so tired. I dread him coming into the room.

HELENA: Why haven't you told him you're going to have a child?

ALISON: I don't know. (*Suddenly anticipating Helena's train of thought.*) Oh, it's his all right. There couldn't be any doubt of that. You see—— (*she smiles*). I've never really wanted anyone else.

HELENA: Listen, darling—you've got to tell him. Either he learns to behave like anyone else, and looks after you——

ALISON: Or?

HELENA: Or you must get out of this mad-house. (*Trumpet crescendo.*) This menagerie. He doesn't seem to know what love or anything else means.

ALISON: (*pointing to chest of drawers up R.*). You see that bear, and that squirrel? Well, that's him, and that's me.

HELENA: Meaning?

ALISON: The game we play: bears and squirrels, squirrels and bears.

Helena looks rather blank.

Yes, it's quite mad, I know. Quite mad. (*Picks up the two animals.*) That's him. . . . And that's me. . . .

HELENA: I didn't realise he was a bit fey, as well as everything else!

ALISON: Oh, there's nothing fey about Jimmy. It's just all we seem to have left. Or had left. Even bears and squirrels seem to have gone their own ways now.

HELENA: Since I arrived?

ALISON: It started during those first months we had alone together—after Hugh went abroad. It was the

one way of escaping from everything—a sort of un-
holy priest-hole of being animals to one another.
We could become little furry creatures with little
furry brains. Full of dumb, uncomplicated affection
for each other. Playful, careless creatures in their
own cosy zoo for two. A silly symphony for people
who couldn't bear the pain of being human beings
any longer. And now, even they are dead, poor little
silly animals. They were all love, and no brains.
(*Puts them back.*)

HELENA: (*gripping her arm*). Listen to me. You've got
to fight him. Fight, or get out. Otherwise, he *will* kill
you.
Enter Cliff.

CLIFF: There you are, dullin'. Hullo, Helena. Tea
ready?

ALISON: Yes, dear, it's all ready. Give Jimmy a call,
will you?

CLIFF: Right. (*Yelling back through door.*) Hey, you
horrible man! Stop that bloody noise, and come and
get your tea! (*Coming in C.*) Going out?

HELENA: (*crossing to L.*). Yes.

CLIFF: Pictures?

HELENA: No. (*Pause.*) Church.

CLIFF: (*really surprised*). Oh! I see. Both of you?

HELENA: Yes. Are you coming?

CLIFF: Well. . . . I—I haven't read the papers properly
yet. Tea, tea, tea! Let's have some tea, shall we?
*He sits at the upstage end of the table. Helena puts
the four plates of salad on it, sits down L., and they
begin the meal. Alison is making up her face at her
dressing table. Presently, Jimmy enters. He places his
trumpet on the bookcase, and comes above the table.*
Hullo, boyo. Come and have your tea. That blinkin'
trumpet—why don't you stuff it away somewhere?

JIMMY: You like it all right. Anyone who doesn't like
real jazz, hasn't any feeling either for music or
people.
He sits R. end of table.

HELENA: Rubbish.

JIMMY: (*to Cliff*). That seems to prove my point fo
    you. Did you know that Webster played the banjo'

CLIFF: No, does he really?

HELENA: He said he'd bring it along next time he came

ALISON: (*muttering*). Oh, no!

JIMMY: Why is it that nobody knows how to treat th
    papers in this place? Look at them. I haven't eve
    glanced at them yet—not the posh ones, anyway.

CLIFF: By the way, can I look at your *New*——

JIMMY: No, you can't! (*Loudly.*) You want anything
    you pay for it. Like I have to. Price——

CLIFF: Price ninepence, obtainable from any book
    stall! You're a mean old man, that's what you are.

JIMMY: What do you want to read it for, anyway'
    You've no intellect, no curiosity. It all just washe
    over you. Am I right?

CLIFF: Right.

JIMMY: What are you, you Welsh trash?

CLIFF: Nothing, that's what I am.

JIMMY: Nothing are you? Blimey you ought to be
    Prime Minister. You must have been talking to som
    of my wife's friends. They're a very intellectual set
    aren't they? I've seen 'em.
    Cliff and Helena carry on with their meal.
    They all sit around feeling very spiritual, with thei
    mental hands on each other's knees, discussing sex a
    if it were the Art of Fugue. If you don't want to be
    an emotional old spinster, just you listen to your dad
    *He starts eating. The silent hostility of the two
    women has set him off on the scent, and he looks
    quite cheerful, although the occasional, thick edge of
    his voice belies it.*
    You know your trouble, son? Too anxious to please.

HELENA: Thank heavens somebody is!

JIMMY: You'll end up like one of those chocolate
    meringues my wife is so fond of. My wife—that's the
    one on the tom-toms behind me. Sweet and sticky
    on the outside, and sink your teeth in it, (*savouring*

every word) inside, all white, messy and disgusting. (*Offering teapot sweetly to Helena.*) Tea?

HELENA: Thank you.

He smiles, and pours out a cup for her.

JIMMY: That's how you'll end up, my boy—black hearted, evil minded and vicious.

HELENA: (*taking cup*). Thank you.

JIMMY: And those old favourites, your friends and mine: sycophantic, phlegmatic, and, of course, top of the bill—pusillanimous.

HELENA: (*to Alison*). Aren't you going to have your tea?

ALISON: Won't be long.

JIMMY: Thought of the title for a new song today. It's called "You can quit hanging round my counter Mildred 'cos you'll find my position is closed". (*Turning to Alison suddenly.*) Good?

ALISON: Oh, very good.

JIMMY: Thought you'd like it. If I can slip in a religious angle, it should be a big hit. (*To Helena.*) Don't you think so? I was thinking you might help me there. (*She doesn't reply.*) It might help you if I recite the lyrics. Let's see now, it's something like this:

> I'm so tired of necking,
> of pecking, home wrecking,
> of empty bed blues—
> just pass me the booze.
> I'm tired of being hetero
> Rather ride on the metero
> Just pass me the booze.
> This perpetual whoring
> Gets quite dull and boring
> So avoid that old python coil
> And pass me the celibate oil.
> You can quit etc.

No?

CLIFF: Very good, boyo.

JIMMY: Oh, yes, and I know what I meant to tell you

—I wrote a poem while I was at the market yester
day. If you're interested, which you obviously are
(*To Helena.*) It should appeal to you, in particular
It's soaked in the theology of Dante, with a good
slosh of Eliot as well. It starts off "There are no dry
cleaners in Cambodia!"

CLIFF: What do you call it?

JIMMY: "The Cess Pool". Myself being a stone
dropped in it, you see——

CLIFF: You should be dropped in it, all right.

HELENA: (*to Jimmy*). Why do you try so hard to be
unpleasant?

*He turns very deliberately, delighted that she should
rise to the bait so soon—he's scarcely in his stride
yet.*

JIMMY: What's that?

HELENA: Do you have to be so offensive?

JIMMY: You mean now? You think I'm being offen
sive? You under-estimate me. (*Turning to Alison.*)
Doesn't she?

HELENA: I think you're a very tiresome young man.

*A slight pause as his delight catches up with him.
He roars with laughter.*

JIMMY: Oh dear, oh dear! My wife's friends! Pass
Lady Bracknell the cucumber sandwiches, will you
*He returns to his meal, but his curiosity about Ali
son's preparations at the mirror won't be denied an*
longer. He turns round casually, and speaks to her.
Going out?

ALISON: That's right.

JIMMY: On a Sunday evening in this town? Where on
earth are you going?

ALISON: (*rising*). I'm going out with Helena.

JIMMY: That's not a direction—that's an affliction.
*She crosses to the table, and sits down C. He leans
forward, and addresses her again.*
I didn't ask you what was the matter with you.
asked you where you were going.

HELENA: (*steadily*). She's going to church.

He has been prepared for some plot, but he is as genuinely surprised by this as Cliff was a few minutes earlier.

JIMMY: You're doing what?

Silence.

Have you gone out of your mind or something? (*To Helena.*) You're determined to win her, aren't you? So it's come to this now! How feeble can you get? (*His rage mounting within.*) When I think of what I did, what I endured, to get you out——

ALISON: (*recognising an onslaught on the way, starts to panic*). Oh yes, we all know what you did for me! You rescued me from the wicked clutches of my family, and all my friends! I'd still be rotting away at home, if you hadn't ridden up on your charger, and carried me off!

The wild note in her voice has re-assured him. His anger cools and hardens. His voice is quite calm when he speaks.

JIMMY: The funny thing is, you know, I really did have to ride up on a white charger—off white, really. Mummy locked her up in their eight bedroomed castle, didn't she. There is no limit to what the middle-aged mummy will do in the holy crusade against ruffians like me. Mummy and I took one quick look at each other, and, from then on, the age of chivalry was dead. I knew that, to protect her innocent young, she wouldn't hesitate to cheat, lie, bully and blackmail. Threatened with me, a young man without money, background or even looks, she'd bellow like a rhinoceros in labour—enough to make every male rhino for miles turn white, and pledge himself to celibacy. But even I under-estimated her strength. Mummy may look over-fed and a bit flabby on the outside, but don't let that well-bred guzzler fool you. Underneath all that, she's armour plated——

He clutches wildly for something to shock Helena with.

She's as rough as a night in a Bombay brothel, and

as tough as a matelot's arms. She's probably in that
bloody cistern, taking down every word we say.
(*Kicks cistern.*) Can you 'ear me, mother. (*Sits on
it, beats like bongo drums.*) Just about get her in
there. Let me give you an example of this lady's
tactics. You may have noticed that I happen to wear
my hair rather long. Now, if my wife is honest, or
concerned enough to explain, she could tell you that
this is not due to any dark, unnatural instincts I pos-
sess, but because (a) I can usually think of better
things than a haircut to spend two bob on, and (b)
I prefer long hair. But that obvious, innocent explanation didn't appeal to Mummy at all. So she hires
detectives to watch me, to see if she can't somehow
get me into the *News of the World*. All so that I
shan't carry off her daughter on that poor old charger
of mine, all tricked out and caparisoned in discred-
ited passions and ideals! The old grey mare that actually once led the charge against the old order—
well, she certainly ain't what she used to be. It was
all she could do to carry me, but your weight (*to
Alison*) was too much for her. She just dropped dead
on the way.

CLIFF: (*quietly*). Don't let's brawl, boyo. It won't do
any good.

JIMMY: Why *don't* we brawl? It's the only thing left
I'm any good at.

CLIFF: Jimmy, boy——

JIMMY: (*to Alison*). You've let this genuflecting sin
jobber win you over, haven't you? She's got you
back, hasn't she?

HELENA: Oh for heaven's sake, don't be such a bully!
You've no right to talk about her mother like that!

JIMMY: (*capable of anything now*). I've got every
right. That old bitch should be dead! (*To Alison.*)
Well? Aren't I right?

*Cliff and Helena look at Alison tensely, but she just
gazes at her plate.*

I said she's an old bitch, and should be dead! What's

the matter with you? Why don't you leap to her defence!

Cliff gets up quickly, and takes his arm.

CLIFF: Jimmy, don't!

*Jimmy pushes him back savagely, and he sits down
helplessly, turning his head away on to his hand.*

JIMMY: If someone said something like that about me,
she'd react soon enough—she'd spring into her well
known lethargy, and say nothing! I say she ought to
be dead. (*He brakes for a fresh spurt later. He's
saving his strength for the knock-out.*) My God,
those worms will need a dose of salts the day they get
through her! Oh what a bellyache you've got coming
to you, my little wormy ones! Alison's mother is on
the way! (*In what he intends to be a comic declama-
tory voice.*) She will pass away, my friends, leaving
a trail of worms gasping for laxatives behind her—
from purgatives to purgatory.

*He smiles down at Alison, but still she hasn't broken.
Cliff won't look at them. Only Helena looks at him.
Denied the other two, he addresses her.*

Is anything the matter?

HELENA: I feel rather sick, that's all. Sick with contempt and loathing.

*He can feel her struggling on the end of his line,
and he looks at her rather absently.*

JIMMY: One day, when I'm no longer spending my
days running a sweet-stall, I may write a book about
us all. It's all here. (*Slapping his forehead.*) Written
in flames a mile high. And it won't be recollected in
tranquillity either, picking daffodils with Auntie
Wordsworth. It'll be recollected in fire, and blood.
My blood.

HELENA: (*thinking patient reasonableness may be
worth a try*). She simply said that she's going to
church with me. I don't see why that calls for this
incredible outburst.

JIMMY: Don't you? Perhaps you're not as clever as I
thought.

HELENA: You think the world's treated you pretty badly, don't you?

ALISON: (*turning her face away L.*). Oh, don't try and take his suffering away from him—he'd be lost without it.

He looks at her in surprise, but he turns back to Helena. Alison can have her turn again later.

JIMMY: I thought this play you're touring in finished up on Saturday week?

HELENA: That's right.

JIMMY: Eight days ago, in fact.

HELENA: Alison wanted me to stay.

JIMMY: What are you plotting?

HELENA: Don't you think we've had enough of the heavy villain?

JIMMY: (*to Alison*). You don't believe in all that stuff. Why you don't believe in anything. You're just doing it to be vindictive, aren't you? Why—why are you letting her influence you like this?

ALISON: (*starting to break*). Why, why, why, why! (*Putting her hands over her ears.*) That word's pulling my head off!

JIMMY: And as long as you're around, I'll go on using it.

He crosses down to the armchair, and seats himself on the back of it. He addresses Helena's back.

JIMMY: The last time she was in a church was when she was married to me. I expect that surprises you, doesn't it? It was expediency, pure and simple. We were in a hurry, you see. (*The comedy of this strikes him at once, and he laughs.*) Yes, we were actually in a hurry! Lusting for the slaughter! Well, the local registrar was a particular pal of Daddy's, and we knew he'd spill the beans to the Colonel like a shot. So we had to seek out some local vicar who didn't know him quite so well. But it was no use. When my best man—a chap I'd met in the pub that morning— and I turned up, Mummy and Daddy were in the church already. They'd found out at the last moment, and had come to watch the execution carried out. How I remember looking down at them, full of beer for breakfast, and feeling a bit buzzed. Mummy was slumped over her pew in a heap—the noble, female rhino, pole-axed at last! And Daddy sat beside her, upright and unafraid, dreaming of his days among the Indian Princes, and unable to believe he'd left his horsewhip at home. Just the two of them in that empty church—them and me. (*Coming out of his remembrance suddenly*.) I'm not sure what happened after that. We must have been married, I suppose. I think I remember being sick in the vestry. (*To Alison*.) Was I?

HELENA: Haven't you finished?

He can smell blood again, and he goes on calmly, cheerfully.

JIMMY: (*to Alison*). Are you going to let yourself be taken in by this saint in Dior's clothing? I will tell you the simple truth about her. (*Articulating with care*.) She is a cow. I wouldn't mind that so much, but she seems to have become a sacred cow as well!

CLIFF: You've gone too far, Jimmy. Now dry up!

HELENA: Oh, let him go on.

JIMMY: (*to Cliff*). I suppose you're going over to that side as well. Well, why don't you? Helena will help to make it pay off for you. She's an expert in the New Economics—the Economics of the Supernatural. It's all a simple matter of payments and penalties. (*Rises*.) She's one of those apocalyptic share pushers who are spreading all those rumours about a transfer of power.

His imagination is racing, and the words pour out.

Reason and Progress, the old firm, is selling out! Everyone get out while the going's good. Those forgotten shares you had in the old traditions, the old beliefs are going up—up and up and up. (*Moves up L.*) There's going to be a change over. A new Board of Directors, who are going to see that the dividends are always attractive, and that they go to the right

people. (*Facing them.*) Sell out everything you've
got: all those stocks in the old, free inquiry. (*Crosses
to above table.*) The Big Crash is coming, you can't
escape it, so get in on the ground floor with Helena
and her friends while there's still time. And there
isn't much of it left. Tell me, what could be more gilt-
edged than the next world! It's a capital gain, and
it's all yours.

He moves round the table, back to his chair R.

You see, I know Helena and her kind so very well.
In fact, her kind are everywhere, you can't move for
them. They're a romantic lot. They spend their time
mostly looking forward to the past. The only place
they can see the light is the Dark Ages. She's moved
long ago into a lovely little cottage of the soul, cut
right off from the ugly problems of the twentieth century altogether. She prefers to be cut off from all the
conveniences we've fought to get for centuries. She'd
rather go down to the ecstatic little shed at the bot-
tom of the garden to relieve her sense of guilt. Our
Helena is full of ecstatic wind—(*he leans across the
table at her*) aren't you?

He waits for her to reply.

HELENA: (*quite calmly*). It's a pity you've been so far
away all this time. I would probably have slapped
your face.

*They look into each other's eyes across the table. He
moves slowly up, above Cliff, until he is beside her.*

You've behaved like this ever since I first came.

JIMMY: Helena, have you ever watched somebody die?

She makes a move to rise.

No, don't move away.

She remains seated, and looks up at him.

It doesn't look dignified enough for you.

HELENA: (*like ice*). If you come any nearer, I will slap
your face.

*He looks down at her, a grin smouldering round his
mouth.*

JIMMY: I hope you won't make the mistake of thinking for one moment that I am a gentleman.

HELENA: I'm not very likely to do that.

JIMMY: (*bringing his face close to hers*). I've no public school scruples about hitting girls. (*Gently.*) If
you slap my face—by God, I'll lay you out!

HELENA: You probably would. You're the type.

JIMMY: You bet I'm the type. I'm the type that detests
physical violence. Which is why, if I find some woman trying to cash in on what she thinks is my defence-
less chivalry by lashing out with her frail little fists, I
lash back at her.

HELENA: Is that meant to be subtle, or just plain Irish?
His grin widens.

JIMMY: I think you and I understand one another all
right. But you haven't answered my question. I said:
have you watched somebody die?

HELENA: No, I haven't.

JIMMY: Anyone who's never watched somebody die
is suffering from a pretty bad case of virginity.
*His good humour of a moment ago deserts him, as
he begins to remember.*
For twelve months, I watched my father dying—
when I was ten years old. He'd come back from the
war in Spain, you see. And certain god-fearing gentlemen there had made such a mess of him, he didn't
have long left to live. Everyone knew it—even I knew
it.
He moves R.
But, you see, I was the only one who cared. (*Turns
to the window.*) His family were embarrassed by the
whole business. Embarrassed and irritated. (*Looking out.*) As for my mother, all she could think about
was the fact that she had allied herself to a man who
seemed to be on the wrong side in all things. My
mother was all for being associated with minorities,
provided they were the smart, fashionable ones.
He moves up C. again.

We all of us waited for him to die. The family sent him a cheque every month, and hoped he'd get on with it quietly, without too much vulgar fuss. My mother looked after him without complaining, and that was about all. Perhaps she pitied him. I suppose she was capable of that. (*With a kind of appeal in his voice.*) But *I* was the only one who cared!

He moves L., behind the armchair.

Every time I sat on the edge of his bed, to listen to him talking or reading to me, I had to fight back my tears. At the end of twelve months, I was a veteran.

He leans forward on the back of the armchair.

All that that feverish failure of a man had to listen to him was a small, frightened boy. I spent hour upon hour in that tiny bedroom. He would talk to me for hours, pouring out all that was left of his life to one, lonely, bewildered little boy, who could barely understand half of what he said. All he could feel was the despair and the bitterness, the sweet, sickly smell of a dying man.

He moves around the chair.

You see, I learnt at an early age what it was to be angry—angry and helpless. And I can never forget it. (*Sits.*) I knew more about—love . . . betrayal . . . and death, when I was ten years old than you will probably ever know all your life.

They all sit silently. Presently, Helena rises.

HELENA: Time we went.

Alison nods.

I'll just get my things together. (*Crosses to door.*) I'll see you downstairs.

EXIT.

A slight pause.

JIMMY: (*not looking at her, almost whispering*). Doesn't it matter to you—what people do to me? What are you trying to do to me? I've given you just everything. Doesn't it mean *anything* to you?

Her back stiffens. His axe-swinging bravado has vanished, and his voice crumples in disabled rage.

You Judas! You phlegm! She's taking you with her, and you're so bloody feeble, you'll let her do it!

Alison suddenly takes hold of her cup, and hurls it on the floor. He's drawn blood at last. She looks down at the pieces on the floor, and then at him. Then she crosses, R., takes out a dress on a hanger, and slips it on. As she is zipping up the side, she feels giddy, and she has to lean against the wardrobe for support. She closes her eyes.

ALISON: (*softly*). All I want is a little peace.

JIMMY: Peace! God! She wants peace! (*Hardly able to get his words out.*) My heart is so full, I feel ill— and she wants peace!

She crosses to the bed to put on her shoes. Cliff gets up from the table, and sits in the armchair R. He picks up a paper, and looks at that. Jimmy has recovered slightly, and manages to sound almost detached.

I rage, and shout my head off, and everyone thinks "poor chap!" or "what an objectionable young man!" But that girl there can twist your arm off with her silence. I've sat in this chair in the dark for hours. And, although she knows I'm feeling as I feel now, she's turned over, and gone to sleep. (*He gets up and faces Cliff, who doesn't look up from his paper.*) One of us is crazy. One of us is mean and stupid and crazy. Which is it? Is it me? Is it me, standing here like an hysterical girl, hardly able to get my words out? Or is it her? Sitting there, putting on her shoes to go out with that—— (*But inspiration has deserted him by now.*) Which is it?

Cliff is still looking down at his paper.

I wish to heaven you'd try loving her, that's all.

He moves up C., watching her look for her gloves.

Perhaps, one day, you may want to come back. I shall wait for that day. I want to stand up in your tears, and splash about in them, and sing. I want to be there when you grovel. I want to be there, I want to watch it, I want the front seat.

Helena enters, carrying two prayer books.

I want to see your face rubbed in the mud—that's all I can hope for. There's nothing else I want any longer.

HELENA: (*after a moment*). There's a 'phone call for you.

JIMMY: (*turning*). Well, it can't be anything good, can it?

HE GOES OUT.

HELENA: All ready?

ALISON: Yes—I think so.

HELENA: You feel all right, don't you? (*She nods.*). What's he been raving about now? Oh, what does it matter? He makes me want to claw his hair out by the roots. When I think of what you will be going through in a few months' time—and all for him! It's as if you'd done *him* wrong! These *men*! (*Turning on Cliff.*) And all the time you just sit there, and do nothing!

CLIFF: (*looking up slowly*). That's right—I just sit here.

HELENA: What's the matter with you? What sort of a man are you?

CLIFF: I'm not the District Commissioner, you know. Listen, Helena—I don't feel like Jimmy does about you, but I'm not exactly on your side either. And since you've been here, everything's certainly been worse than it's ever been. This has always been a battlefield, but I'm pretty certain that if I hadn't been here, everything would have been over between these two long ago. I've been a—a no-man's land between them. Sometimes, it's been still and peaceful, no incidents, and we've all been reasonably happy. But most of the time, it's simply a very narrow strip of plain hell. But where I come from, we're used to brawling and excitement. Perhaps I even enjoy being in the thick of it. I love these two people very much. (*He looks at her steadily, and adds simply*) And I pity all of us.

HELENA: Are you including me in that? (*But she goes on quickly to avoid his reply.*) I don't understand him, you or any of it. All I know is that none of you seems to know how to behave in a decent, civilised way. (*In command now.*) Listen, Alison—I've sent your father a wire.

ALISON: (*numbed and vague by now*). Oh!

Helena looks at her, and realizes quickly that everything now will have to depend on her own authority. She tries to explain patiently.

HELENA: Look, dear—he'll get it first thing in the morning. I thought it would be better than trying to explain the situation over the 'phone. I asked him to come up, and fetch you home tomorrow.

ALISON: What did you say?

HELENA: Simply that you wanted to come home, and would he come up for you.

ALISON: I see.

HELENA: I knew that would be quite enough. I told him there was nothing to worry about, so they won't worry and think there's been an accident or anything. I had to do something, dear. (*Very gently.*) You didn't mind, did you?

ALISON: No, I don't mind. Thank you.

HELENA: And you will go when he comes for you?

ALISON: (*Pause.*) Yes. I'll go.

HELENA: (*relieved*). I expect he'll drive up. He should be here about tea-time. It'll give you plenty of time to get your things together. And, perhaps, after you've gone—Jimmy (*saying the word almost with difficulty*) will come to his senses, and face up to things.

ALISON: Who was on the 'phone?

HELENA: I didn't catch it properly. It rang after I'd sent the wire off—just as soon as I put the receiver down almost. I had to go back down the stairs again. Sister somebody, I think.

ALISON: Must have been a hospital or something. Unless he knows someone in a convent—*that* doesn't seem very likely, does it? Well, we'll be late, if we don't hurry. (*She puts down one of the prayer books on the table.*)

Enter Jimmy. He comes down C., between the two women.

CLIFF: All right, boyo?

JIMMY: (*to Alison*). It's Hugh's mum. She's—had a stroke.

Slight pause.

ALISON: I'm sorry.

Jimmy sits on the bed.

CLIFF: How bad is it?

JIMMY: They didn't say much. But I think she's dying.

CLIFF: Oh dear. . . .

JIMMY: (*rubbing his fist over his face*). It doesn't make any sense at all. Do you think it does?

ALISON: I'm sorry—I really am.

CLIFF: Anything I can do?

JIMMY: The London train goes in half an hour. You'd better order me a taxi.

CLIFF: Right. (*He crosses to the door, and stops.*) Do you want me to come with you, boy?

JIMMY: No thanks. After all, you hardly knew her. It's not for you to go.

Helena looks quickly at Alison.

She may not even remember me, for all I know.

CLIFF: O.K.

EXIT.

JIMMY: I remember the first time I showed her your photograph—just after we were married. She looked at it, and the tears just welled up in her eyes, and she said: "But she's so beautiful! She's so beautiful!" She kept repeating it as if she couldn't believe it. Sounds a bit simple and sentimental when you repeat it. But it was pure gold the way she said it.

He looks at her. She is standing by the dressing table, her back to him.

She got a kick out of you, like she did out of everything else. Hand me my shoes, will you?

She kneels down, and hands them to him. (looking down at his feet.) You're coming with me, aren't you? She *(he shrugs)* hasn't got anyone else now. I . . . need you . . . to come with me.

He looks into her eyes, but she turns away, and stands up. Outside, the church bells start ringing. Helena moves up to the door, and waits watching them closely. Alison stands quite still, Jimmy's eyes burning into her. Then, she crosses in front of him to the table where she picks up the prayer book, her back to him. She wavers, and seems about to say something, but turns upstage instead, and walks quickly to the door.

ALISON: *(hardly audible)*. Let's go.

She goes out, Helena following. Jimmy gets up, looks about him unbelievingly, and leans against the chest of drawers. The teddy bear is close to his face, and he picks it up gently, looks at it quickly, and throws it downstage. It hits the floor with a thud, and it makes a rattling, groaning sound—as guaranteed in the advertisement. Jimmy falls forward on to the bed, his face buried in the covers.

QUICK CURTAIN

END OF SCENE ONE

ACT II

ACT II

SCENE TWO

The following evening. When the curtain rises, ALI-
SON is discovered R., going from her dressing table
to the bed, and packing her things into a suitcase.
Sitting down L. is her father, COLONEL REDFERN, a
large handsome man, about sixty. Forty years of
being a soldier sometimes conceals the essentially
gentle, kindly man underneath. Brought up to command respect, he is often slightly withdrawn and uneasy now that he finds himself in a world where his
authority has lately become less and less unquestion-
able. His wife would relish the present situation, but
he is only disturbed and bewildered by it. He looks
around him, discreetly scrutinising everything.

COLONEL: (*partly to himself*). I'm afraid it's all be-
yond me. I suppose it always will be. As for Jimmy
—he just speaks a different language from any of us.
Where did you say he'd gone?
ALISON: He's gone to see Mrs. Tanner.
COLONEL: Who?
ALISON: Hugh Tanner's mother.
COLONEL: Oh, I see.
ALISON: She's been taken ill—a stroke. Hugh's abroad,
as you know, so Jimmy's gone to London to see her.
He nods.
He wanted me to go with him.
COLONEL: Didn't she start him off in this sweet-stall
business?
ALISON: Yes.
COLONEL: What is she like? Nothing like her son, I
trust?

64

ALISON: Not remotely. Oh—how can you describe her? Rather—ordinary. What Jimmy insists on calling working class. A charwoman who married an actor, worked hard all her life, and spent most of it struggling to support her husband and her son. Jimmy and she are very fond of each other.

COLONEL: So you didn't go with him?

ALISON: No.

COLONEL: Who's looking after the sweet-stall?

ALISON: Cliff. He should be in soon.

COLONEL: Oh yes, of course——Cliff. Does he live here too?

ALISON: Yes. His room is just across the landing.

COLONEL: Sweet-stall. It does seem an extraordinary thing for an educated young man to be occupying himself with. Why should he want to do that, of all things. I've always thought he must be quite clever in his way.

ALISON: (*no longer interested in this problem*). Oh, he tried so many things—journalism, advertising, even vacuum cleaners for a few weeks. He seems to have been as happy doing this as anything else.

COLONEL: I've often wondered what it was like—where you were living, I mean. You didn't tell us very much in your letters.

ALISON: There wasn't a great deal to tell you. There's not much social life here.

COLONEL: Oh, I know what you mean. You were afraid of being disloyal to your husband.

ALISON: Disloyal! (*She laughs.*) He thought it was high treason of me to write to you at all! I used to have to dodge downstairs for the post, so that he wouldn't see I was getting letters from home. Even then I had to hide them.

COLONEL: He really does hate us doesn't he?

ALISON: Oh yes—don't have any doubts about that. He hates all of us.

COLONEL: (*sighs*). It seems a great pity. It was all so unfortunate—unfortunate and unnecessary. I'm afraid I can't help feeling that he must have had a certain amount of right on his side.

ALISON: (*puzzled by this admission*). Right on his side?

COLONEL: It's a little late to admit it, I know, but your mother and I weren't entirely free from blame. I have never said anything—there was no point afterwards—but I have always believed that she went too far over Jimmy. Of course, she was extremely upset at the time—we both were—and that explains a good deal of what happened. I did my best to stop her, but she was in such a state of mind, there was simply nothing I could do. She seemed to have made up her mind that if he was going to marry you, he must be a criminal, at the very least. All those inquiries, the private detectives—the accusations. I hated every moment of it.

ALISON: I suppose she was trying to protect me—in a rather heavy-handed way, admittedly.

COLONEL: I must confess I find that kind of thing rather horrifying. Anyway, I try to think now that it never happened. I didn't approve of Jimmy at all, and I don't suppose I ever should, but, looking back on it, I think it would have been better, for all concerned, if we had never attempted to interfere. At least, it would have been a little more dignified.

ALISON: It wasn't your fault.

COLONEL: I don't know. We were all to blame, in our different ways. No doubt Jimmy acted in good faith. He's honest enough, whatever else he may be. And your mother—in her heavy-handed way, as you put it—acted in good faith as well. Perhaps you and I were the ones most to blame.

ALISON: You and I!

COLONEL: I think you may take after me a little, my dear. You like to sit on the fence because it's comfortable and more peaceful.

ALISON: Sitting on the fence! I married him, didn't I.

COLONEL: Oh yes, you did.

ALISON: In spite of all the humiliating scenes and the threats! What did you say to me at the time? Wasn't I letting you down, turning against you, how could I do this to you etcetera?

COLONEL: Perhaps it might have been better if you hadn't written letters to us—knowing how we felt about your husband, and after everything that had happened. (*He looks at her uncomfortably.*) Forgive me, I'm a little confused, what with everything— the telegram, driving up here suddenly. . . .

He trails off rather helplessly. He looks tired. He glances at her nervously, a hint of accusation in his eyes, as if he expected her to defend herself further. She senses this, and is more confused than ever.

ALISON: Do you know what he said about Mummy? He said she was an overfed, overprivileged old bitch. "A good blow-out for the worms" was his expression, I think.

COLONEL: I see. And what does he say about me?

ALISON: Oh, he doesn't seem to mind you so much. In fact, I think he rather likes you. He likes you because he can feel sorry for you. (*Conscious that what she says is going to hurt him.*) "Poor old Daddy— just one of those sturdy old plants left over from the Edwardian Wilderness that can't understand why the sun isn't shining any more." (*Rather lamely.*) Something like that, anyway.

COLONEL: He has quite a turn of phrase, hasn't he? (*Simply, and without malice.*) Why did you ever have to meet this young man?

ALISON: Oh, Daddy, please don't put me on trial now. I've been on trial every day and night of my life for nearly four years.

COLONEL: But why should he have married you, feeling as he did about everything?

ALISON: That is the famous American question—you know, the sixty-four dollar one! Perhaps it was revenge.

He looks up uncomprehendingly.

Oh yes. Some people do actually marry for revenge. People like Jimmy, anyway. Or perhaps he should have been another Shelley, and can't understand now why I'm not another Mary, and you're not William Godwin. He thinks he's got a sort of genius for love and friendship—on his own terms. Well, for twenty years, I'd lived a happy, uncomplicated life, and suddenly, this—this spiritual barbarian—throws down the gauntlet at me. Perhaps only another woman could understand what a challenge like that means— although I think Helena was as mystified as you are.

COLONEL: I am mystified. (*He rises, and crosses to the window R.*) Your husband has obviously taught you a great deal, whether you realise it or not. What any of it means, I don't know. I always believed that people married each other because they were in love. That always seemed a good enough reason to me. But apparently, that's too simple for young people nowadays. They have to talk about challenges and revenge. I just can't believe that love between men and women is really like that.

ALISON: Only some men and women.

COLONEL: But why you? My daughter. . . . No. Perhaps Jimmy is right. Perhaps I am a—what was it? an old plant left over from the Edwardian Wilderness. And I can't understand why the sun isn't shining any more. You can see what he means, can't you? It was March, 1914, when I left England, and, apart from leaves every ten years or so, I didn't see much of my own country until we all came back in '47. Oh, I knew things had changed, of course. People told you all the time the way it was going—going to the dogs, as the Blimps are supposed to say. But it seemed very unreal to me, out there. The England I remembered was the one I left in 1914, and I was happy to go on remembering it that way. Besides, I had the Maharajah's army to command—that was my world, and I loved it, all of it. At the time, it looked like going on forever. When I think of it now,

it seems like a dream. If only it could have gone on
forever. Those long, cool evenings up in the hills,
everything purple and golden. Your mother and I
were so happy then. It seemed as though we had
everything we could ever want. I think the last day
the sun shone was when that dirty little train steamed
out of that crowded, suffocating Indian station, and
the battalion band playing for all it was worth. I
knew in my heart it was all over then. Everything.

ALISON: You're hurt because everything is changed.
Jimmy is hurt because everything is the same. And
neither of you can face it. Something's gone wrong
somewhere, hasn't it?

COLONEL: It looks like it, my dear.

*She picks up the squirrel from the chest of drawers,
is about to put it in her suitcase, hesitates, and then
puts it back. The Colonel turns and looks at her.
She moves down towards him, her head turned away.
For a few moments, she seems to be standing on the
edge of choice. The choice made, her body wheels
round suddenly, and she is leaning against him,
weeping softly.*

(*presently*). This is a big step you're taking. You've
made up your mind to come back with me? Is that
really what you want?

Enter Helena.

HELENA: I'm sorry. I came in to see if I could help
you pack, Alison. Oh, you look as though you've
finished.

*Alison leaves her father, and moves to the bed, push-
ing down the lid of her suitcase.*

ALISON: All ready.

HELENA: Have you got everything?

ALISON: Well, no. But Cliff can send the rest on sometime, I expect. He should have been back by now.
Oh, of course, he's had to put the stall away on his
own today.

COLONEL: (*crossing and picking up the suitcase*).
Well, I'd better put this in the car then. We may as

well get along. Your mother will be worried, I know.
I promised her I'd ring her when I got here. She's
not very well.

HELENA: I hope my telegram didn't upset her too
much. Perhaps I shouldn't have——

COLONEL: Not at all. We were very grateful that you
did. It was very kind of you, indeed. She tried to
insist on coming with me, but I finally managed to
talk her out of it. I thought it would be best for
everyone. What about your case, Helena? If you
care to tell me where it is, I'll take it down with this
one.

HELENA: I'm afraid I shan't be coming tonight.

ALISON: (*very surprised*). Aren't you coming with us?
Enter Cliff.

HELENA: I'd like to, but the fact is I've an appointment
tomorrow in Birmingham—about a job. They've just
sent me a script. It's rather important, and I don't
want to miss it. So it looks as though I shall have to
stay here tonight.

ALISON: Oh, I see. Hullo, Cliff.

CLIFF: Hullo there.

ALISON: Daddy—this is Cliff.

COLONEL: How do you do, Cliff.

CLIFF: How do you do, sir.
Slight pause.

COLONEL: Well, I'd better put this in the car, hadn't
I? Don't be long, Alison. Good-bye, Helena. I expect
we shall be seeing you again soon, if you're not busy.

HELENA: Oh, yes, I shall be back in a day or two.
Cliff takes off his jacket.

COLONEL: Well, then—good-bye, Cliff.

CLIFF: Good-bye, sir.
*The Colonel goes out. Cliff comes down L. Helena
moves C.*
You're really going then?

ALISON: Really going.

CLIFF: I should think Jimmy would be back pretty
soon. You won't wait?

ALISON: No, Cliff.

CLIFF: Who's going to tell him?

HELENA: I can tell him. That is, if I'm here when he
comes back.

CLIFF: (*quietly*). You'll be here. (*To Alison.*) Don't
you think you ought to tell him yourself?
*She hands him an envelope from her handbag. He
takes it.*
Bit conventional, isn't it?

ALISON: I'm a conventional girl.
He crosses to her, and puts his arms round her.

CLIFF: (*back over his shoulder, to Helena*). I hope
you're right, that's all.

HELENA: What do you mean? You hope *I'm* right?

CLIFF: (*to Alison*). The place is going to be really
cock-eyed now. You know that, don't you?

ALISON: Please, Cliff——
He nods. She kisses him.
I'll write to you later.

CLIFF: Good-bye, lovely.

ALISON: Look after him.

CLIFF: We'll keep the old nut-house going somehow.
*She crosses C., in between the two of them, glances
quickly at the two armchairs, the papers still left
around them from yesterday. Helena kisses her on
the cheek, and squeezes her hand.*

HELENA: See you soon.
*Alison nods, and goes out quickly. Cliff and Helena
are left looking at each other.*
Would you like me to make you some tea?

CLIFF: No, thanks.

HELENA: Think I might have some myself, if you don't
mind.

CLIFF: So you're staying?

HELENA: Just for tonight. Do you object?

CLIFF: Nothing to do with me. (*Against the table C.*)
Of course he may not be back until later on.
She crosses L., to the window, and lights a cigarette.

HELENA: What do you think he'll do? Perhaps he'll

look out one of his old girl friends. What about this Madeline?

CLIFF: What about her?

HELENA: Isn't she supposed to have done a lot for him? Couldn't he go back to her?

CLIFF: I shouldn't think so.

HELENA: What happened?

CLIFF: She was nearly old enough to be his mother. I expect that's something to do with it! Why the hell should I know!

For the first time in the play, his good humour has completely deserted him. She looks surprised.

HELENA: You're his friend, aren't you? Anyway, he's not what you'd call reticent about himself, is he? I've never seen so many souls stripped to the waist since I've been here.

He turns to go.

HELENA: Aren't you staying?

CLIFF: No, I'm not. There was a train in from London about five minutes ago. And, just in case he may have been on it, I'm going out.

HELENA: Don't you think you ought to be here when he comes?

CLIFF: I've had a hard day, and I don't think I want to see anyone hurt until I've had something to eat first, and perhaps a few drinks as well. I think I might pick up some nice, pleasant little tart in a milk bar, and sneak her in past old mother Drury. Here! (*Tossing the letter at her.*) You give it to him! (*Crossing to door.*) He's all yours. (*At door.*) And I hope he rams it up your nostrils!

EXIT.

She crosses to the table, and stubs out her cigarette. The front door downstairs is heard to slam. She moves to the wardrobe, opens it idly. It is empty, except for one dress, swinging on a hanger. She goes over to the dressing table, now cleared but for a framed photograph of Jimmy. Idly, she slams the empty drawers open and shut. She turns upstage to the chest of drawers, picks up the toy bear, and sits on the bed, looking at it. She lays her head back on the pillow, still holding the bear. She looks up quickly as the door crashes open, and Jimmy enters. He stands looking at her, then moves down C., taking off his raincoat, and throwing it over the table. He is almost giddy with anger, and has to steady himself on the chair. He looks up.

JIMMY: That old bastard nearly ran me down in his car! Now, if he'd killed me, that really would have been ironical. And how right and fitting that my wife should have been a passenger. A passenger! What's the matter with everybody? (*Crossing up to her.*) Cliff practically walked into me, coming out of the house. He belted up the other way, and pretended not to see me. Are you the only one who's not afraid to stay?

She hands him Alison's note. He takes it.

Oh, it's one of these, is it? (*He rips it open.*)

He reads a few lines, and almost snorts with disbelief.

Did you write this for her! Well, listen to this then! (*Reading.*) "My dear—I must get away. I don't suppose you will understand, but please try. I need peace so desperately, and, at the moment, I am willing to sacrifice everything just for that. I don't know what's going to happen to us. I know you will be feeling wretched and bitter, but try to be a little patient with me. I shall always have a deep, loving need of you—Alison." Oh, how could she be so bloody wet! Deep loving need! That makes me puke! (*Crossing to R.*) She couldn't say "You rotten bastard! I hate your guts, I'm clearing out, and I hope you rot!" No, she has to make a polite, emotional mess out of it! (*Seeing the dress in the wardrobe, he rips it out, and throws it in the corner up L.*) Deep, loving need! I never thought she was capable of being as phoney as that! What is that—a line from one of those plays you've been in? What are you doing here anyway? You'd better keep out of my way, if you don't want your head kicked in.

HELENA: (*calmly*). If you'll stop thinking about yourself for one moment, I'll tell you something I think you ought to know. Your wife is going to have a baby.

He just looks at her.

Well? Doesn't that mean anything? Even to you?

He is taken aback, but not so much by the news, as by her.

JIMMY: All right—yes. I am surprised. I give you that. But, tell me. Did you honestly expect me to go soggy at the knees, and collapse with remorse! (*Leaning nearer.*) Listen, if you'll stop breathing your female wisdom all over me, I'll tell you something: I don't care. (*Beginning quietly.*) I don't care if she's going to have a baby. I don't care if it has two heads! (*He knows her fingers are itching.*) Do I disgust you? Well, go on—slap my face. But remember what I told you before, will you? For eleven hours, I have been watching someone I love very much going through the sordid process of dying. She was alone, and I was the only one with her. And when I have to walk behind that coffin on Thursday, I'll be on my own again. Because that bitch won't even send her a bunch of flowers—I know! She made the great mistake of all her kind. She thought that because Hugh's mother was a deprived and ignorant old woman, who said all the wrong things in all the wrong places, she couldn't be taken seriously. And you think I should be overcome with awe because that cruel, stupid girl is going to have a baby! (*Anguish in his voice.*) I can't believe it! I can't. (*Grabbing her shoulders.*) Well, the performance is over. Now leave me alone, and *get out,* you evil-minded little virgin.

She slaps his face savagely. An expression of horror and disbelief floods his face. But it drains away, and

*all that is left is pain. His hand goes up to his head,
and a muffled cry of despair escapes him. Helena
tears his hand away, and kisses him passionately,
drawing him down beside her.*

CURTAIN

END OF ACT II

ACT III

SCENE ONE

Several months later. A Sunday evening. ALISON's personal belongings, such as her make-up things on the dressing table, for example, have been replaced by HELENA's.

At rise of curtain, we find JIMMY and CLIFF sprawled in their respective armchairs, immersed in the Sunday newspapers. HELENA is standing down L. leaning over the ironing board, a small pile of clothes beside her. She looks more attractive than before, for the setting of her face is more relaxed. She still looks quite smart, but in an unpremeditated, careless way; she wears an old shirt of JIMMY's.

CLIFF: That stinking old pipe!
Pause.
JIMMY: Shut up.
CLIFF: Why don't you do something with it?
JIMMY: Why do I spend half of Sunday reading the papers?
CLIFF: (*kicks him without lowering his paper*). It stinks!
JIMMY: So do you, but I'm not singing an aria about it. (*Turns to the next page.*) The dirty ones get more and more wet round the mouth, and the posh ones are more pompous than ever. (*Lowering paper, and waving pipe at Helena.*) Does this bother you?
HELENA: No. I quite like it.
JIMMY: (*to Cliff*). There you are—she likes it!
He returns to his paper. Cliff grunts.
Have you read about the grotesque and evil practices going on in the Midlands?

76

CLIFF: Read about the what?

JIMMY: Grotesque and evil practices going on in the Midlands.

CLIFF: No, what about 'em?

JIMMY: Seems we don't know the old place. It's all in here. Startling Revelations this week! Pictures too. Reconstructions of midnight invocations to the Coptic Goddess of fertility.

HELENA: Sounds madly depraved.

JIMMY: Yes, it's rather us, isn't it? My gosh, look at 'em! Snarling themselves silly. Next week a well-known debutante relates how, during an evil orgy in Market Harborough, she killed and drank the blood of a white cockerel. Well—I'll bet Fortnums must be doing a roaring line in sacrificial cocks! (*Thoughtful.*) Perhaps that's what Miss Drury does on Sunday evenings. She puts in a stint as evil high priestess down at the Y.W.—probably having a workout at this very moment. (*To Helena.*) You never dabbled in this kind of thing did you?

HELENA: (*laughs*). Not lately!

JIMMY: Sounds rather your cup of tea—cup of blood, I should say. (*In an imitation of a midlands accent.*) Well, I mean, it gives you something to do, doesn't it? After all, it wouldn't do if we was all alike, would it? It'd be a funny world if we was all the same, that's what *I* always say! (*Resuming in his normal voice.*) All I know is that somebody's been sticking pins into *my* wax image for years.

(*Suddenly.*) Of course: Alison's mother! Every Friday, the wax arrives from Harrods, and all through the week-end, she's stabbing away at it with a hatpin! Ruined her bridge game, I dare say.

HELENA: Why don't *you* try it?

JIMMY: Yes, it's an idea. (*Pointing to Cliff.*) Just for a start, we could roast him over the gas stove. Have we got enough shillings for the meter? It seems to be just the thing for these Autumn evenings. After all the whole point of a sacrifice is that you give up something you never really wanted in the first place. You know what I mean? People are doing it around you all the time. They give up their careers, say— or their beliefs—or sex. And everyone thinks to themselves: how wonderful to be able to do that. If only I were capable of doing that! But the truth of it is that they've been kidding themselves, and they've been kidding you. It's not awfully difficult—giving up something you were incapable of ever really wanting. We shouldn't be admiring them. We should feel rather sorry for them. (*Coming back from this sudden, brooding excursion, and turning to Cliff.*) You'll make an admirable sacrifice.

CLIFF: (*mumbling*). Dry up! I'm trying to read.

JIMMY: Afterwards, we can make a loving cup from his blood. Can't say I fancy that so much. I've seen it—it looks like cochineal, ever so common. (*To Helena.*) Yours would be much better—pale Cambridge blue, I imagine. No? And afterwards, we could make invocations to the Coptic Goddess of fertility. Got any idea how you do that? (*To Cliff.*) Do you know?

CLIFF: Shouldn't have thought *you* needed to make invocations to the Coptic whatever-she-is!

JIMMY: Yes, I see what you mean. (*To Helena.*) Well, we don't want to *ask* for trouble, do we? Perhaps it might appeal to the lady here—she's written a long letter all about artificial insemination. It's headed: Haven't we tried God's patience enough! (*Throws the paper down.*) Let's see the other posh one.

CLIFF: Haven't finished yet.

JIMMY: Well, hurry up. I'll have to write and ask them to put hyphens in between the syllables for you. There's a particularly savage correspondence going on in there about whether Milton wore braces or not. I just want to see who gets shot down this week.

CLIFF: Just read that. Don't know what it was about,

but a Fellow of All Souls seems to have bitten the dust, and the Athenaeum's going up in flames, so the Editor declares that this correspondence is now closed.

JIMMY: I think you're actually acquiring yourself a curiosity, my boy. Oh yes, and then there's an American professor from Yale or somewhere, who believes that when Shakespeare was writing *The Tempest,* he changed his sex. Yes, he was obliged to go back to Stratford because the other actors couldn't take him seriously any longer. This professor chap is coming over here to search for certain documents which will prove that poor old W.S. ended up in someone else's second best bed—a certain Warwick-shire farmer's, whom he married after having three children by him.

Helena laughs. Jimmy looks up quizzically.

Is anything the matter?

HELENA: No, nothing. I'm only beginning to get used to him. I never (*this is to Cliff*) used to be sure when he was being serious, or when he wasn't.

CLIFF: Don't think he knows himself half the time. When in doubt, just mark it down as an insult.

JIMMY: Hurry up with that paper, and shut up! What are we going to do tonight? There isn't even a decent concert on. (*To Helena.*) Are you going to Church?

HELENA: (*rather taken aback*). No. I don't think so. Unless you want to.

JIMMY: Do I detect a growing, satanic glint in her eyes lately? Do you think it's living in sin with me that does it? (*To Helena.*) Do you feel very sinful my dear? Well? Do you?

She can hardly believe that this is an attack, and she can only look at him, uncertain of herself.

Do you feel sin crawling out of your ears, like stored up wax or something? Are you wondering whether I'm joking or not? Perhaps I ought to wear a red nose and funny hat. I'm just curious, that's all.

She is shaken by the sudden coldness in his eyes, but

before she has time to fully realise how hurt she is,
he is smiling at her, and shouting cheerfully at Cliff.
Let's have that paper, stupid!

CLIFF: Why don't you drop dead!

JIMMY: (*to Helena*). Will you be much longer doing
that?

HELENA: Nearly finished.

JIMMY: Talking of sin, wasn't that Miss Drury's Rev-
erend friend I saw you chatting with yesterday.
Helena darling, I said wasn't that. . . .

HELENA: Yes it was.

JIMMY: My dear, you don't have to be on the defensive you know.

HELENA: I'm not on the defensive.

JIMMY: After all, there's no reason why we shouldn't
have the parson to tea up here. Why don't we? Did
you find that you had much in common?

HELENA: No I don't think so.

JIMMY: Do you think that some of this spiritual beefcake would make a man of me? Should I go in for
this moral weight lifting and get myself some over-
developed muscle? I was a liberal skinny weakling. I
too was afraid to strip down to my soul, but now
everyone looks at my superb physique in envy. I can
perform any kind of press there is without betraying
the least sign of passion or kindliness.

HELENA: All right Jimmy.

JIMMY: Two years ago I couldn't even lift up my head
—now I have more uplift than a film starlet.

HELENA: Jimmy, can we have one day, just one day,
without tumbling over religion or politics?

CLIFF: Yes, change the record old boy, or pipe down.

JIMMY: (*rising*). Thought of the title for a new song
today. It's called "My mother's in the madhouse—
that's why I'm in love with you." The lyrics are
catchy too. I was thinking we might work it into the
act.

HELENA: Good idea.

JIMMY: I was thinking we'd scrub Jock and Day, and

call ourselves something else. "And jocund day stands tiptoed on the misty mountain tops." It's too intellectual! Anyway, I shouldn't think people will want to be reminded of that peculiar man's plays after Harvard and Yale have finished with him. How about something bright and snappy? I know——— What about—T. S. Eliot and Pam!

CLIFF: (*casually falling in with this familiar routine*). Mirth, mellerdy and madness!

JIMMY: (*sitting at the table R. and "strumming" it*). Bringing quips and strips for you!

They sing together.

"For we may be guilty, darling. . . .
But we're both insane as well!"

Jimmy stands up, and rattles his lines off at almost unintelligible speed.

Ladies and gentlemen, as I was coming to the theatre tonight, I was passing through the stage door, and a man comes up to me, and 'e says:

CLIFF: 'Ere! Have you seen nobody?

JIMMY: Have I seen who?

CLIFF: Have you seen nobody?

JIMMY: Of course, I haven't seen nobody! Kindly don't waste my time! Ladies and gentlemen, a little recitation entitled "She said she was called a little Gidding, but she was more like a gelding iron!" Thank you. "She said she was called little Gidding———"

CLIFF: Are you quite sure you haven't seen nobody?

JIMMY: Are you still here?

CLIFF: I'm looking for nobody!

JIMMY: *Will* you kindly go away! "She said she was called little Gidding———"

CLIFF: Well, I can't find nobody anywhere, and I'm supposed to give him this case!

JIMMY: Will you kindly stop interrupting per*lease!* Can't you see I'm trying to entertain these ladies and gentlemen? Who is this nobody you're talking about?

CLIFF: I was told to come here and give this case to nobody.

JIMMY: You were told to come here and give this case to nobody.

CLIFF: That's right. And when I gave it to him, nobody would give me a shilling.

JIMMY: And when you gave it to him, nobody would give you a shilling.

CLIFF: That's right.

JIMMY: Well, what about it?

CLIFF: Nobody's not here!

JIMMY: Now, let me get this straight: when you say nobody's here, you don't mean nobody's here?

CLIFF: No.

JIMMY: No.

JIMMY: You mean—nobody's here.

CLIFF: That's right.

JIMMY: Well, why didn't you say so before?

HELENA: (*not quite sure if this is really her cue*). Hey! You down there!

JIMMY: Oh, it goes on for hours yet, but never mind. What is it, sir?

HELENA: (*shouting*). I think your sketch stinks! I say —I think your sketch stinks!

JIMMY: He thinks it stinks. And, who, pray, might you be?

HELENA: Me? Oh—(*with mock modesty*) I'm nobody.

JIMMY: Then here's your bloody case!

He hurls a cushion at her, which hits the ironing board.

HELENA: My ironing board!

The two men do a Flanagan and Allen, moving slowly in step, as they sing.

Now there's a certain little lady, and you all know who I mean,

She may have been to Roedean, but to me she's still a queen.

Someday I'm goin' to marry her,

When times are not so bad,
Her mother doesn't care for me
So I'll 'ave to ask 'er dad.
We'll build a little home for two,
And have some quiet menage,
We'll send our kids to public school
And live on bread and marge.
Don't be afraid to sleep with your sweetheart,
Just because she's better than you.
Those forgotten middle-classes may have
    fallen on their noses,
But a girl who's true blue,
Will still have something left for you,
The angels up above, will know that you're in
    love
So don't be afraid to sleep with your sweetheart,
Just because she's better than you. . . .
          They call me Sydney,
Just because she's better than you.

*But Jimmy has had enough of this gag by now, and
he pushes Cliff away.*

JIMMY: Your damned great feet! That's the second
time you've kicked my ankle! It's no good—Helena
will have to do it. Go on, go and make some tea,
and we'll decide what we're going to do.

CLIFF: Make some yourself!

*He pushes him back violently, Jimmy loses his bal-
ance, and falls over.*

JIMMY: You rough bastard!

*He leaps up, and they grapple, falling on to the floor
with a crash. They roll about, grunting and gasping.
Cliff manages to kneel on Jimmy's chest.*

CLIFF: (*breathing heavily*). I want to read the papers!

JIMMY: You're a savage, a hooligan! You really are!
Do you know that! You don't deserve to live in the
same house with decent, sensitive people!

CLIFF: Are you going to dry up, or do I read the
papers down here?

Jimmy makes a supreme effort, and Cliff topples to the floor.

JIMMY: You've made me wrench my guts!

He pushes the struggling Cliff down.

CLIFF: Look what you're doing! You're ripping my shirt. Get *off!*

JIMMY: Well, what do you want to wear a shirt for? (*Rising.*) A tough character like you! Now go and make me some tea.

CLIFF: It's the only clean one I've got. Oh, you big oaf! (*Getting up from the floor, and appealing to Helena.*) Look! It's filthy!

HELENA: Yes, it is. He's stronger than he looks. If you like to take it off now, I'll wash it through for you. It'll be dry by the time we want to go out.

Cliff hesitates.

What's the matter, Cliff?

CLIFF: Oh, it'll be all right.

JIMMY: Give it to her, and quit moaning!

CLIFF: Oh, all right.

He takes it off, and gives it to her.

Thanks, Helena.

HELENA: (*taking it*). Right. I won't be a minute with it.

She goes out. Jimmy flops into his armchair. R.

JIMMY: (*amused*). You look like Marlon Brando or something. (*Slight pause.*) You don't care for Helena, do you?

CLIFF: You didn't seem very keen yourself once. (*Hesitating, then quickly.*) It's not the same, is it?

JIMMY: (*irritably*). No, of course it's not the same, you idiot! It never is! Today's meal is always different from yesterday's and the last woman isn't the same as the one before. If you can't accept that, you're going to be pretty unhappy, my boy.

CLIFF: (*sits on the arm of his chair, and rubs his feet*). Jimmy—I don't think I shall stay here much longer.

JIMMY: (*rather casually*). Oh, why not?

CLIFF: (*picking up his tone*). Oh, I don't know. I've

just thought of trying somewhere different. The sweet-stall's all right, but I think I'd like to try something else. You're highly educated, and it suits you, but I need something a bit better.

JIMMY: Just as you like, my dear boy. It's your business, not mine.

CLIFF: And another thing—I think Helena finds it rather a lot of work to do with two chaps about the place. It won't be so much for her if there's just the two of you. Anyway, I think I ought to find some girl who'll just look after me.

JIMMY: Sounds like a good idea. Can't think who'd be stupid enough to team themselves up with you though. Perhaps Helena can think of somebody for you—one of her posh girl friends with lots of money, and no brains. That's what you want.

CLIFF: Something like that.

JIMMY: Any idea what you're going to do?

CLIFF: Not much.

JIMMY: That sounds like you all right! Shouldn't think you'll last five minutes without me to explain the score to you.

CLIFF: (*grinning*). Don't suppose so.

JIMMY: You're such a scruffy little beast—I'll bet some respectable little madam from Pinner or Guildford gobbles you up in six months. She'll marry you, send you out to work, and you'll end up as clean as a new pin.

CLIFF: (*chuckling*). Yes, I'm stupid enough for that too!

JIMMY: (*to himself*). I seem to spend my life saying good-bye.
Slight pause.

CLIFF: My feet hurt.

JIMMY: Try washing your socks. (*Slowly.*) It's a funny thing. You've been loyal, generous and a good friend. But I'm quite prepared to see you wander off, find a new home, and make out on your own. And all because of something I want from that girl down-stairs, something I know in my heart she's incapable of giving. You're worth a half a dozen Helenas to me or to anyone. And, if you were in my place, you'd do the same thing. Right?

CLIFF: Right.

JIMMY: Why, why, why, why do we let these women bleed us to death? Have you ever had a letter, and on it is franked "Please Give Your Blood Gener-ously"? Well, the Postmaster-General does that, on behalf of all the women of the world. I suppose people of our generation aren't able to die for good causes any longer. We had all that done for us, in the thirties and the forties, when we were still kids. (*In his familiar, semi-serious mood.*) There aren't any good, brave causes left. If the big bang does come, and we all get killed off, it won't be in aid of the old-fashioned, grand design. It'll just be for the Brave New-nothing-very-much-thank-you. About as pointless and inglorious as stepping in front of a bus. No, there's nothing left for it, me boy, but to let yourself be butchered by the women.

Enter Helena.

HELENA: Here you are, Cliff. (*Handing him the shirt.*)

CLIFF: Oh, thanks, Helena, very much. That's decent of you.

HELENA: Not at all. I should dry it over the gas—the fire in your room would be better. There won't be much room for it over that stove.

CLIFF: Right, I will. (*Crosses to door.*)

JIMMY: And hurry up about it, stupid. We'll all go out, and have a drink soon. (*To Helena.*) O.K.?

HELENA: O.K.

JIMMY: (*shouting to Cliff on his way out*). But make me some tea first, you madcap little Charlie.

She crosses down L.

JIMMY: Darling, I'm sick of seeing you behind that damned ironing board!

HELENA: (*wryly*). Sorry.

JIMMY: Get yourself glammed up, and we'll hit the town. See you've put a shroud over Mummy, I think you should have laid a Union Jack over it.

HELENA: Is anything wrong?

JIMMY: Oh, don't frown like that—you look like the presiding magistrate!

HELENA: How should I look?

JIMMY: As if your heart stirred a little when you looked at me.

HELENA: Oh, it does that all right.

JIMMY: Cliff tells me he's leaving us.

HELENA: I know. He told me last night.

JIMMY: Did he? I always seem to be at the end of the queue when they're passing information out.

HELENA: I'm sorry he's going.

JIMMY: Yes, so am I. He's a sloppy, irritating bastard, but he's got a big heart. You can forgive somebody almost anything for that. He's had to learn how to take it, and he knows how to hand it out. Come here. *He is sitting on the arm of his chair. She crosses to him, and they look at each other. Then she puts out her hand, and runs it over his head, fondling his ear and neck.*

Right from that first night, you have always put out your hand to me first. As if you expected nothing, or worse than nothing, and didn't care. You made a good enemy, didn't you? What they call a worthy opponent. But then, when people put down their weapons, it doesn't mean they've necessarily stopped fighting.

HELENA: (*steadily*). I love you.

JIMMY: I think perhaps you do. Yes, I think perhaps you do. Perhaps it means something to lie with your victorious general in your arms. Especially, when he's heartily sick of the whole campaign, tired out, hungry and dry.

His lips find her fingers, and he kisses them.

She presses his head against her.

You stood up, and came out to meet me. Oh, Helena—

His face comes up to hers, and they embrace fiercely.

Don't let anything go wrong!

HELENA: (*softly*). Oh, my darling——

JIMMY: Either you're with me or against me.

HELENA: I've always wanted you—always!

They kiss again.

JIMMY: T. S. Eliot and Pam, we'll make a good double. If you'll help me. I'll close that damned sweet-stall, and we'll start everything from scratch. What do you say? We'll get away from this place.

HELENA: (*nodding happily*). I say that's wonderful.

JIMMY: (*kissing her quickly*). Put all that junk away, and we'll get out. We'll get pleasantly, joyfully tiddly, we'll gaze at each other tenderly and lecherously in "The Builder's Arms", and then we'll come back here, and I'll make such love to you, you'll not care about anything else at all.

She moves away L., after kissing his hand.

HELENA: I'll just change out of your old shirt. (*Folding ironing board.*)

JIMMY: (*moving U.S. to door*). Right. I'll hurry up the little man.

But before he reaches the door, it opens and Alison enters. She wears a raincoat, her hair is untidy, and she looks rather ill. There is a stunned pause.

ALISON: (*quietly*). Hullo.

JIMMY: (*to Helena, after a moment*). Friend of yours to see you.

He goes out quickly, and the two women are left looking at each other.

QUICK CURTAIN

END OF SCENE ONE

ACT III

ACT III

SCENE TWO

It is a few minutes later. From CLIFF's room, across the landing, comes the sound of JIMMY's jazz trumpet.

At rise of the curtain, HELENA is standing L. of the table, pouring out a cup of tea. ALISON is sitting on the armchair R. She bends down and picks up JIMMY's pipe. Then she scoops up a little pile of ash from the floor, and drops it in the ashtray on the arm of the chair.

ALISON: He still smokes this foul old stuff. I used to hate it at first, but you get used to it.

HELENA: Yes.

ALISON: I went to the pictures last week, and some old man was smoking it in front, a few rows away. I actually got up, and sat right behind him.

HELENA: (*coming down with cup of tea*). Here, have this. It usually seems to help.

ALISON: (*taking it*). Thanks.

HELENA: Are you sure you feel all right now?

ALISON: (*nods*). It was just—oh, everything. It's my own fault—entirely. I must be mad, coming here like this. I'm sorry, Helena.

HELENA: Why should you be sorry—you of all people?

ALISON: Because it was unfair and cruel of me to come back. I'm afraid a sense of timing is one of the things I seem to have learnt from Jimmy. But it's something that can be in very bad taste. (*Sips her tea.*) So many times, I've just managed to stop myself coming here—right at the last moment. Even today, when I went to the booking office at St.

89

Pancras, it was like a charade, and I never believed
that I'd let myself walk on to that train. And when I
was on it, I got into a panic. I felt like a criminal.
I told myself I'd turn round at the other end, and
come straight back. I couldn't even believe that this
place existed any more. But once I got here, there
was nothing I could do. I had to convince myself
that everything I remembered about this place had
really happened to me once.

*She lowers her cup, and her foot plays with the
newspapers on the floor.*

How many times in these past few months I've
thought of the evenings we used to spend here in this
room. Suspended and rather remote. You make a
good cup of tea.

HELENA: (*sitting L. of table*). Something Jimmy taught
me.

ALISON: (*covering her face*). Oh, why am I here! You
must all wish me a thousand miles away!

HELENA: I don't wish anything of the kind. You've
more right to be here than I.

ALISON: Oh, Helena, don't bring out the book of
rules——

HELENA: You are his wife, aren't you? Whatever I
have done, I've never been able to forget that fact.
You have all the rights——

ALISON: Helena—even I gave up believing in the
divine rights of marriage long ago. Even before I
met Jimmy. They've got something different now—
constitutional monarchy. You are where you are by
consent. And if you start trying any strong arm stuff,
you're out. And I'm out.

HELENA: Is that something you learnt from him?

ALISON: Don't make me feel like a blackmailer or
something, please! I've done something foolish, and
rather vulgar in coming here tonight. I regret it, and
I detest myself for doing it. But I did not come here
in order to gain anything. Whatever it was—hysteria

or just macabre curiosity, I'd certainly no intention of making any kind of breach between you and Jimmy. You must believe that.

HELENA: Oh, I believe it all right. That's why everything seems more wrong and terrible than ever. You didn't even reproach me. You should have been outraged, but you weren't. (*She leans back, as if she wanted to draw back from herself.*) I feel so—*ashamed.*

ALISON: You talk as though he were something you'd swindled me out of——

HELENA: (*fiercely*). And you talk as if he were a book or something you pass around to anyone who happens to want it for five minutes. What's the matter with you? You sound as though you were quoting *him* all the time. I thought you told me once you couldn't bring yourself to believe in him.

ALISON: I don't think I ever believed in your way either.

HELENA: At least, I still believe in right and wrong! Not even the months in this madhouse have stopped me doing that. Even though everything I have done is wrong, at least I have known it was wrong.

ALISON: You loved him, didn't you? That's what you wrote, and told me.

HELENA: And it was true.

ALISON: It was pretty difficult to believe at the time. I couldn't understand it.

HELENA: I could hardly believe it myself.

ALISON: Afterwards, it wasn't quite so difficult. You used to say some pretty harsh things about him. Not that I was sorry to hear them—they were rather comforting then. But you even shocked me sometimes.

HELENA: I suppose I was a little over-emphatic. There doesn't seem much point in trying to explain everything, does there?

ALISON: Not really.

HELENA: Do you know—I have discovered what is wrong with Jimmy? It's very simple really. He was born out of his time.

ALISON: Yes. I know.

HELENA: There's no place for people like that any longer—in sex, or politics, or anything. That's why he's so futile. Sometimes, when I listen to him, I feel he thinks he's still in the middle of the French Revolution. And that's where he ought to be, of course. He doesn't know where he is, or where he's going. He'll never do anything, and he'll never amount to anything.

ALISON: I suppose he's what you'd call an Eminent Victorian. Slightly comic—in a way. . . . We seem to have had this conversation before.

HELENA: Yes, I remember everything you said about him. It horrified me. I couldn't believe that you could have married someone like that. Alison—it's all over between Jimmy and me. I can see it now. I've got to get out. No—listen to me. When I saw you standing there tonight, I knew that it was all utterly wrong. That I didn't believe in any of this, and not Jimmy or anyone could make me believe otherwise. (*Rising.*) How could I have ever thought I could get away with it! He wants one world and I want another, and lying in that bed won't ever change it! I believe in good and evil, and I don't have to apologise for that. It's quite a modern, scientific belief now, so they tell me. And, by everything I have ever believed in, or wanted, what I have been doing is wrong and evil.

ALISON: Helena—you're not going to leave him?

HELENA: Yes, I am. (*Before Alison can interrupt, she goes on.*) Oh, I'm not stepping aside to let you come back. You can do what you like. Frankly, I think you'd be a fool—but that's your own business. I think I've given you enough advice.

ALISON: But he—he'll have no one.

HELENA: Oh, my dear, he'll find somebody. He'll

probably hold court here like one of the Renaissance popes. Oh, I know I'm throwing the book of rules at you, as you call it, but, believe me, you're never going to be happy without it. I tried throwing it away all these months, but I know now it just doesn't work. When you came in at that door, ill and tired and hurt, it was all over for me. You see—I didn't know about the baby. It was such a shock. It's like a judgment on us.

ALISON: You saw me, and I had to tell you what had happened. I lost the child. It's a simple fact. There is no judgment, there's no blame——

HELENA: Maybe not. But I feel it just the same.

ALISON: But don't you see? It isn't logical!

HELENA: No, it isn't. (*Calmly.*) But I know it's right.
The trumpet gets louder.

ALISON: Helena, (*going to her*) you mustn't leave him. He needs you, I know he needs you——

HELENA: Do you think so?

ALISON: Maybe you're not the right one for him—we're neither of us right——

HELENA: (*moving upstage*). Oh, why doesn't he stop that damned noise!

ALISON: He wants something quite different from us. What it is exactly I don't know—a kind of cross between a mother and a Greek courtesan, a henchwoman, a mixture of Cleopatra and Boswell. But give him a little longer——

HELENA: (*wrenching the door open*). Please! Will you stop that! I can't think!
There is a slight pause, and the trumpet goes on. She puts her hands to her head.
Jimmy, for God's sake!
It stops.
Jimmy, I want to speak to you.

JIMMY: (*off*). Is your friend still with you?

HELENA: Oh, don't be an idiot, and come in here!
She moves down L.

ALISON: (*rising*). He doesn't want to see me.

HELENA: Stay where you are, and don't be silly. I'm
sorry. It won't be very pleasant, but I've made up
my mind to go, and I've got to tell him now.
Enter Jimmy.

JIMMY: Is this another of your dark plots? (*He looks
at Alison.*) Hadn't she better sit down? She looks a
bit ghastly.

HELENA: I'm so sorry, dear. Would you like some
more tea, or an aspirin or something?
*Alison shakes her head, and sits. She can't look at
either of them.*
(*to Jimmy, the old authority returning*). It's not
very surprising, is it? She's been very ill, she's——

JIMMY: (*quietly*). You don't have to draw a diagram
for me—I can see what's happened to her.

HELENA: And doesn't it mean anything to you?

JIMMY: I don't exactly relish the idea of anyone being
ill, or in pain. It was my child too, you know. But
(*he shrugs*) it isn't my first loss.

ALISON: (*on her breath*). It was mine.
He glances at her, but turns back to Helena quickly.

JIMMY: What are you looking so solemn about?
What's she doing here?

ALISON: I'm sorry, I'm—— (*Presses her hand over
her mouth.*)
Helena crosses to Jimmy C., and grasps his hand.

HELENA: Don't please. Can't you see the condition
she's in? She's done nothing, she's said nothing, none
of it's her fault.
*He takes his hand away, and moves away a little
downstage.*

JIMMY: What isn't her fault?

HELENA: Jimmy—I don't want a brawl, so please——

JIMMY: Let's hear it, shall we?

HELENA: Very well. I'm going downstairs to pack my
things. If I hurry, I shall just catch the 7.15 to London.
*They both look at him, but he simply leans forward
against the table, not looking at either of them.*

This is not Alison's doing—you must understand
that. It's my own decision entirely. In fact, she's just
been trying to talk me out of it. It's just that suddenly, tonight, I see what I have really known all
along. That you can't be happy when what you're
doing is wrong, or is hurting someone else. I suppose
it could never have worked, anyway, but I do love
you, Jimmy. I shall never love anyone as I have
loved you. (*Turns away L.*) But I can't go on.
(*Passionately and sincerely.*) I can't take part—in
all this suffering. I can't!

*She appeals to him for some reaction, but he only
looks down at the table, and nods. Helena recovers,
and makes an effort to regain authority.*

(*to Alison*). You probably won't feel up to making
that journey again tonight, but we can fix you up at
an hotel before I go. There's about half an hour. I'll
just make it.

*She turns up to the door, but Jimmy's voice stops
her.*

JIMMY: (*in a low, resigned voice*). They all want to
escape from the pain of being alive. And, most of
all, from love. (*Crosses to the dressing table.*) I
always knew something like this would turn up—
some problem, like an ill wife—and it would be too
much for those delicate, hot-house feelings of yours.
*He sweeps up Helena's things from the dressing
table, and crosses over to the wardrobe. Outside, the
church bells start ringing.*
It's no good trying to fool yourself about love. You
can't fall into it like a soft job, without dirtying up
your hands. (*Hands her the make-up things, which
she takes. He opens the wardrobe.*) It takes muscle
and guts. And if you can't bear the thought (*takes
out a dress on a hanger*) of messing up your nice,
clean soul, (*crossing back to her*) you'd better give
up the whole idea of life, and become a saint. (*Puts
the dress in her arms.*) Because you'll never make it
as a human being. It's either this world or the next.

She looks at him for a moment, and then goes out quickly. He is shaken, and he avoids Alison's eyes, crossing to the window. He rests against it, then bangs his fist against the frame.

Oh, those bells!

The shadows are growing around them. Jimmy stands, his head against the window pane. Alison is huddled forward in the armchair R. Presently, she breaks the stillness, and rises to above the table.

ALISON: I'm . . . sorry. I'll go now.

She starts to move upstage. But his voice pulls her up.

JIMMY: You never even sent any flowers to the funeral. Not—a little bunch of flowers. You had to deny me that too, didn't you?

She starts to move, but again he speaks.

The injustice of it is almost perfect! The wrong people going hungry, the wrong people being loved, the wrong people dying.

She moves to the gas stove. He turns to face her.

Was I really wrong to believe that there's a—a kind of—burning virility of mind and spirit that looks for something as powerful as itself? The heaviest, strongest creatures in this world seem to be the loneliest. Like the old bear, following his own breath in the dark forest. There's no warm pack, no herd to comfort him. That voice that cries out doesn't *have* to be a weakling's, does it?

He moves in a little.

Do you remember that first night I saw you at that grisly party? You didn't really notice me, but I was watching you all the evening. You seemed to have a wonderful relaxation of spirit. I knew that was what I wanted. You've got to be really brawny to have that kind of strength—the strength to relax. It was only after we were married that I discovered that it wasn't relaxation at all. In order to relax, you've first got to sweat your guts out. And, as far as you were concerned, you'd never had a hair out of place, or a bead of sweat anywhere.

A cry escapes from her, and her fist flies to her mouth. She moves down to below the table, leaning on it.

I may be a lost cause, but I thought if you loved me, it needn't matter.

She is crying silently. He moves down to face her.

ALISON: It doesn't matter! I was wrong, I was wrong! I don't want to be neutral, I don't want to be a saint. I want to be a lost cause. I want to be corrupt and futile!

All he can do is watch her helplessly. Her voice takes on a little strength, and rises.

Don't you understand? It's gone! It's gone! That— that helpless human being inside my body. I thought it was so safe, and secure in there. Nothing could take it from me. It was mine, my responsibility. But it's lost.

She slides down against the leg of the table to the floor.

All I wanted was to die. I never knew what it was like. I didn't know it could be like that! I was in pain, and all I could think of was you, and what I'd lost. (*Scarcely able to speak.*) I thought: if only— if only he could see me now, so stupid, and ugly and ridiculous. That is what he's been longing for me to feel. This is what he wants to splash about in! I'm in the fire, and I'm burning, and all I want is to die! It's cost him his child, and any others I might have had! But what does it matter—this is what he wanted from me!

She raises her face to him.

Don't you see! I'm in the mud at last! I'm grovelling! I'm crawling! Oh, God——

She collapses at his feet. He stands, frozen for a moment, then he bends down and takes her shaking body in his arms. He shakes his head, and whispers:

JIMMY: Don't. Please don't. . . . I can't——
She gasps for her breath against him.
You're all right. You're all right now. Please, I—
I. . . . Not any more. . . .
*She relaxes suddenly. He looks down at her, full of
fatigue, and says with a kind of mocking, tender
irony:*
We'll be together in our bear's cave, and our squirrel's drey, and we'll live on honey, and nuts—lots
and lots of nuts. And we'll sing songs about ourselves—about warm trees and snug caves, and lying
in the sun. And you'll keep those big eyes on my fur,
and help me keep my claws in order, because I'm a
bit of a soppy, scruffy sort of a bear. And I'll see
that you keep that sleek, bushy tail glistening as it
should, because you're a very beautiful squirrel, but
you're none too bright either, so we've got to be
careful. There are cruel steel traps lying about everywhere, just waiting for rather mad, slightly satanic,
and very timid little animals. Right?
Alison nods.
(*pathetically*). Poor squirrels!
ALISON: (*with the same comic emphasis*). Poor bears!
*She laughs a little. Then looks at him very tenderly,
and adds very, very softly.* Oh, poor, poor bears!
Slides her arms around him.

CURTAIN

THE
ENTERTAINER

NOTE

The music hall is dying, and, with it, a significant part of England. Some of the heart of England has gone; something that once belonged to everyone, for this was truly a folk art. In writing this play, I have not used some of the techniques of the music hall in order to exploit an effective trick, but because I believe that these can solve some of the eternal problems of time and space that face the dramatist, and, also, it has been relevant to the story and setting. Not only has this technique its own traditions, its own convention and symbol, its own mystique, it cuts right across the restrictions of the so-called naturalistic stage. Its contact is immediate, vital, and direct.

CAST

BILLY RICE

JEAN RICE

ARCHIE RICE

PHOEBE RICE

FRANK RICE

WILLIAM (BROTHER BILL) RICE

GRAHAM DODD

The first performance in Great Britain of THE ENTER-TAINER was given at the Royal Court Theatre, Sloane Square, London, on 10th April 1957 by the English Stage Company. It was directed by Tony Richardson and the decor was by Alan Tagg. The cast was as follows:

BILLY RICE	George Relph
JEAN RICE	Dorothy Tutin
PHOEBE RICE	Brenda de Banzie
ARCHIE RICE	Laurence Olivier
FRANK RICE	Richard Pasco
GORGEOUS GLADYS	Vivienne Drummond
WILLIAM (BROTHER BILL) RICE	Aubrey Dexter
GRAHAM	Stanley Meadows

CONTENTS

OVERTURE

Setting: The action takes place in a large coastal resort. The house where the Rice family live is one of those tall ugly monuments built by a prosperous business man at the beginning of the century. Only twenty-five minutes in the brougham to the front. Now, trolley buses hum past the front drive, full of workers from the small factories that have grown up round about. This is a part of the town the holiday makers never see—or, if they do, they decide to turn back to the pleasure gardens. This is what they have spent two or three hours in a train to escape. They don't even have to pass it on their way in from the central station, for this is a town on its own, and it has its own station, quite a large one, with acres of goods sheds and shunting yards. However, the main line trains don't stop there. It is not residential, it is hardly industrial. It is full of dirty blank spaces, high black walls, a gas holder, a tall chimney, a main road that shakes with dust and lorries. The shops are scattered at the corners of narrow streets. A newsagent's, a general grocer's, a fish-and-chip shop.

OVERTURE

During the Intermissions, an advertising sheet is lowered.

NUMBER ONE

At the back a gauze. Behind it, a part of the town.
In front of it, a high rostrum with steps leading to
it. Knee-high flats and a door frame will serve for a
wall. The sight-lines are preserved by swagging. Different swags can be lowered for various scenes to
break up the acting areas. Also, ordinary, tatty backcloth and draw-tabs. There are two doors L. and R.
of the apron. The lighting is the kind you expect to
see in the local Empire—everything bang-on, bright
and hard, or a simple follow-spot. The scenes and
interludes must, in fact, be lit as if they were simply
turns on the bill. Furniture and props are as basic as
they would be for a short sketch. On both sides of
the proscenium is a square in which numbers—the
turn numbers—appear. The problems involved are
basically the same as those that confront any resi-
dent stage-manager on the twice nightly circuit every Monday morning of his working-life.
Music. The latest, the loudest, the worst. A gauzed
front-cloth. On it are painted enormous naked young
ladies, waving brightly coloured fans, and kicking
out gaily. Written across it in large letters are the
words "ROCK'N ROLL NEW'D LOOK."
Behind the up-stage gauze, light picks out an old
man. He walks across the stage from L. to R. As he
reaches C. he pauses and looks up. There are shouts
and screams. The noise of a woman trying to sepa-
rate two men—her son and her lover perhaps. Cries
of "Oh leave him alone! Don't! Please don't! Leave
him *alone.*" He walks off R. and reappears beside
the swagging, walking in C. There is a crash and

the sounds of blows. He pauses again, then goes on. The woman screams, loudly this time. He pauses again, turns back, and shouts down over the banister rail "Do you mind being quiet down there, please." He pauses, but there is no response. *"Will you* kindly stop making all that noise!" He manages to sound dignified, but he has a powerful voice and the noise stops for a moment. He nods and starts moving. A voice shouts "Why don't you shut your great big old gob, you poor, bloody old fool!" A woman's sob stabs the end of the sentence and the old man hesitates, turns back and calls over the stairs "Are you all right, Mrs. ——?" A man's voice is heard, urgent and heated. A door bangs, and the noise is muffled. The sobbing is still audible but the situation seems to be more controlled. The old man returns C. and enters through the door-frame.

BILLY RICE is a spruce man in his seventies. He has great physical pride, the result of a life-time of being admired as a "fine figure of a man." He is slim, upright, athletic. He glows with scrubbed well-being. His hair is just grey, thick and silky from its vigorous daily brush. His clothes are probably twenty-five years old—including his pointed patent leather shoes—but well-pressed and smart. His watch chain gleams, his collar is fixed with a tie-pin beneath the tightly knotted black tie, his brown homburg is worn at a very slight angle. When he speaks it is with a dignified Edwardian diction—a kind of repudiation of both Oxford and cockney that still rhymes "cross" with "force," and yet manages to avoid being exactly upper-class or effete. Indeed, it is not an accent of class but of period. One does not hear it often now.

Take up front gauze.

He walks down C., laying down a folded newspaper, two quart bottles of beer, and a telegram, which he glances at quickly. He crosses to the fore-stage door

R., and goes through it singing sonorously but cheerfully:

> "Rock of Ages cleft for me
> Let me hide myself in thee!"

He reappears in his shirt sleeves pulling on a heavy woollen cardigan over his waistcoat. Still singing, he sits down, pours himself out a glass of beer, and starts to unlace his shoes. He puts these in a box with tissue paper up-stage C. The noise starts up again from downstairs. He drinks from his glass of beer, takes out a nail file and stands cleaning his nails expertly. This is like flicking off the old, imaginary speck of dust. There is a yell from downstairs. BILLY speaks, gravely, with forethought.

BILLY: Bloody Poles and Irish!

He sits down and puts on his carpet slippers. Front door slams, he takes spectacles from his case and puts them on.

I hate the bastards.

He unfolds his newspaper, the doorbell is still ringing. He looks irritated, but he has his feet up and is too comfortable to move. He sings cheerfully, as if to drown the noise of the doorbell.

BILLY: Nearer my God to Thee
Nearer to Thee!

He listens and then goes on.

Even though it be a cross
That raiseth me

He picks up the newspaper and peers at it gravely.

Still all my song would be
Nearer my God to Thee,
Nearer to Thee!

He puts down his paper.

(*Standing*). Why don't they answer the bloody door!

He leans his arms on the chair, wondering whether he will have to go after all.

Ought to be locked up, some of these people.

It looks as though he won't have to go after all, and
he settles back cheerfully.

Dirty, filthy lot. (*Picks up paper. Pushes paper*
down suddenly.)

My God, there's a draught!

Gets up and goes to door and looks out.

I'll bet they've left the front door open. Born in
fields, they are.

Takes a rug and arranges it against the door.

Probably were born in fields. Animals. (*Back to*
chair and sits down.) Like animals. Wild animals.

He settles down. Across from up L. comes a young
girl.

Billy pours himself out some more beer. The girl
knocks on the door. He listens.

Who is it?

The girl knocks again.

Who is it? Can't get any peace in this damned house.

GIRL: Is that you, Grandad?

BILLY: What?

GIRL: It's Jean.

BILLY: (*rising*). Who is it?

JEAN: It's me—Jean.

BILLY: (*goes to door and stands behind it*). Can't
even read the paper in peace. Who?

JEAN: It's your granddaughter.

Jean tries to push the door open but the rug pre-
vents it.

BILLY: Just a minute! Just a minute! Hold your horses!
(*He bends down*).

JEAN: Sorry.

BILLY: Hold your horses!

He releases the rug and opens the door, revealing
Jean Rice. She is about twenty-two, dark, with slight-
ly protruding teeth and bad eyesight. She is what
most people would call plain, but already humour
and tenderness have begun to stake their small

claims around her nose and eyes. Her mouth is large, generous.

JEAN: Hello, Grandad.

BILLY: I wondered who the hell it was.

JEAN: I'm sorry.

BILLY: I thought it was some of that mad lot carrying on. Well, come in if you're coming, it's draughty standing about in the doorway. I've only just sat down.

JEAN: (*coming in*). Did I disturb you, I am sorry.

BILLY: I'd just sat down to read the evening paper. It's a bloody farm-yard this place.

JEAN: Well, how are you?

BILLY: Bloody farm-yard. They want locking up. And you know what now, don't you? You know who she's got upstairs, in Mick's old room, don't you? Some black fellow. It's true. I tell you, you've come to a mad-house this time.

JEAN: You're looking very well. How do you feel?

BILLY: I'm all right. You expect a few aches and pains when you get to my age. Phoebe's at the pictures, I think. She didn't tell me you were coming.

JEAN: I didn't tell her.

BILLY: No, well she didn't say anything. So I wasn't expecting a knock on the door.

JEAN: I only decided to come up this morning.

BILLY: I'd only just sat down to read the evening paper.

JEAN: I'm sorry. I disturbed you.

She has picked up her cue neatly. The fact that his evening has been disturbed is established. His air of distracted irritation relaxes and he smiles a little. He is pleased to see her anyway.

BILLY: Well, give your Grandad a kiss, come on.

She does so.

JEAN: It's good to see you.

BILLY: Well, it's nice to see you, my darling. Bit of a surprise. Go on, take your things off.

Jean undoes her coat, and throws a packet of ciga-
rettes on the table.

JEAN: Got you those.

BILLY: Phoebe won't be long. What she went out for
I don't know.

JEAN: Gone to the pictures has she?

BILLY: She's mad. Oh, that's very kind of you. Very
kind. Thank you. Yes, she said she was going early
I don't know why she can't stay in.

JEAN: Well, you know—she's always been like that
She enjoys it.

BILLY: Well, she'll have to learn. She's not a youngster
any more. When she gets to my age, she won't want
to do it.

He unwraps the cigarettes and takes out an ivory
holder from his waistcoat.

Oh, this is nice of you. Thank you. Still, if she stays
in she only gets irritable. And I can't stand rows.
Not any more. (*He stares in front of him.*) No use
arguing with Phoebe anyway. Would you like some
beer?

She shakes her head.

She just won't listen to you. Are you sure you won't?
There's a damn great crate out in the kitchen, Frank
brought it in this morning.

JEAN: No thanks, Grandad.

BILLY: No, when she gets in that mood, I just go out.

JEAN: Where do you go?

BILLY: I go for a walk. Or I go to the Club. You
haven't been to the Club. Oh, I must take you then.
It's very quiet, mind you. Except at week-ends. You
get some of the wives then. But they're mostly old-
timers like me.

JEAN: Sounds fun.

BILLY: Well, it's somewhere to go when you're fed up
with the place. Don't suppose it would appeal much
to youngsters like yourself. I expect you go in more
for these jazz places.

JEAN: I'd like to go. You must take me.

BILLY: Would you really? Would you? All right. But, I warn you, there's none of your boogie-woogie. How long are you here for?

JEAN: Just the week-end.

BILLY: We'll go tomorrow night. It's a good night, Sunday. I sing them some of the old songs, sometimes, when I feel like it. Haven't done it lately, not for a long time. Don't seem to feel like it.

JEAN: Where's Dad?

BILLY: He's at the theatre. He's playing here—at the Grand this week, you know.

JEAN: Oh, yes, of course.

BILLY: I don't seem to feel like it these days. You get a bit depressed sometimes sitting here. Oh, then there's the Cambridge down the road. I go there, of course. But there's not the old crowd there, you know. What about the news, eh? That's depressing. What d'you make of all this business out in the Middle East? People seem to be able to do what they like to us. Just what they like. I don't understand it. I really don't. Archie goes to that damned place down by the clock tower.

JEAN: The Rockliffe.

BILLY: Yes, the Rockliffe. Every tart and pansy boy in the district are in that place at a week-end. Archie tried to get me there the other day. No thank you. It's just a meat-market.

JEAN: How is Dad?

BILLY: He's a fool.

JEAN: Oh?

BILLY: Putting money into a road-show.

JEAN: I didn't know.

BILLY: Oh, it's another of his cock-eyed ideas. He won't listen to me. He spends half his time in that Rockliffe.

JEAN: I see. What show is it this time?

BILLY: Oh, I don't remember what it's called.

JEAN: Have you seen it?

BILLY: No, I haven't seen it. I wouldn't. These nudes.

They're killing the business. Anyway, I keep telling him—it's dead already. Has been for years. It was all over, finished, dead when I got out of it. I saw it coming. I saw it coming, and I got out. They don't want real people any more.

JEAN: No, I suppose they don't.

BILLY: They don't want human-beings. Not any more. Wish he wouldn't get stuck in that Rockliffe. Gets half his posing girls in there if you ask me. (*Warming up.*) Well, why should a family man take his wife and kids to see a lot of third-class sluts standing about in the nude? It's not even as if they got the figures nowadays. They're all skin and bone.

JEAN: (*smiles*). Like me.

BILLY: Well, you don't stand around with nothing on for everyone to gaup at and God bless you for it. But you never see a woman with a really good figure now. I could tell you something about beautiful women now, I could. And it wasn't all make-up either. They were ladies. Ladies, and you took off your hat before you dared speak to them. Now! why, half the time you can't tell the women from the men. Not from the back. And even at the front you have to take a good look, sometimes.

JEAN: Like the Government and the Opposition.

BILLY: What's that? Like the Government and the Opposition. Don't talk to me about the Government. Or that other lot. Grubby lot of rogues. Want locking up. No, old Archie's a fool. He won't even listen to you. That's why I put up with old Phoebe. She's had to cope I can tell you. But I don't have to tell you. He's going to come a cropper I'm afraid. And pretty soon too. He's bitten off more than he can chew.

JEAN: With this new show you mean. Has he really put money into it?

BILLY: Put money into it! Don't make me laugh! He hasn't got two halfpennies for a penny. It's all credit

Credit, if you please! How he gets it beats me, after that last business. Still, he could always talk, your Dad. And that's about all. Do you know, I spent thousands of pounds on his education. Went to the same school as me. And his brother. Thousands of pounds. He wasn't one of these scholarship people, like you. And where's it got 'em? (*He takes a drink.*) That Rockliffe. They should close the place. Someone should write to the Council about it. I'm surprised nobody hasn't. There's a lot of gentry here, you know—Besides the riff-raff round here. Retired people. They don't want that kind of thing going on. Are you all right? You look as though you've been keeping late nights or something. What have you been doing with yourself? Lots of these parties, eh?

JEAN: No, not really.

BILLY: Well, you've got to have a good time while you're young. You won't get it later on. I'll bet he won't be in till all hours tonight.

JEAN: Dad?

BILLY: I'm pleased to see you, Jean. Are you all right? They're treating you right?

JEAN: Oh, yes.

BILLY: They're doing right by you, I hope. You're not in any trouble, are you?

JEAN: No, Grandad. I'm not in any trouble.

BILLY: I just wondered why you came up to see us like this suddenly.

JEAN: Oh, it's just——

BILLY: I'm not asking you to tell me. You do as you like, my darling. I 'spect you're hungry are you?

JEAN: I ate on the train.

BILLY: You shouldn't have done that. It's extravagant, and all they give you is a lot of rubbish. You're not extravagant, are you?

JEAN: I don't think so.

BILLY: No, I didn't think so. You're a good girl, Jean. You'll get somewhere. I know you'll get somewhere.

You're not like the lot in this house. You'll do something for yourself. You take after your old grandfather.

She smiles at him affectionately.

Don't you? Jean, if ever you're in any kind of trouble, you will come to me now won't you?

JEAN: I will.

BILLY: I mean it. Now look—there's just the two of us here. Promise me you'll come and tell me.

JEAN: Of course I will, but there's nothing——

BILLY: I'm not fooling about, I'm serious. Phoebe will be back any minute, and I don't want her to know. I want you to promise me.

JEAN: I promise you. If there is anything——

BILLY: If it's money, mind——

JEAN: Well I tell you I've just——

BILLY: I've got a few pounds in the Post Office. Not much, mind you, but I've got a few pounds. Nobody knows, so not to say a word, mind.

JEAN: No.

BILLY: Not even the pension people. I don't tell them my business. But, as I say——

JEAN: Grandad, I promise. If I want anything——

BILLY: Probably don't give you much in that job, do they? You tell 'em what you're worth, they're robbers.

JEAN: They pay pretty well.

BILLY: How much was your fare up here? (*He is getting slightly carried away.*)

JEAN: No, Grandad, please—I don't want it.

BILLY: Hold your bloody noise. If I want to give it to you, you shall have it. Here just a minute——

JEAN: Please——

BILLY: What's the matter? Isn't it good enough for you?

JEAN: It isn't that——

BILLY: Well then. Do as you're told and take it. I wouldn't have dared argue with my grandfather. Even at your age. (*Counting out his money.*) Um.

Well, I don't seem to have enough just now. How much is it?

JEAN: I don't remember.

BILLY: Of course you remember. Look, there's half a quid. You take that towards it for now, and on Monday I'll go to the Post Office and get it out for you.

JEAN: Darling, you'll need that for the week-end. There's cigarettes and papers, and you're taking me to the Club, remember?

BILLY: Oh. Yes. I'd forgotten that. Well, we'll call it a loan, mind?

JEAN: A loan?

BILLY: Yes, a loan. You know what a loan is.

JEAN: Oh, all right.

BILLY: You mustn't go short. We all need looking after. And you've got to look after your own kind. No use leaving it to the Government for them to hand out to a lot of bleeders who haven't got the gumption to do anything for themselves. I want to look after you, Jean. I do, I do really. You're a good girl and I know you'll do something with your life, you'll *be* somebody. You won't waste it away and be silly.

JEAN: Bless you.

BILLY: Don't waste it. Do something good with it. Don't waste it. Sit down, for God's sake. You look as if you're going to put on your hat and coat and go. Sit down and talk to your Grandad. I don't get much chance to talk to anyone. They think you're a bit soft. Just because you can remember things when they were a bit different. Go on, have a glass.

JEAN: Thank you.

BILLY: Like that barmaid in the Cambridge. I don't go there so much. I've seen her laughing up her sleeve. She thinks I haven't seen her, but I am not soft. She's a common bit of goods, too. Great bosoms sticking out here. As if you want to see that, when you lean over for your drink. Enough to put you off your beer. And she gives short measure. You've got

to watch them. They think they can have it ove
you.

JEAN: What time does the second house finish?

BILLY: I don't know. About eleven I suppose. You'
wait up all night if you wait for him. They wouldn'
have employed someone like that in the old days
Like a common prostitute.

JEAN: Perhaps I should go and meet him.

BILLY: Do as you like, my girl. But I shouldn't
They've got a television in that bar now. A televi
sion. Now who do you think would want a televisio
in a pub? Blaring away, you can't hear yoursel
think. D'you know? Do you know I asked them t
turn it down, the other night. That cow with th
bosom. Well, you'd expect her to be insolent. Bu
then I asked the Gov'nor—Charlie Rowse. He's
pal of mine. I've known him for years. And do yo
know—he wouldn't hear of it! I don't know what'
happening to everyone. I don't. Do you know?

JEAN: (*she isn't listening*). No, Grandad I don't.

BILLY: It makes you sad—sometimes. Old Charli
Rowse of all people. I haven't been able to go i
there since, somehow. I got these in the off-licenc
over the way. (*He looks at her shrewdly.*) I suppos
you've no right to expect people to listen to you. Jus
because you've had your life. It's all over for you
Why should anyone listen to you? (*Pause.*) Hav
you been drinking?

JEAN: Yes.

BILLY: I always know when a woman's been drinking

JEAN: I'm sorry.

BILLY: That's all right, my girl. I dare say you know
what you're doing. I should put your feet up, an
close your eyes. You'll feel better in a minute.

JEAN: I had four gins. Four large gins. I'll be all righ
What's the business like?

BILLY: At the theatre? I don't know. I don't ask. Bu
I'll bet there's more in the saloon bar of the Cam

bridge than he's got in there. I know how you feel, girl. You just relax.

JEAN: I like listening to you. I always have.

BILLY: Yes, you always used to like coming to see me, didn't you? You used to enjoy yourself with me when you were a little girl. You were a pretty little thing. With your dark curls and your little dresses. (*Quickly.*) Not that looks are everything. Not even for a woman. Don't you believe it. You don't look at the mantelpiece when you poke the fire.

She sits down and leans back.

No, I'll say this for Archie—he always saw that you looked nicely turned out. You looked a little picture always. Spent too much I daresay. He was a smart little boy himself. Used to dress them in sailor suits then. He was a pretty little boy. Funny how they all turn out. (*Pause, then softly, sincerely*) I feel sorry for you people. You don't know what it's really like. You haven't lived, most of you. You've never known what it was like, you're all miserable really. You don't know what life can be like.   ← CUE 4

The light fades, a tatty backcloth descends.

NUMBER TWO

Front cloth. Darkened stage. Spotlight hits the
prompt corner. Music strikes up. ARCHIE RICE makes
his entrance.

ARCHIE: Good evening, ladies and gentlemen—Archie
Rice is the name. Archie Rice. Mrs. Rice's favourite
boy. We're going to entertain you for the next two
and a half hours and you've really had it now. All
the exit doors locked. Talking about being locked
in, some of these people ought to be locked up.
Locked up. They did, honest. I'll give you a case in
point. A case in point. My wife—my wife. Old
Charlie knows her, don't you, Charlie? Old Charlie
knows her. A real road-mender's job she is—isn't
she, Charlie? It's all right. I've taken his drill away
from him now. I have. Haven't I, Charlie. He's the
only boy soprano in the Musicians' Union. I know
what you're waiting for. I know what you're waiting
for and who isn't? Just keep your peckers up—they'll
be on in a minute. You've got to put up with me first.
And now—now, to open the show. I'm going to sing
a little song I wrote myself. I hope you like it.

"Why should I care?
Why should I let it touch me!
Why shouldn't I, sit down and try
To let it pass over me?
Why should they stare,
Why should I let it get me?
What's the use of despair,
If they call you a square?
You're a long time dead——
So why, oh why should I bother to care?"

122

He goes into his dance routine. ← *COLOR CHANGE*

> "Why should I care?
> Why should I let it touch me!
> Why shouldn't I, sit down and try
> To let it pass over me?
> Why should they stare,
> Why should I let it get me?
> What's the use of despair,
> If they call you a square?
> If they see that you're blue, they'll—look
>   down on you
>   So why should I bother to care? (Thank
>   God I'm normal!)
> So why should I bother to care?"

EXIT

NUMBER THREE

The music fades. The backcloth goes up, revealing
BILLY, JEAN and PHOEBE. PHOEBE is about sixty,
with fair hair that was attractive once, and still has
a great deal of care spent on it. Her face is made up,
though not very skilfully. She is never still, she
never listens—like most of the people in this house.
Or, if she is obliged to sit and listen to anyone, she
usually becomes abstracted and depressed, sitting on
the edge of her chair, twisting her fingers round her
hair. Just now, she is flushed, like a child, prepared
to be excited.

PHOEBE: Oh, he will be so glad to see you. (*To Billy.*)
Won't he? But why didn't you let us know? I'd have
got you something prepared. Are you sure you won't
have something? I've got a bit of York ham in—I
bought it this morning. Wouldn't you like a bit of
that?

JEAN: No thank you, dear. I told you I just came up
on the spur of the moment.

PHOEBE: That's right, you did. But you said something
in your letter about going away for the week-end.
Did something go wrong?

JEAN: I changed my mind.

PHOEBE: Oh, well it's lovely to see you. Isn't it, Dad?
He's pleased. He doesn't have anyone much to talk
to. Do you? I say you don't have much chance for a
talk. He's on his own here half the time. It's not my
fault. He won't come to the pictures with me. But
you've got to go somewhere, as I say to him. You
get bored stiff just sitting indoors. He likes to listen
to a play on the wireless sometimes. You *like* a nice

124

play. But I can't sit for long, I'd rather have a spot of pictures.

BILLY: I'm all right.

PHOEBE: Well, I suppose that's sitting down too, but it's not the same somehow, is it? Let's open this, shall we? (*She indicates bottle on the table.*) You shouldn't have bought gin. She's naughty, isn't she?

BILLY: She ought to have more sense—spending her money.

PHOEBE: Never mind, she's big hearted, that's the main thing. Hand me a couple of glasses. You're going to have one with me, aren't you? I don't want one on my own.

JEAN: All right—just a small one.

PHOEBE: Oh, sorry, Dad—do you want one?

BILLY: No thank you.

PHOEBE: Well, this is nice. What a shame—I'd have been in earlier but I stayed and saw a bit of the big picture round again.

BILLY: I know better than to overdo it.

JEAN: What was it like?

PHOEBE: The picture? Oh, wasn't up to much. But there was that nice fellow in it, what's his name? Oh, he sings sometimes, got very deep set eyes, dark. You'd know who I mean.

JEAN: Is he American or British?

PHOEBE: Oh, I don't know. American I should think.

JEAN: What was the picture called?

PHOEBE: (*laughs*). Blimey, you should know better than to ask me that! You know what a rotten memory I've got. Well, cheerio! (*She drinks.*) Oooh, that's a nice drop of gin—some of the muck they give you nowadays—tastes like cheap scent. You should hear him going on about the beer. No, they've a lot of rubbish on at the pictures these days. I haven't seen a decent picture for ages. It seems to be all bands or singing. Either that or Westerns. He doesn't mind them so much. But I can't stand all that shooting. It gives me a headache. But I'm dreadful—if there's nothing else on, I still go just the same, don't I? Even if it is just to the bug house round the corner. I get myself six penn'orth of sweets and have a couple of hours whatever's on. I hear they're closing that place down, by the way. Everything's doing badly. That's what I tell Archie. 'Course he gets worried because the business is bad. Still, that's how it is; people haven't got the money, have they? I'm at Woolworth's now, did I tell you? I'm on the electrical counter. It's not bad. Girls are a bit common, that's all. Oh, it is nice to see you. Archie will be so pleased. She looks a bit peaky. Round the face, don't you think? Don't you think she looks a bit peaky?

BILLY: She looks all right.

PHOEBE: I don't suppose she's eating properly. You know what these young girls are. They worry about their figures. So, you didn't go away for the weekend after all?

JEAN: No.

PHOEBE: Graham's all right, is he?

JEAN: Yes, he's all right.

PHOEBE: There's nothing wrong there, is there?

BILLY: Why don't you mind your bloody business? She'll tell you if she wants to.

PHOEBE: All right, I know. She doesn't mind telling me if there's anything, do you?

JEAN: We had a slight disagreement. Nothing more, that's all.

PHOEBE: After all, she may not be my own, but I did help to bring her up a little, didn't I? After all, she's Archie's daughter. Be a bit strange if I wasn't interested whether she was happy or not. Oh, well, dear, don't take any notice. You'll soon make it up. Men are funny. You don't want to take any notice of them.

JEAN: (*smiling*). Wish I didn't.

PHOEBE: That's right. Have another drink. You'll soon feel better. What did you have a row about? Some-

thing silly I'll bet. You haven't broken off your engagement?

JEAN: I don't know. Probably.

PHOEBE: Oh dear, I'm sorry.

JEAN: I went to the Rally in Trafalgar Square last
Sunday.

BILLY: You did what?

JEAN: I went to the Rally in Trafalgar Square.

BILLY: What for, for God's sake?

JEAN: Because, Grandad, somehow—with a whole lot
of other people, strange as it may seem—I managed
to get myself steamed up about the way things were
going.

BILLY: And you went to Trafalgar Square?

PHOEBE: Well she said so didn't she?

BILLY: Well I should think you want your bloody head
read!

JEAN: That was more or less Graham's feeling about
it. Only he happens to be about fifty years younger
than you, and he put it a bit differently. It all really
started over something I wanted to do, and then
it all came out, lots of things. All kinds of bitterness
—things I didn't even know existed.

BILLY: I didn't know you were interested in politics.

JEAN: Neither did I. I've always found the whole thing
rather boring.

BILLY: Good God! I've heard some things in my time.
This is what comes of giving them the bloody vote.
They start breaking their engagements, just because
they believe every shiftless lay-about writing for the
papers.

PHOEBE: Oh, shut up, just for a minute, Dad. You had
a row because of something you wanted to do?

JEAN: Well, it's—oh, it's a complicated story. I think
I wrote and told you I was teaching Art to a bunch
of Youth Club kids.

PHOEBE: Oh, yes. That was ages ago.

JEAN: Nearly a year. I knew someone who had been
doing it—a young man Graham knew. He said it was

too much for him, and he couldn't stick it any longer. "They're little bastards the lot of them," he said. "If anyone believes you can teach those monsters to create anything, they're crazy. They're a lot of little bastards." That's what he said. But—something, something, made me want to have a go at it. There wasn't any money in it. Just a few shillings for a few nights a week. But it was something I knew a little about—or thought I knew about. I'd never been good enough to paint myself, but I thought this was something I really could do. Even if it was just battling a gang of moronic teenagers. The Club leader thought I was mad, and so did Graham.

PHOEBE: I can't say I blame him really. It doesn't sound a very nice job at all. Not for a young girl like you, Jean. They sound like a real tough crowd to me.

JEAN: They were. Too tough for either of the young men who had taken them on before.

PHOEBE: Well if they don't want to learn, why do they go for heaven's sake?

JEAN: It was an obligatory class, if they attended one of my classes a week, they could take part in the Club's other activities—the dances and so on. I fought those kids back—and some of them were eight feet tall. Most of the time I've loathed it, and I loathed them. I pretended to myself that I didn't, but I did. I hated them, but I think I was getting somewhere. And now Graham wants me to marry him. Now, before he's qualified but I wouldn't. He doesn't want me to try something for myself. He doesn't want me to threaten him or his world, he doesn't want me to succeed. I refused him. Then it all came out—Trafalgar Square and everything. You know, I hadn't realized—it just hadn't occurred to me that you could love somebody, that you could want them, and want them twenty-four hours of the day and then suddenly find that you're neither of you even living in the same world. I don't understand that. I just don't understand it. I wish I could understand it. It's frightening. Sorry, Phoebe, I shouldn't be drinking your gin. I bought this for you.

BILLY: Well we only need a few pigeons for it to be like Trafalgar Square in here. I've never known such a draughty bloody place. Everybody leaves the windows and doors open. I don't believe that's healthy. I tell you, you come in one door and you get blown out the other.

JEAN: How's young Mick—have you heard from him?

PHOEBE: Oh, yes. Of course. He's out there—you knew that, didn't you?

JEAN: Yes. I knew.

PHOEBE: Archie worries about him. He doesn't say so, but I know he does. It's funny really because they never seemed to hit it off so well, in lots of ways. Not like you and him, or Frank. He's a very sensible boy, young Mick. He's very straight. I've lost some sleep this week, I can tell you.

BILLY: He's a fine boy. When they called him, he went. No arguments, nothing. He just went.

JEAN: (*suddenly*). And when they called Frank, he refused, and he went to jail for it—for six months. Young Frank full of doubts about himself, and everybody, with a cold in his head half the year, and a weak chest. Lucky to pass C3. Poor Frank. (*To Phoebe.*) He's not very strong, you always said. You went without to buy him little luxuries to eat, why you wouldn't let him even clean his own shoes. No, you'd do it for him. But he went and said no, and, what's more, he went to jail for it. Oh, he gave in eventually, but he said no for six months of his poor protected life—he said no! I think that's something. You don't have to measure up young Mick against Frank, Grandad. Now, don't look hurt. I'm not getting at you. I love you very much—both of you, but I probably shouldn't have started drinking gin on the train.

Pause.

PHOEBE: Well, we'll shut up about it now.

BILLY: I just said that Mick was a good boy.

JEAN: He is. He's a very good boy. He's a gallant young nineteen year old who's fighting for us all, who never somehow learnt to say no, who never wanted to, and I hope to God he comes back safely.

PHOEBE: Oh dear, Jean, you think he'll be all right, don't you? I don't know why they send these boys out to do the fighting. They're just kids, that's all. That's all he is, a kid.

BILLY: You can't turn against your own people, Jean. You can't do it.

JEAN: Where is Frank? My own people—who are my people?

PHOEBE: He plays the piano in one of these late-night drinking places. He doesn't seem to know what to do with himself. Since he came out of that place. That damned prison. I'll never forget it. Making him go to prison. I'll never forget it. I can't get over it—ever.

JEAN: Well, it's all over now. Have some more of that gin. I bought it for you.

PHOEBE: I won't. And making him do that job. A boy like him shouldn't be doing it. Hospital porter. D'you know they made him stoke the boilers?

JEAN: Yes. He'd have been better off in the Army—sticking a bayonet into some wog.

PHOEBE: He doesn't say a word to me about it. I wish he hadn't done it all the same. I wonder whether Mick isn't better off after all. I mean—they do look after them, don't they?

JEAN: Oh, yes they look after them all right.

BILLY: Look after them better now than they did, when I was in it. I haven't read the evening paper yet. The Dardanelles—I went through that without a scratch. Not a scratch on me.

JEAN: They're all looking after us. We're all right, all of us. Nothing to worry about. *We're* all right. God save the Queen!

Blackout. Draw tabs.   CUE 6

ARCHIE IN TROUBLE – LIKE JOHNNY CARSON WITH ~~DEBAD~~ MONOLEVE

NUMBER FOUR

Spotlight on ARCHIE at microphone.

ARCHIE: I've played in front of them all! "The Queen,"
"The Duke of Edinburgh," "The Prince of Wales,"
and the—what's the name of that other pub? Blimey,
that went better first house. (*Pause.*) I've taken my
glasses off. I don't want to see you suffering. What
about these crooners, eh? What about these crooners?
I don't know what we're coming to. I don't, honest.
Look at the stuff they sing. Look at the songs they
sing! "The Dark Town Strutters' Ball," "The Wood-
choppers' Ball," "The Basin Street Ball"—it's a lot
of rubbish, isn't it? I'll bet you thought I was a
rotten act before I come on, didn't you? What about
these girls? (*Indicates up stage.*) What about them?
Smashin'. I bet you think I have a marvellous time
up here with all these posing girls, don't you? You
think I have a smashin' time don't you? (*Pause.*)
You're dead right! You wouldn't think I was sexy
to look at me, would you! No, lady. To look at me
you wouldn't think I was sexy, would you! (*Pause.*)
You ask him! (*Points to conductor's stand.*) Ask
him! (*Staring out at audience.*) You think I'm like
that, don't you? You think I am! Well, I'm not. But
he is! (*Points to conductor's stand again.*) I'd rather
have a glass of beer any day! And now I'm going
to sing you a little song, a little song, a little song
written by the wife's sister, a little song entitled "The
Old Church bell won't ring tonight, as the Verger's
dropped a clanger!" Thank you, Charlie.

132

"We're all out for good old number one,
  Number one's the only one for me!
  Good old England, you're my cup of tea,
  But I don't want no drab equality.
  Don't let your feelings roam,
  But remember that charity begins at home.
  For Britons shall be free!
  The National Health won't bring you wealth
  Those wigs and blooming spectacles are
        bought by you and me.
  The Army, the Navy and the Air Force,
  Are all we need to make the blighters see
  It still belongs to you, the old red, white and
        blue
Drop Union Jack ← DN LFS ↑ FULL
  Those bits of red still on the map ← CUE B
  We won't give up without a scrap. FOLLOW SP
  What we've got left back   NC
  We'll keep—and blow you, Jack!
  Oh, number one's the only one for me!
  We're all out for good old number one,
  Yes number one's the only one for me——
  God bless you!
  Number one's the only one for me!
  Number one's the only one for me!"

B.O. ——————— EXIT →
      CUE 9

NUMBER FIVE

JACK R ONLY - SWEET

BILLY, PHOEBE, JEAN.

BILLY: They were graceful, they had mystery and dignity. Why when a woman got out of a cab, she descended. Descended. And you put your hand out to her smartly to help her down. Look at them today. Have you ever seen a woman get out of a car? Well, have you? I have, and I don't want to see it again, thank you very much. Why I never saw a woman's legs until I was nineteen. Didn't know what they looked like. Nineteen. I was married when I was nineteen, you know. I was only twenty when Archie's brother was born. Old Bill. He's got on, anyway. I remember the first time I set eyes on your grandmother. She was just eighteen. She had a velvet coat on, black it was, black with fur round the edge. They were all the fashion just about then. It was so tight round her figure. And with her little fur cap on and muff, she looked a picture.

CUE 11

ARCHIE rushes in, his arms full with a carrier bag and bottles, briskly distracted. ARCHIE RICE is about fifty. His hair is brushed flat, almost grey. He wears glasses and has a slight stoop, from a kind of offhand pedantry which he originally assumed thirty years ago when he left one of those minor public day schools in London, which have usually managed to produce some raffish middle class adventurers as well as bank managers and poets. Landladies adore and cosset him because he is so friendly, and obviously such a gentleman. Some of his fellow artists even call him "Professor" occasionally, as they might call a retired Army Captain "Colonel." He smiles

LTS 4

kindly at this simplicity, knowing himself to belong to no class and plays the part as well as he knows how. He lightly patronizes his father, whom he admires deeply. He patronizes his wife, Phoebe, whom he pities wholeheartedly. It is this which has prevented him from leaving her twenty years ago. Or, is it simply because, as many people would suggest, he lacks the courage? Anyway, he makes no secret of his perennial affairs with other women— real and fictitious: It is part of his pity, part of his patronage, part of his personal myth. He patronizes his elder son Frank, who lacks his own brand of indulgence, stoicism and bravura, and for whom he has an almost unreal, pantomime affection. In contrast, his patronage of his daughter Jean is more wary, sly, unsure. He suspects her intelligence, aware that she may be stronger than the rest of them. Whatever he says to anyone is almost always very carefully "thrown away." Apparently absent minded, it is a comedian's technique, it absolves him seeming committed to anyone or anything.   ← LEGS LIGHT UP

ARCHIE: Ay, ay, women's legs again! (*To the others.*) That's what Sterne calls riding your tit with sobriety. I think it was Sterne, anyway. Or was it George Robey? Um? Hello, dear, this is nice. (*He kisses Jean.*) I haven't got my glasses on. I thought you were the Income Tax man sitting there. I thought we had shaken him off. All right, are you?

JEAN: Thank you. I have had too much gin waiting for you.

ARCHIE: Never mind, you can have some more in a minute. You haven't fixed an hotel or anything respectable, have you?

JEAN: No, but——

ARCHIE: Jolly good. I'm sleeping alone tonight. The back of my legs ache as it is. You and Phoebe can sleep up in my room, and I'll kip on the sofa. I've just been talking to our coloured friend on the stairs.

PHOEBE: He's a student.

ARCHIE: No he's not. He's a ballet dancer.

PHOEBE: (*astonished*). Is he! (*To Jean.*) He's a big fellow.

ARCHIE: Playing the Winter Gardens for a fortnight.

BILLY: A ballet dancer!

ARCHIE: He was telling me if you drop your hat outside there now, you have to kick it down to the promenade before you can pick it up. (*Pauses quickly, then goes on expertly.*) They're not all coloured, I saw a couple of 'em on the bus on the way home yesterday. They were talking together all the way, everybody listening. I just got up to press the bell, and a woman shouted out, "I lost two boys in the war for the likes of you!" I thought she meant me for a moment, so I turned round, and there she was, beating them with her umbrella like crazy.

BILLY: Don't like to see a man dancing like that.

ARCHIE: I was in a show with a couple of male dancers once. And wherever we went, on the Monday night some woman used to complain about their tights bulging. Wherever we went. Every Monday night. I'm sure it was the same woman each time. I used to call her the Camp Follower. Now, what are we going to have? Let's see what we've got. (*Rummages in carrier and pockets.*)

BILLY: There's a telegram come for you.

PHOEBE: Don't you think she's looking a bit peaky.

ARCHIE: Looks all right to me. Needs a drink that's all.

BILLY: (*beginning to get tired and irritable*). There's a telegram come for you!

ARCHIE: Have you been on the batter, you old gubbins!

BILLY: No I haven't! I've been sitting here talking to Jean.

ARCHIE: I should go to bed if you're tired.

BILLY: I'm not tired—I could see you out any day!

ARCHIE: (*picks up telegram*). You've been giving him that beastly gin. He sounds like a toast-master with DTs. One of my creditors. It'll wait. (*Throws it back on the table.*) You'd think they'd know better by this time! I've got some gin too—and dubonnet. Old Phoebe likes that don't you, dear! She thinks she's being awfully U when she drinks that, don't you?

PHOEBE: I like it. It seems to suit me. I can't drink gin on its own—not like he can. (*To Archie.*) What's all this for? Was it—was it all right at the theatre?

ARCHIE: No it wasn't all right at the theatre. Monday night there were sixty sad little drabs in, and tonight there were about two hundred sad little drabs. If we can open on Monday night at West Hartlepool, it will be by very reluctant agreement of about thirty angry people, but I'm not thinking about that tonight.

PHOEBE: Oh, Archie!

ARCHIE: Go on, have your dubonnet, dear. Don't get all emotional. Jean, that's yours. Billy, wake up!

BILLY: I am awake!

ARCHIE: Well stop yelling then. You're like one of those television commercials. There's a drink for you.

BILLY: I don't want a bloody drink.

ARCHIE: You look as though you're going to sing a hymn.

BILLY: I'm tired.

ARCHIE: Well that's better—have a drink and go to bed.

BILLY: I haven't seen the evening paper yet.

ARCHIE: Well if you've won the pools, we can read about it in the morning.

BILLY: I don't want to sit here and stagnate even if you do. I want to know what's going on in the world.

ARCHIE: Yes, you're amazingly well informed. (*To the others.*) He's quite well-read for an ignorant old pro.

BILLY: I'm not an ignorant old pro!

ARCHIE: Yes you are, now don't argue and drink up. I'm having a celebration.

BILLY: Celebration! What have you got to celebrate about?

ARCHIE: Oh dear.

BILLY: (*stands up*). You haven't got a thing you can call your own. And as sure as God made little apples, I'll lay a sovereign to a penny piece, you'll end up in the bankruptcy court again before Christmas, and you'll be lucky if you don't land up in jail as well.

PHOEBE: Get 'im to go to bed, Archie. He's overtired.

ARCHIE: Go to bed. You're overtired.

BILLY: I'm not overtired. I don't relish the idea of another jail-bird in the family.

PHOEBE: Be quiet, Dad. You've had too much to drink.

BILLY: I could drink you lot under the table.

ARCHIE: Oh dear, he's getting religious now.

BILLY: I used to have half a bottle of three star brandy for breakfast——

ARCHIE: And a pound of steak and a couple of chorus girls. He'll tell you the whole story at the drop of a hat.

BILLY: (*in rage*). I leave chorus girls to *you*!

ARCHIE: Nothing like slicing yourself off a nice piece of bacon.

BILLY: I know what you mean.

ARCHIE: Don't get excited, Father. You'll wake the Poles up.

BILLY: Don't talk to me about that bunch of greasy tom-cats! One Britisher could always take on half a dozen of that kind. Or used to. Doesn't look like it now.

ARCHIE: Well never mind, don't spoil the party——

BILLY: I pay my way, which is more than you've ever done. And I'll tell you that I was educated at one of the finest schools in England.

ARCHIE: It produced one Field Marshal with strong Fascist tendencies, one Catholic poet who went bonkers and Archie Rice.

BILLY: D'you know what James Agate said about me?

ARCHIE: Oh yes—that you and Mrs. Pat Campbell were his favourite female impersonators.

BILLY: You know bloody well what he said.

Archie knows by long experience how far he can go and he manages gently to turn the situation.

ARCHIE: We all know what he said, and every word of it was true.

Billy glares at him, and grabs his glass.

ARCHIE: Well, as I was saying, before my ignorant old Father interrupted——

BILLY: There's nothing to be ashamed of in being an old pro. It's more than you'll ever be. You don't know the meaning of the word!

PHOEBE: Oh go to bed, Dad—you're getting silly now.

BILLY: You had to have personality to be a comedian then. You had to *really be somebody*!

ARCHIE: The reason for this little celebration is that tomorrow—oh it's today now—today is my twentieth anniversary.

PHOEBE: Twentieth anniversary? Anniversary of what?

ARCHIE: The twentieth anniversary of my not paying income tax. The last time I paid income tax was in 1936.

BILLY: They'll get you all right, they always get you in the end. You see!

ARCHIE: All right, love, you can sing us a hymn later. I think that is a very significant achievement, and I deserve some kind of tribute for it. (*To Jean.*) Don't you think your old man deserves a tribute?

JEAN: I was just wondering how you came to pay income tax in 1936.

ARCHIE: Bad luck that's all. I was trapped in hospital with a double hernia. Very nasty it was too. Terribly complicated. I even thought all my plans for the future were going to be finished at one point. Anyway, that's another story. I'll tell you sometime. I was lying there on my back, wondering whether draught bass on its own was enough to make life worth living, when two men in bowlers and rain-coats sprang at me from behind the screens. That was Archie's one downfall. Could have happened to anyone. I think the ward-sister must have tipped them off. She used to tell me she was very spiritual, so she probably did. I'd gone legit, for a while just then, and I'd been in "The Tale of Two Cities." When I told her she said, "Oh, yes I think I've heard of that——" (*To Billy.*) She was an Irish lady. "A Tale of Two Cities—isn't it about Sodom and Gomorrah?"

Jean smiles. Billy and Phoebe are no longer listening.

ARCHIE: A lady in the pit thought that was quite funny tonight.

PHOEBE: Jean's had an upset with Graham.

ARCHIE: Have you? Oh I'm sorry. I should have asked, shouldn't I? I'm sorry dear. I'm afraid I'm a wee bit slewed. (*Looks round.*) I think everyone is. You are.

PHOEBE: She's broken off her engagement.

ARCHIE: Have you really? Well, I should have thought engagements were a bit suburban for intellectuals like you anyway. You'll be getting a motor-cycle and side-car next.

PHOEBE: Oh stop poking fun at her, Archie. Be sensible. You can see she's upset.

JEAN: I'm not upset, and I haven't made a decision about anything yet. I just came up because I wanted to see you all, and see how you are. And because I miss you.

PHOEBE: Oh, did you really? That's very sweet of you, dear. I appreciate that, I do really.

ARCHIE: She knows I'm not poking fun at her.

PHOEBE: Oh, I wish I knew what's going to happen.

JEAN: Never mind about me. You haven't heard from young Mick?

ARCHIE: No, old Mick can look after himself, he's a boy without problems, that one. I expect he's screwing himself silly. I hope he is anyway. What's happened with you and Graham?

BILLY: Your daughter went to that Trafalgar Square circus last Sunday, if you please!

ARCHIE: Oh, really? Are you one of those who don't like the Prime Minister? I think I've grown rather fond of him. I think it was after he went to the West Indies to get Noel Coward to write a play for him. Still, perhaps only someone of my generation could understand that. Does he bring you out in spots?

PHOEBE: Oh, Christ, I wish I knew what was going to happen to us!

ARCHIE: I feel rather like that about that horrible dog downstairs. It brings me out in a rash every time I look at it. There are three things that do that to me, three things. Nuns, clergymen and dogs.

PHOEBE: I don't want to always have to work. I mean you want a bit of life before it's all over. It takes all the gilt off if you know you've got to go on and on till they carry you out in a box. It's all right for him, he's all right. He's still got his women. While it lasts anyway. But I don't want to end up being laid out by some stranger in some rotten stinking little street in Gateshead, or West Hartlepool or another of those dead-or-alive holes!

JEAN: Phoebe, don't upset yourself, please. Let's enjoy ourselves——

PHOEBE: Enjoy yourself! D'you think I don't want to enjoy myself! I'm just sick of being with down and outs, I'm sick of it, and people like him.
She is crying.

ARCHIE: I wish women wouldn't cry. I wish they wouldn't. Try and say something to her, Jean.

JEAN: (*going to Phoebe*). Why don't you?

ARCHIE: I wish I could. I only wish I could.

JEAN: (*to Phoebe*). Come on, dear, would you like to go to bed?

PHOEBE: Yes, I think so, dear, if you don't mind. I think I've overdone it a bit. Archie knows what I'm like. I never could stand too much excitement. I think perhaps I got over-excited seeing you. It was such a nice surprise. And I'm probably worrying about young Mick underneath. I keep thinking of all that fighting——

ARCHIE: Get some sleep, love, you'll feel better when you wake up.

PHOEBE: (*rising*). All right, dear, I'll get along, it's late anyway. Dad should have been in bed hours ago. He'll be awful tomorrow. Make him go to bed, Archie, will you?

ARCHIE: I will. (*To Jean.*) See her up.

PHOEBE: (*stopping*). Would you come and say good night to me, Archie?

ARCHIE: Yes. I'm just going to finish my little celebration. It's my anniversary, remember?

PHOEBE: (*smiles*). He's funny.

Exit with Jean.

ARCHIE: (*to Billy*). Want another before you turn in?

BILLY: No thank you. I have had sufficient.

ARCHIE: Go on you old gubbins. (*Pours out a drink.*) I know that expression. That's your hymn look.

BILLY: You think I won't!

ARCHIE: I'm damn sure you will. All right, let's have a good heart warmer. Then drink up your beer and go to bed.

BILLY: All right. I will.

He sits upright and sings.

> "Onward Christian soldiers
>   Marching as to war
>   With the Cross of Jesus
>   Going on before.
>   Christ the Royal Master
>   Fights against the foe
>   Forward into battle . . ."

Jean has come back into the room and Billy is too weary to go on. He starts to move down to his room.

BILLY: Good night, Jean. It was good to see you. We'll have a talk tomorrow.

JEAN: Yes, we will. And you're taking me to the Club, remember.

BILLY: Good night, son.

ARCHIE: Good night, Dad.

Exit Billy.

JEAN: Dad——

ARCHIE: Yes.

JEAN: You're keeping something to yourself.

ARCHIE: You never miss a thing, do you? Observation —is the basis of all Art.

JEAN: What is it? I've had a strange sick feeling in my stomach all day. As if something was going to happen. You know the feeling.

ARCHIE: Yes. I know the feeling. Mick's been taken prisoner. Nobody here seemed to know. It's in the paper actually. There was no point in breaking it tonight. Tomorrow's soon enough. (*He tears open the telegram.*) They usually get these things before the people who really matter. I know what this must be. (*He hands it to her and picks up the paper.*) He seems to have been shooting up quite a lot of wogs, doesn't he? There's a picture of your friend here too, the one who gives you a rash. He's looking rather serious this time. Perhaps he's worrying about young Mick.

JEAN: I think I will have some of that.

He pushes her glass towards her.

ARCHIE: Well, Mick wouldn't want us to cut the celebration short. We'll drink to Mick, and let's hope to God he manages. Mick and the income tax man. With you it's Prime Ministers, with me it's dogs. Nuns, clergymen and dogs. Did I ever tell you the greatest compliment I had paid to me—the greatest compliment I always treasure? I was walking along the front somewhere—I think it was here actually— one day, oh, it must be twenty-five years ago, I was quite a young man. Well, there I was walking along the front, to meet what I think we used to call a piece of crackling. Or perhaps it was a bit of fluff. No, that was earlier. Anyway, I know I enjoyed it afterwards. But the point is I was walking along the front, all on my own, minding my own business,

(*Pause*) and two nuns came towards me—(*Pause*)
two nuns——

*He trails off, looking very tired and old. He looks
across at Jean and pushes the bottle at her.*

ARCHIE: Talk to me.

CURTAIN

END OF ACT ONE

LTS↓o

∴

FOLLOW SPOT POPS ON

INTERMISSION

NUMBER SIX

BILLY, PHOEBE and JEAN. PHOEBE is flushed with drink.

BILLY: I knew they couldn't keep him. They wouldn't dare.

PHOEBE: Home in a couple of days—I just can't believe it.

BILLY: They wouldn't dare, not even nowadays—cockeyed bunch they are. I remember 'em from before the war. I was with that show, you remember, Phoebe——

PHOEBE: Well what would they want to keep a boy like that for? That's what I kept asking myself. Can't do them any good. It couldn't do them any good, could it?

BILLY: Grubby lot of rogues. I was a guest at the Ambassadors, you know. Gave me a box of Romeo and Juliet cigars.

JEAN: (*surrounded by pile of newspapers*). Well, the name of Rice is famous once again.

BILLY: This long they were. Haven't had a cigar like that for years.

PHOEBE: He likes a cigar. I buy those cheroots sometimes. They're only cheap things, but he doesn't mind them, does he?

BILLY: Course I don't mind them. Jeannie gave me some didn't she? What's the matter with you?

PHOEBE: Oh yes, I was forgetting.

BILLY: Got a mind like a bloody sieve!

PHOEBE: I was always a dunce at school. I keep thinking of Archie. I'm so afraid that he's going to be disappointed. That everything will go wrong, and they won't let Mick come home after all.

BILLY: Pardon me, Phoebe, but you do talk the most almighty rubbish I've ever had to sit and listen to.

JEAN: They've given a formal undertaking.

BILLY: Formal undertaking, my backside—if I thought that boy's future depended on their "formal undertaking" we could say "thank you very much and good night."

PHOEBE: (*paper in her lap*). We've got an aeroplane standing by all ready to rush him home.

BILLY: "Formal undertaking"—proper politicians' words they are. They'd mean damn all if they were said by one of ours.

JEAN: (*reading*). "Bring him home"—in a matter of a few hours Sergeant Rice should be speeding homewards in a specially allocated Dakota.

BILLY: They know damn well they daren't do anything else.

JEAN: We're going to have ourselves a hero, you can see that——

BILLY: Any one of us would have done the same thing. There's nothing wrong with any of us, never has been. You can't all get to the top. You can't make your own luck. Me, I was always lucky, always was. Mind you, I was good too. That Ambassador, Sir Somebody Pearson his name was, charming, absolutely, the real best type, absolutely the best type. He told me I was his favourite artist. Barring George Robey.

PHOEBE: What good would it do them, hanging on to a kid. That's all he is.

JEAN: This one says——

BILLY: He's lucky. I was always lucky. Mind you, I was good too.

JEAN: (*reading*). "Lieut. Pearson, of Leicester, who had been with Sergeant Rice until a few minutes before he was captured, said he must have killed at least seven of the attackers."

BILLY: Was that Pearson you said——

JEAN: "Before he was overwhelmed, 'he must have run out of ammunition,' said Pearson. Young Rice wasn't the type to give up."

Pause.

PHOEBE: I don't want Archie to be disappointed, that's all. On top of everything else. He's had enough of disappointments. I don't think he ever really gets used to them.

BILLY: You see, a couple of days, and Mick'll be sitting down here talking about it.

PHOEBE: I remember once my Mum promised to take us kids to the pantomime, and then something happened, she couldn't take us. I don't know what it was, she didn't have the money I expect. You could sit up in the gallery then for sixpence. Poor old Mum—she took us later, but it didn't seem the same to me. I was too disappointed. I'd been thinking about that pantomime for weeks. You shouldn't build things up. You're always disappointed really. That's Archie's trouble. He always builds everything up. And it never turns out.

BILLY: He's a fool.

PHOEBE: He's too good for them, that's his trouble. People don't appreciate you properly. Let's finish this up shall we? Archie'll bring some more in with him when he comes.

BILLY: It's all over, finished. I told him years ago. But he won't listen. He won't listen to anybody.

PHOEBE: You can't help giving Archie his own way. Not really. No, all they're out for is a cheap thrill. (*To Jean.*) Come on, have half of this with me. We've all got to—what's the word?

BILLY: I dunno what you're talking about.

JEAN: Compromise?

PHOEBE: She knows what I mean. That's right, dear.

You keep on and on, try your best, and then a time comes when you can't go on any longer. It's not giving in—or I suppose it is. It's just being sensible. (*To Jean.*) Has he said anything to you?

JEAN: What about?

PHOEBE: Oh, about anything. He never tells me anything now, he just tells me not to worry, and says nothing. Frank told me the company only got half salary on Saturday night, and he thinks these scenery people must have caught up with him because——

BILLY: He said he'd bring me back some cigarettes. I could have got them myself by this time. I suppose he's in that Rockliffe.

PHOEBE: Whenever there's a ring at the door, I daren't answer it, in case it's a policeman standing there with another summons.

JEAN: (*offering cigarettes to Billy*). Have one of these.

BILLY: That bloody meat market.

PHOEBE: It's not a nice feeling when you can't go and answer the door.

BILLY: There'll be a policeman at the door all right——

PHOEBE: (*weary, not peevish*). Oh, don't keep interrupting while I'm talking to Jean.

BILLY: (*to Jean, politely*). Thank you, my dear. (*Picks up his newspaper.*)

PHOEBE: I've upset him now.

JEAN: No you haven't. He's just reading. Aren't you, Grandad?

PHOEBE: Oh well, it's no good worrying. Is it? It says in the papers Mick's coming home, and they ought to know about these things, and that's all that really matters. Have a drop of this, dear.

BILLY: No thank you.

PHOEBE: (*to Jean*). Pour him out a glass. There's one over there. Oh, Dad, he exaggerates everything, don't you? He exaggerates everything, but he's right, you know. He's right about Archie. He hasn't got an enemy in the world who's done him the harm he's done himself.

JEAN: There you are, Grandad.

BILLY: Thank you, Jean. I'll have it later.

JEAN: Don't have it later. Have it now. This is the time to celebrate. Come on then. Let's drink to Mick.

PHOEBE: Yes, we mustn't sit here, getting morbid. We're a bit short on the drink, aren't we? I hope Archie won't be long in that place.

JEAN: Frank's gone with him. He won't be long.

PHOEBE: Oh, Frank'll see he doesn't get home too late. Frank's a sensible boy—sometimes he is anyway. (*To Jean.*) I think you're the only really sensible one of us lot.

JEAN: Grandad doesn't think so, do you?

BILLY: She's just as bloody daft as the rest of you.

PHOEBE: He's a fool to himself. Always some big idea he's got to make money. A while back it was female impersonators. We were going to make a packet. That's what Archie said anyway. But by the time Archie got started with it it had all petered out. Now it's rock and roll. Oh well. It's like the women. They get tired of him. They come back here a few times, and that's that——

BILLY: Why don't you hold your bloody noise!

PHOEBE: He doesn't like me talking about it. As if she didn't know what's been going on all this time.

BILLY: Well there's no reason to talk about it.

PHOEBE: She's not soft, are you, dear?

BILLY: I don't want to hear about it, and I shouldn't think she does.

PHOEBE: All right, all right.

BILLY: She's used to be with people who know how to behave. She doesn't want to hear about your troubles.

PHOEBE: No of course she doesn't.

BILLY: Well then—the trouble with you people is you don't know how to carry on properly, that's your trouble. Give the girl a chance, she's got her own life to lead.

PHOEBE: I was only telling her——

BILLY: And I'm telling you don't! There's nothing you can tell her. So hold your noise——

JEAN: Grandad, please——

BILLY: Why don't you go back to London to your friends?

JEAN: Don't let's argue——

BILLY: We're no good to you——

JEAN: I don't think I want to go back to London——

PHOEBE: I was only talking to her about Archie. You don't want to leave, do you, dear?

JEAN: Of course I don't.

PHOEBE: I was just saying, in the course of ordinary conversation, that Archie wasn't very lucky that's all.

JEAN: Here——(*She has put a small bottle of gin on the table.*)

PHOEBE: And if I mention the women, it was just because it's been the same thing with them. It's never bothered me, that, so much. It never meant a great deal to me, not even when I was young. Still, I suppose men are different. It's more important to them. Oh, look what she's done!

JEAN: I thought I'd better get some in, in case Dad was late.

BILLY: What do you think you're supposed to be—a millionairess?

JEAN: But you're not to have any, till you've had something to eat first, you've had nothing but tea and cigarettes for days.

PHOEBE: I couldn't eat anything, dear. Honestly.

JEAN: I'll get something for you.

PHOEBE: No, I couldn't. I couldn't—hold it down.

JEAN: (*moving*). I'm not going to argue——

PHOEBE: Jean, I've asked you—I can't! I don't want it!

JEAN: But people have got to eat, dear. If you don't have something——

PHOEBE: (*laughing slightly*). People have to eat, she says. That's a good one!

JEAN: You can't carry on, dear.

Billy gets up humming "Rock of Ages" and goes off L.

PHOEBE: People have to eat, she says. D'you hear that? Where's he got to?

JEAN: He's just gone into the kitchen.

PHOEBE: That's not all they have to do. They have to do a whole lot of things, a lot of things you don't even know about, and it's nothing to do with being educated and all that. Why should you know about it?

JEAN: I know, love. Things have been tough. But be sensible, you've got to keep on.

PHOEBE: Don't tell me to be sensible, Jean.

JEAN: I'm sorry, dear. I didn't mean it like that——

PHOEBE: Don't tell me to be sensible! You're a sweet girl, Jean, and I'm very fond of you. But you're not even my own daughter. I wouldn't take that from Mick or Frank, and they're my own.

JEAN: All right, forget it. We'll forget it. We haven't had our drink to Mick yet.

PHOEBE: Don't—don't presume too much.

JEAN: Phoebe please—I just——

PHOEBE: Don't presume too much. What's he doing out there?

JEAN: He's probably getting him something to eat, I expect.

PHOEBE: I don't want him messing about out there. He knows I don't like him going out there. He leaves everything in such a mess.

JEAN: Here, have this.

PHOEBE: Why doesn't Archie come back? You'd think he'd come back here and celebrate after hearing his son is safe and on his way home. I don't know— you people——

JEAN: Come along, Phoebe, don't let's have a row. And over nothing—it's silly.

PHOEBE: It's not silly. Anyway, who said we're having a row? All I said was I wasn't hungry, and you start getting at me.

JEAN: I wasn't getting at you.

PHOEBE: You people—you're all alike.

JEAN: Believe me, Phoebe. I wasn't——

PHOEBE: I can't eat because I feel sick.

JEAN: Well, all right then.

PHOEBE: You don't know what it's like. You don't know what it's like because we tried to do our best by you. Oh, Archie tried to do his best by you, even if it didn't add up to very much. Not that you weren't a good girl, you worked hard. You deserved it, you've always tried, and you've got what it takes. And that's more than any of us have got, my dear. You're the only one of us who has. You and young Mick. And the old man of course. He had it. Not that it's any use to him now. He's just a has-been, I suppose. Still—it's better to be a has-been than a never-was. His other son's the same—Old Bill. Archie's brother. Not that you'd think he was. Now he's really a big pot. He's really a big pot. There's no flies on brother Bill.

JEAN: (*trying to turn the conversation*). He's a barrister—that's why you like him so much. He's like that actor on the pictures who's always in a wig and gown in every other——

PHOEBE: I like him because he's a gentleman. He's different from your father, even if they did go to the same posh school and all that. I like him because of the way he treats me. He talks to me beautifully, the way he calls me "Phoebe." You should hear the way he calls me "Phoebe."

JEAN: I only saw him a couple of times.

PHOEBE: Well, of course you did. He didn't approve of the way Archie carried on. He never did. Sometimes, in the early days he'd come and see us. He always slipped a couple of fivers in my hand before he left, and he'd just say "Not a word to Archie, now." I just never used to know what to say to him. We'd always be living in some bloody digs some-

where, and I didn't like him coming. I'd feel awful.
He could never bring his wife, and I never knew
what to say. Then he and Archie would always have
a row over something Archie had been doing. Either
he'd lost money, or he was out of work. I remember
he came once, and Archie and me didn't have a
bean. We'd been living on penny pieces of bacon
from the butcher's, and what we got then from the
Tribunal. (*She pronounces it Tribbunel.*) You and
the boys were staying with the Old Man then. Archie
wouldn't take money from his Dad then—perhaps
it was professional jealousy, I don't know. Anyway,
Bill heard that Archie was in trouble again—I don't
remember what it was. But it was something serious
this time, I think. Oh, he tried to pass a dud cheque
and he'd picked the wrong person or something. That
wasn't like Archie, I must admit, because he never
did anything really dishonest like that, whatever else
he might have done. He must have been drunk. Anyway, Old Bill came over—we were living at Brixton
at that time, and the kids in the street made a terrible
mess of his car. They didn't see many cars in that
street except when it was the doctor. Not that he said
a word about it. When we went to the door, and I
saw what they'd done to it, I just stood there, I felt
so ashamed, and I burst out crying. He patted my arm
in that way of his and he just said "I'm so sorry,
Phoebe. I really am. I'm afraid it's always going to
be like this." Well, he got Archie out of whatever it
was, and that was that. It wasn't the money, or his
helping Archie—although I was grateful for that, of
course. It was the way he spoke to me in that quiet
gentlemanly way, and the way he patted my arm.
JEAN: Yes, I can see him doing it.
PHOEBE: What do you mean—what do you mean by
    that remark?
JEAN: Oh nothing, dear. Let's not talk about it——
PHOEBE: What do you mean by that remark?

JEAN: Oh, it's just that I can see brother Bill patting your arm, slipping that ten pounds in your hand, and then driving off to have dinner at his Club. That's all, Phoebe. Now let's not talk about it any more.

PHOEBE: You mean he was just sorry for me, don't you?

JEAN: No, I don't.

PHOEBE: Come on, say it—you mean he was just sorry for me, don't you?

JEAN: I didn't say that and I didn't mean that. Now come on——

Enter ARCHIE *with* FRANK. FRANK *is a pale, shy boy of about nineteen. He has allowed himself to slip into the role of* ARCHIE's *"feed" because this seems to be a warm, reasonable relationship substitute that suits them both. He is impulsive, full of affection that spills over easily. He is young, and will probably remain so.*

PHOEBE: I want to know what you meant.

ARCHIE: My dear, nobody can tell you what they mean. You ought to know that by now.

PHOEBE: Shut up a minute, Archie—I'm talking to Jean. She knows what I mean. You know what I meant, don't you?

ARCHIE: Do you know what she means? I wish to God I did. (*To Frank.*) I can see we should have stayed.

PHOEBE: Shall I tell you something?

JEAN: Phoebe, what are you doing?

PHOEBE: Shall I?

JEAN: It's just that I know exactly how Uncle Bill patted your arm—just in the same way as he'd wait on the men at Christmas when he was in the army. So democratic, so charming, and so English.

ARCHIE: Oh, Bill's all right. Just doesn't understand people like us, that's all. And what's more he doesn't want to. Can't blame him really.

PHOEBE: (*to Jean*). You don't like him, do you? I knew you didn't like him.

ARCHIE: Like now. Oh, brother Bill wouldn't understand all this at all. He'd be frightfully embarrassed, wouldn't he? Give us over that carrier, Frankie love.

PHOEBE: You can't afford not to like him. You owe him too much.

ARCHIE: Sounds a pretty good reason for not liking anyone, I should say.

PHOEBE: He's something you'll never be.

ARCHIE: And I'm something he'll never be—good Old Bill. He may be successful, but he's not a bad sort. Do you know that my brother Bill has had one wife, no love affair, he's got three charming gifted children. Two of them took honours degrees at Cambridge, and all of them have made what these people call highly successful marriages.

FRANK: What on earth's everybody talking about? Hullo, Jean, love. I thought we were going to have a party.

He throws his arms around her and kisses her.

ARCHIE: It's perfectly true. I read it in the *Telegraph* today. I got bored reading about young Mick, and there, tucked away in the middle——

JEAN: (*eagerly*). Don't tell me you read——

ARCHIE: Of course, I read it. How else would I know whether my relations were getting married, or dying, or having babies. As I was saying——

FRANK: Before you were so rudely interrupted.

Kissing Jean affectionately once again.

ARCHIE: Yes, before that. Young Sonia is getting married.

JEAN: Who to?

ARCHIE: Oh, the son of some industrialist, Capt. Charlie Double-back-Action hyphen-breech loading Gore of Elm Lodge, Shrewkesbury, Glos. Where are all the glasses, for God's sake? Good ole Bill—he's got everything he wants now, including Captain Charlie Double-back-Action Gore.

PHOEBE: Archie, I'm talking to Jean.

ARCHIE: Yes, I thought that's what you were doing. I sized the situation up in a flash.

PHOEBE: Oh, it's easy for people like you to make fun. I left school when I was twelve years old.

ARCHIE: Christ, if she tells me that once more I shall get up on the roof, drunk as I am, I shall get up on the roof and scream. I've never done that before.

PHOEBE: You had to pay sixpence a week then.

FRANK: Leave her alone, you old bastard. Come on, Mum, we're going to have a party.

PHOEBE: I'm talking to Jean.

ARCHIE: Yes, we were in on that. Why don't we all talk to Jean. We don't see much of her. Frank—talk to Jean.

FRANK: Dad——

He nods towards PHOEBE, *distressed to see her like this, but* ARCHIE, *who has come in prepared to be gay, is tired and has begun to give up the situation.*

ARCHIE: Let's have a drink first. If I'm going to be either very diplomatic, or very tactful, I must have plenty to drink first.

PHOEBE: We had to pay sixpence a week, and most weeks my mother couldn't find it——

ARCHIE: This is a welfare state, my darling heart. Nobody wants, and nobody goes without, all are provided for.

PHOEBE: I was out scrubbing a dining hall for——

ARCHIE: Everybody's all right. Young Mick's all right. Bill's all right. Why, he never even got himself jailed by a lot of wogs. Frank's all right—he won't be stoking boilers much longer, will you, boy?

FRANK: I wish you'd both shut up.

ARCHIE: Jean's all right. She'll make it up with Graham, and forget about silly old Trafalgar Square, and Prime Ministers who look like dogs downstairs. Here you are, dear. (*Offers drink to Phoebe.*)

PHOEBE: You don't understand——

ARCHIE: I know. Phoebe scrubbed a dining hall floor for five hundred kids when she was twelve years old, didn't you?

PHOEBE: Oh——

ARCHIE: Didn't you? Have you any idea, any of you, have you any idea how often she's told me about those five hundred kids and that dining hall?

FRANK: Oh, shut up.

ARCHIE: Yes, son, I'll shut up. Pass this to Jean. She looks as though she can use it.

(*Rises and gives drink to Jean. Remain standing by D.L. chair.*)

JEAN: I can.

FRANK: You've been away too long. Every night is party night.

ARCHIE: And do you know why? Do you know why? Because we're dead beat and down and outs. We're drunks, maniacs, we're crazy, we're bonkers, the whole flaming bunch of us. Why, we have problems that nobody's ever heard of, we're characters out of something that nobody believes in. We're something that people make jokes about, because we're so remote from the rest of ordinary everyday, human experience. But we're not really funny. We're too boring. Simply because we're not like anybody who ever lived. We don't get on with anything. We don't ever succeed in anything. We're a *nuisance,* we do nothing but make a God almighty fuss about anything we ever do. All the time we're trying to draw someone's attention to our nasty, sordid, unlikely little problems. Like that poor, pathetic old thing there. Look at her. What has she got to do with people like you? People of intellect and sophistication. She's very drunk, and just now her muzzy, under-developed, untrained mind is racing because her blood stream is full of alcohol I can't afford to give her, and she's going to force us to listen to all sorts of dreary embarrassing things we've all heard a hundred times before. She's getting old, and she's worried about who's going to keep her when she can't work any longer. She's afraid of ending up in a long box in somebody else's front room in Gateshead, or was it West Hartlepool?

PHOEBE: What's he talking about?

ARCHIE: She's going to tell you that old brother Bill paid for all your education. That's what she wants to tell you, Jean. That scholarship didn't pay for the things that really mattered, you know. The books, the fares, the clothes, and all the rest of it. Bill paid for that. For all of you. Frank knows that, don't you, Frank? I'm sorry, Phoebe. I've killed your story. Old Archie could always kill anybody's punch line if he wanted.

PHOEBE: She doesn't know about Mick and you and me. I know she doesn't.

ARCHIE: She'll find out. We always find these things out in time. (*To Frank and Jean.*) She's tired and she's getting old. She's tired, and she's tired of me. Nobody ever gave her two pennyworth of equipment except her own pretty unimpressive self to give anything else to the rest of the world. All it's given her is me, and my God she's tired of that! Aren't you, my old darling? You're tired of that, aren't you?

PHOEBE: (*fiercely*). I tried to make something of myself. I tried, I really did try. I was nothing much to look at, but what I was I made myself. I was a plain kid—no I wasn't. I wasn't even plain. I was the ugliest bloody kid you ever saw in your life. You've never seen anyone as ugly as I was. But I made something of myself. I did try to do something. I made him want me anyway.

FRANK: Everyone shouts! Please, somebody speak quietly, just for once. Those bloody Poles will be up here in a minute. Let's have a row. It looks as if we're going to have one anyway. But please can we have a *quiet* row!

ARCHIE: It was a long time ago. They knew it was a long time ago. (*To Frank.*) I wish you'd stop yelling, I can't hear myself shout. Sing one of your songs, there's a good boy. Where's the old man?

JEAN: He's in the kitchen.

ARCHIE: Billy! Come out of there! Who's he got in

there? Something you picked up in the Cambridge!
Have you ever had it on a kitchen table? Like a piece
of meat on a slab. Slicing pieces of bacon. Don't you
wish you were back with old Graham? (*To Jean.*)

PHOEBE: Frank, he's going to bring up one of those
women, isn't he? In here, isn't he?

ARCHIE: Leave her alone, son.

Sits L. of D.R. sofa.

PHOEBE: Do you think I don't lie awake upstairs, and
hear it going on?

ARCHIE: Of course they know. They know what sort of a
bastard I am, love. I think they know almost as well
as you do. Well, almost as well. She'll be all right,
won't you, love? Where's the old man? (*To Frank
and Jean.*) Now don't pretend you're not used to it.

Billy appears.

There you are, you old has-been! Have you brought
us a slice of bacon in?

BILLY: What's the matter with you lot?

ARCHIE: We're all just waiting for the little yellow van
to come——

BILLY: Did you get my cigarettes?

ARCHIE: Except for Jean. There's still hope for her. You
wait, you old Gubbins, you'll be reading about your
granddaughter and Mr. Graham Thing of Elm Lodge,
Shrewkesbury, Glos. Here you are. (*Tosses cigarettes
to Billy and gives him a drink.*)

PHOEBE: (*to Billy*). You've been at that cake.

BILLY: What?

PHOEBE: You've been at my cake. You've been at my
cake, haven't you?

BILLY: (*flushing*). I was hungry——

PHOEBE: That cake was for Mick. It was for Mick, it
wasn't for you.

BILLY: I'm sorry——

PHOEBE: I bought it for Mick. It was for when he comes
home.

ARCHIE: Well, never mind.

PHOEBE: What do you mean—never mind!

ARCHIE: Mick wouldn't mind.

PHOEBE: Well I mind! I don't want him in that kitchen. Tell him to keep out of it. It's not much, and it's not mine, but I mind very much. Why couldn't you leave it alone?

BILLY: I just fancied——

PHOEBE: Couldn't you leave it alone? It wasn't for you. What's the matter with you? I feed you, don't I? Don't think you give me all that much money every week, because you don't!

ARCHIE: Phoebe, forget it!

PHOEBE: I don't forget, I don't forget anything. I don't forget anything even if you do.

ARCHIE: We'll buy another one.

PHOEBE: Oh, you'll buy another one! You're so rich! You're such a great big success! What's a little cake —we'll order a dozen of 'em! I bought that cake, and it cost me thirty shillings, it was for Mick when he comes back, because I want to give him something, something I know he'll like, after being where he's been, and going through what he has—and now, that bloody *greedy* old pig—that old pig, as if he hadn't had enough of everything already—he has to go and get his great fingers into it!

Unable to top this, she bursts into tears. BILLY stands, ashamed and deeply hurt by what she has said, even though he vaguely realizes the condition she is in. He puts down the drink he has been holding, and the cigarettes.

BILLY: Excuse me, Jean.

He crosses down to his room and goes out.

PHOEBE: Archie, you haven't got anybody coming tonight, have you?

ARCHIE: I suppose he has had more than any of us, and he's enjoyed it. Good luck to him. All the same, you needn't have done that. No, there's nobody coming.

PHOEBE: Oh, I'm sorry, Archie. Try and forgive me——

ARCHIE: Not that I don't wish there were. But then you know that. Come on love, pull yourself together.

That's what we should have done years ago. Pulled ourselves together. Let's pull ourselves together. (*Sings.*) Let's pull ourselves together, together, together. Let's pull ourselves together, and the happier we'll be!

FRANK: That's right chaps—remember we're British!

ARCHIE: That's what everybody does. Perfectly simple. I've always known it. That's what my old brother Bill used to tell me. Now let's fill up and be happy. What about old Mick, eh?

FRANK: Yes, what about old Mick? Don't look so glum, Jean. You know what everybody's like.

JEAN: Do I?

ARCHIE: Never mind, there's no reason why she should, as Phoebe would say. We're all a bit slewed, which means that we're a bit more sub-human even than we usually are. (*To Frank.*) Isn't that right, you great weedy boiler stoker you! I'll bet the patients in that hospital all freeze to death—he must be saving the National Health thousands.

FRANK: (*to Phoebe*). Feel all right now?

PHOEBE: Perhaps Jean doesn't want to have a drink, and do you know why?

ARCHIE: No, why?

PHOEBE: Because I don't think she even likes him. I don't think she likes Mick.

ARCHIE: There's no reason why she should. But that won't stop her. Or me. Frank, go in and talk to the old man, and get him to come back. (*Crosses to D.R. proscenium arch.*) We'll try to be a little normal just for once, and pretend we're a happy, respectable, decent family. For Mick's sake. You know, I really think that's what he'd like, somehow. I'm sure he thinks we're rather dreadful. Worse than the wogs really. Don't worry, Jean, you won't have to put up with this kind of thing for long—any more than Mick. And this is Mick's party. Phoebe, let's see you do your dance. (*This is thrown off in the usual casual, studied Archie manner.*) She dances jolly well, don't

you, you poor old thing. I wonder if she'll make me
cry tonight. We'll see. Frank, sing us your song.

JEAN: I don't even know what I'm feeling. I don't even
know if I do at all.

ARCHIE: Never mind, dear. I didn't know that for years,
either. You're a long time dead, Mrs. Murphy, let's
make it a party, Mick the soldier's coming back, let's
just whoop it up!

CUE 16

CURTAIN

NUMBER SEVEN

Music. ARCHIE *rises, his face held open by a grin, and dead behind the eyes. Just now and then, for a second or two, he gives the tiniest indication that he is almost surprised to find himself where he is.*

ARCHIE: Here, here! Here, I've just seen a man with a lemon stuck in his ear! A lemon stuck in his ear! So I went up to him, I said: "What are you doing with that lemon stuck in your ear?" and he says: "Well, you know that man with a hearing aid—well, I'm the man with the lemonade." Thank you for that burst of heavy breathing. You should have heard what James Agate said about *me*! (*Back again.*) But I have a go, lady, don't I? I 'ave a go. I do. You think I am, don't you? Well, I'm not. But *he* is! Here, here! Did I tell you about the wife? Did I? My wife —not only is she stupid, not only is she stupid, but she's cold as well. Oh yes, cold. She may look sweet, but she's a very cold woman, my wife. Very cold. Cold and stupid. She's what they call a moron glacee. Don't clap too hard—it's a very old building. Well, I 'ave a go, don't I? I do—I 'ave a go. Look at me— it's all real, you know. Me—all real, nothing shoddy. You don't think I'm real, do you? Well, I'm not. (*Stumbling.*) I'm not going to deprive you of the treat I know you've all been waiting for. Yes, I'm going to sing to you. I'm going to sing to you a little song, a little song written by myself. I haven't recorded it, so if you like it, you tell 'em. They won't listen, but you tell 'em. A little song called "My girl's always short of breath, but she don't mind a good blow through."

He sings.
    Now I'm just an ordinary bloke

COLOR
CHANGE
    The same as you out there.
    Not mad for women, I'm not a soak,
    I never really care.
    I'm what you call a moderate,
    I weigh all the pros. and the cons.
    I don't push and shove
    At the thing they call love,
    I never go in for goings on.
    Thank God I'm normal, normal, normal.
    Thank God I'm normal,
    I'm just like the rest of you chaps.

    Thank God I'm normal,
    I'm just like the rest of you chaps,
    Decent and full of good sense,
    I'm not one of these extremist saps,
    For I'm sure you'll agree,
    That a fellow like me
    Is the salt of our dear old country,
            of our dear old country.
Bang on appropriate lighting. Speaking:
    But when our heritage is threatened
    At home or cross the sea.
Play "Land of Hope and Glory."
    It's chaps like us—yes you and me,
    Who'll march again to victory.
    Some people say we're finished,

BRIT. ↑
    Some people say we're done.
    But if we all stand
Spotlight behind gauze reveals a nude in Britannia's
helmet and holding a bulldog and trident.
    By this dear old land,
    The battle will be won.

    Thank God we're normal, normal, normal.
    Thank God we're normal.
    We are the country's flower,

And when the great call comes,
Someone will gaze down on us,
And say: They made no fuss——
For this was their finest shower.
Yes, this was their finest shower!
Thank God we're normal, normal, normal,
Thank God we're normal,
Yes, this is our finest shower!

EXIT ARCHIE.

NUMBER EIGHT

ARCHIE, FRANK, PHOEBE, JEAN, BILLY.

ARCHIE: She'd steal your knickers and sell 'em for dusters.

FRANK: Who?

ARCHIE: Mrs. Roberts, No. 7, Claypit Lane, always used to say that.

FRANK: Who are you talking about, you bloody right-wing old poup?

ARCHIE: I'm talking about that blonde bitch in the Cambridge, the one who's always upsetting your Grandad. And don't call me a right-wing old poup.

PHOEBE: I remember Mrs. Roberts. She was very nice to us.

ARCHIE: I may be an old poup, but I'm not a right-wing.

FRANK: That's strictly for cigar smokers like Grandad. (*Dancing.*) "Oh, the end of me old cigar, cigar, the end of me old cigar, I turned 'em round and touched 'em up with the end of me old cigar! The end of me old cigar, cigar, the end of me old cigar——"

ARCHIE: There was a chap at my school who managed to get himself into the Labour Government, and they always said he was left of centre. Then he went into the House of Lords, and they made him an honourable fishmonger. Well, that just about wraps up the Left of Centre, doesn't it?

FRANK: You know, you don't know what you're talking about.

BILLY: I used to have digs in Claypit Lane—ten shillings a week all-in.

PHOEBE: Frank, I thought you were going to sing.

168

ARCHIE: If you can dodge all the clichés dropping like bats from the ceiling, you might pick up something from me.

FRANK: Well, plenty of others have picked it up from you.

ARCHIE: Just you remember I'm your father.

FRANK: When did you ever remember it?

PHOEBE: Frank! Come on now, be a good boy.

ARCHIE: You want to be more like Jean——

FRANK: She's just not used to us any more. Are you, love? Are you all right?
Puts his arm around her.

JEAN: I'm all right.

FRANK: Are you really? Bet you'd forgotten what this was like, didn't you?

PHOEBE: Course she hadn't forgotten. She doesn't forget as easy as that, do you, dear?

JEAN: No—I don't think so.

FRANK: (*to Phoebe*). You're feeling better?

PHOEBE: Yes, thank you, dear. Come over here and give me a kiss. (*He does so.*) He's a good boy to me, aren't you, dear? Even when I act a bit daft. We all act a bit daft sometimes, I suppose.

ARCHIE: Except Jean——

JEAN: Will you please stop trying to make me feel as if I were from another planet or something.

PHOEBE: Archie's just pulling your leg, aren't you Archie? I didn't have my Beecham's Pills yesterday. D'you know my mother never had a doctor in her life—except when we were born, of course. And all she ever took was two pennorth of Beecham's, peroxide, and Dutch drops.

JEAN: Peroxide?

FRANK: She used to drink it like Guinness.

PHOEBE: Well, she lived to be ninety-three and never cost the Government a penny. (*To Billy.*) All right?

BILLY: Yes, thank you, Phoebe.

PHOEBE: (*to Archie*). Put something in his glass, Archie. It's nearly empty.

BILLY: I was just trying to remember the name of the woman.

PHOEBE: What woman?

BILLY: The one in Claypit Lane. She used to give us bacon every morning for breakfast, and she'd melt cheese over it. First time I'd ever had it.

PHOEBE: Don't like anything like that much. Here, did you—pardon my interruption but I just remembered it—did you see that picture of the Duchess of Porth's daughter in the paper today?

FRANK: Should we?

PHOEBE: I wouldn't have seen it. I was only really reading about Mick, of course, but I couldn't help noticing it. She looked so fascinating. Did you see it, Archie?

ARCHIE: Oh yes. She was next to Captain Breech-Loading Gore.

PHOEBE: Didn't you think she looked magnificent?

ARCHIE: I thought she looked like Dad's barmaid in the Cambridge.

FRANK: Yes—in drag.

PHOEBE: Frank!

ARCHIE: (*quickly*). Phoebe's very keen on the Duchess of Porth, aren't you, love? She says she thinks she's natural.

PHOEBE: I suppose it's a bit silly, but I've always taken an interest in her. Oh, ever since she was quite young. I feel she must be very nice somehow. (*Pause.*) (*To Archie.*) Is he all right? (*Nodding to Billy.*)

ARCHIE: He's all right. You're all right, aren't you?

BILLY: She always used to put cheese over the bacon.

ARCHIE: He's thinking about the landlady in Claypit Lane. You know, that barmaid in the Cambridge reminds me of a bloke—(*To Jean*)—this'll interest you because it's Prime Ministers and Dogs—he was Irish, he did a trampoline act and they called him "Lady Rosie Bothways." Actually, he was a devout sort of a lad. He gave it all up later and went into Public Relations or something. Well, Rosie knew more dirty words than you'll hear in any place on any Saturday night. He could go on for ten minutes without pausing for breath, or repeating himself once. He was an artist. But to Rosie the most deadly four-letter word in the English—or any other—language, was Tory. He'd apply it to anything, provided he thought it was really bad enough.

BILLY: I'll bet he was bloody Irish.

ARCHIE: I've just said so. Do try and listen.

PHOEBE: I thought Frank was going to sing.

ARCHIE: If you gave him a plate of badly cooked chips, he'd hold 'em up and say: "Who done these no-good, blank, blank, stinking, Tory chips?"

FRANK: You've told that story before.

ARCHIE: I'll bodge you in a minute.

FRANK: I'll bodge *you* in a minute. It's not even a very good story.

ARCHIE: When you learn to tell a story as well as I do, you'll be all right——

FRANK: I'll never look *old* enough, to tell your stories.

ARCHIE: I think you'd better sing, don't you?

FRANK: All right, all right, I will. I'll sing for Jean, because she hasn't heard me. I'm going to sing one of Billy's. It's British——

BILLY: What's that? What song?

FRANK: And very religious.

BILLY: What song's he singing?

FRANK: So there's something in it for you all.

He sings and dances.

> When you've shouted Rule Britannia,
> When you've sung God Save the Queen,
> When you've finished killing Kruger with your mouth,
> Will you kindly drop a shilling in my little tambourine
> For a gentleman in khaki ordered south.

> He's an absent-minded beggar, and his weaknesses are great

> But we informers take him as we find him,
> For he's out on active service, wiping something
>   off a slate
> And he's left a lot of little things behind him.
> Cook's son, duke's son, son of a belted earl——
>
> Fifty thousand horse and foot ordered to Table
>   Bay.
> Each of 'em's doing his country work——
> And who's to look after the girl?
> Pass the hat for your credit's sake, and pay, pay,
>   pay!

BILLY: Pass the hat for your credit's sake, and pay, pay, pay.

ARCHIE: Not bad for an amateur.

BILLY: Last time I sang that was in a pub, some place in Yorkshire. If you bought a pint of beer, you could get a plateful of Yorkshire Pudding then, as much as you could eat. All for tuppence.

ARCHIE: Come off it, Dad. Nobody ever gave away stuff like that, not even when you remember.

BILLY: I tell you, you got a plate of Yorkshire Pudding——

ARCHIE: You're getting really old.

BILLY: As much as you could eat.

ARCHIE: Your mind's going, Dad. I should sit down.

BILLY: I *am* sitting down.

ARCHIE: Getting feeble.

PHOEBE: Archie—don't tease him.

BILLY: I'm not feeble! I'm not half as bloody feeble as you are—thank God! (*Suddenly sees them smiling at him.*) Thank God I'm not, that's all. You think you have it over me all right. Give me some of that!

FRANK: When there isn't a girl about you feel so lonely. When there isn't a girl about you're on your only——

ARCHIE: Be quiet a minute, will you? I'm trying to think. Ah! yes. Yes. The girl I love is up in the lavatory, the girl I love is looking down on me.

PHOEBE: No don't do that, Archie. Don't sing it like

that! (*To Jean and Frank.*) He always used to sing that song, didn't you? It was his favourite, I think.

JEAN: You sing it.

PHOEBE: Me—Oh I can't sing. I don't know even if I can remember the words.

FRANK: Go on, love, have a go.

PHOEBE: (*to Archie*). Shall I? (*He nods shortly.*) All right, then.

She sings:

> Oh the boy I love he's up in the gallery
> The boy I love is looking down at me.
> Where is he?
> There is he,
> Waving of his handkerchee,
> Happy as the robin
> That sings on the tree.

JEAN: Thank you, Phoebe. Thank you.

PHOEBE: It sounded bloody awful, I expect.

BILLY: Well, I'm going to bed.

PHOEBE: Going already?

BILLY: (*going down to his room*). Yes, I only sat up to drink a toast to young Mick. I'm going to bed before you get those bloody Poles up here. Good night, everybody.

They all call out: "Good night."

PHOEBE: I suppose I ought to go in a minute. I feel a bit tired. Still, I shan't go in to work tomorrow. Well, I shouldn't think they'll expect me to, would you?

JEAN: Of course not.

PHOEBE: Probably be too excited to sleep anyway. (*To Jean.*) Did I show you the letter I had from Clare?

JEAN: Who's Clare?

ARCHIE: (*to Phoebe*). I should go to bed, dear.

PHOEBE: Just a minute. I'm going to read her Clare's letter. Clare's my niece—that's the one in Toronto. I'd better read it to you, her writing's not very good. She's my brother John's daughter. They're all over there now, my brother John as well. They started off in the restaurant business four years ago with five hundred dollars—that's their little girl. (*Hands photograph to Jean.*) Now they've got a hotel in Toronto, and they're going to open another one.

ARCHIE: (*to Jean*). You don't have to look interested, dear. (*To Phoebe.*) She's not interested in all that horse manure about Canada.

PHOEBE: Of course she's interested. She doesn't mind listening, do you?

ARCHIE: Why doesn't Frank sing another song?

PHOEBE: I'm only trying to explain to her. They've opened one in Toronto, and now they're going to open another hotel in Ottawa. My brother John is managing the one in Toronto for them, but they want us to go out there, and for Archie to manage the hotel in Ottawa.

ARCHIE: What do I know about hotels? All I've lived in is digs.

PHOEBE: He gets cross if I mention it.

ARCHIE: For God's sake don't say I get cross if you mention it once more. You've mentioned it, haven't you? And I'm not cross! I just think it's a bloody pointless idea.

JEAN: When did they write this to you?

PHOEBE: About a fortnight now. Oh, she says we needn't make a decision for another month or two.

JEAN: What about the boys?

PHOEBE: They can come too if they want. I don't know about Mick, but Frank likes the idea, don't you?

JEAN: Do you, Frank?

FRANK: Look around you. Can you think of any good reason for staying in this cosy little corner of Europe? Don't kid yourself anyone's going to let you do anything, or try anything here, Jeannie. Because they're not. You haven't got a chance. Who are you—you're nobody. You're nobody, you've no money, and you're young. And when you end up it's pretty certain you'll still be nobody, you'll still have no money —the only difference is you'll be *old*! You'd better start thinking about number one, Jeannie, because nobody else is going to do it for you. Nobody else is going to do it for you because nobody believes in that stuff any more. Oh, they may say they do, and may take a few bob out of your pay packet every week and stick some stamps on your card to prove it, but don't believe it—nobody will give you a second look. They're all so busy, speeding down the middle of the road together, not giving a damn where they're going, as long as they're in the bloody middle! (*Chirpily, almost singing.*) *The rotten bastards!* "Oh when there isn't a girl about you feel so lonely. When there isn't a girl about you're on your only."

ARCHIE: Ssh, you'll wake up the Poles.

FRANK: Somebody should wake you up. "You're on your only!"

ARCHIE: You should go to bed.

FRANK: You and that blonde bitch in the Cambridge. You and her.

Like a monkey up a tree, I don't think!

I'm going to bed.

He goes out singing, laying an arm on Archie's shoulder, and waving to the others.

ARCHIE: Good night, boy.

FRANK: (*singing*).

"Rock of Ages cleft for me,
Let me hide myself in thee!"

Exit.

ARCHIE: Anyway you can't buy draught Bass in Toronto.

PHOEBE: Here, this is what she says: She talks about us coming out, and paying our fare, etc., and then the job in Ottawa. Experience isn't necessary, it's having your own people. She says: "We have a twenty-one inch T.V. set, a radio, etc. and now we have a 1956 Chevrolet Bel Air car complete with automatic shift and all the fancy gadgets everyone goes in for over here. I'm quite sure that you and Archie would settle down in no time, and everything would work out fine." (*She folds the letter up carefully.*) I thought you'd like to hear what she said.

JEAN: Yes, thank you.

PHOEBE: (*after a slight pause*). Are you staying up much longer, Archie?

ARCHIE: I'm just going.

PHOEBE: I think we're all tired. I can't take all this excitement any more. (*To Jean.*) Good night, dear. Forgive me being a bit silly, won't you?

JEAN: Forget it. Good night. I shan't wake you up.

PHOEBE: Good night, Archie.

ARCHIE: I'll come up and say good night.

PHOEBE: Thank you, dear. We'll have to find him somewhere to sleep, won't we?

ARCHIE: Mick? Oh, he can bed down here with me.

PHOEBE: Yes, I expect he'll be fagged out, poor kid. Oh, well, he won't be long now.
Exit.

ARCHIE: I went to Canada during the war.

JEAN: I remember.

ARCHIE: Couldn't get any draught Bass, not even in Toronto, and they seemed to reckon that was pretty English. (*Pause.*) Didn't seem very English to me. Can't get over you going to Trafalgar Square. Did you really care about all that?

JEAN: I thought I did at the time.

ARCHIE: Like draught Bass and women, eh? Did I ever tell you my nuns story? They just took one look at me—I can remember their white, unhealthy faces, and their little eyes—they took one look at me, and, together, at the same time, quite, quite spontaneously, they crossed themselves. They crossed themselves. And that was the biggest compliment I ever had paid to me in my whole life. Let's have some more of this, shall we?

JEAN: Sure.

ARCHIE: You were having trouble with Phoebe tonight.

JEAN: It was nothing much. She just seemed to suddenly turn on me.

ARCHIE: Your mother caught me in bed with Phoebe. (*Pause.*)

JEAN: I didn't know.

ARCHIE: I don't know what I really expected, but somehow I expected you to say something more than that.

JEAN: What do you expect me to do—hold a rally in Trafalgar Square?

ARCHIE: All my children think I'm a bum. I've never bothered to hide it, I suppose—that's the answer.

JEAN: Perhaps we should go to bed.

ARCHIE: No, stay up for a while. I think we're both in the mood. You'd just been born and your mother found poor old Phoebe and me together. Poor old Phoebe, she's never even enjoyed it very much. Your mother walked out, she walked out just like that. She was what you'd call a person of—a person of principle. She knew how people should behave, and there were no two ways about it. She never forgave me anyway.

JEAN: You didn't love her——

ARCHIE *is drunk, and he sings and orchestrates his speech as only a drunken man can, almost objectively and fastidiously, like a conductor controlling his own sound.* ➝ FOLLOW SPOT AS SPECIAL

ARCHIE: Yes, I loved her. I was in love with her, whatever that may mean. I don't know. Anyway, a few months later she was dead and that was that. She felt everything very deeply, your mother. Much more deeply than I did. Perhaps we could have worked it out between us. Did I ever tell you the most moving thing that I ever heard? It was when I was in Canada —I managed to slip over the border sometimes to some people I knew, and one night I heard some Negress singing in a bar. *Now you're going to smile at this,* you're going to smile your educated English head off, because I suppose you've never sat lonely and half slewed in some bar among strangers a thousand miles from anything you think you understand. But if ever I saw any hope or strength in the human race, it was in the face of that old fat Negress getting up to sing about Jesus or something like that. She was poor and lonely and oppressed like nobody you've ever known. Or me, for that matter. I never even liked that kind of music, but to see that old black whore singing her heart out to the whole world, you knew somehow in your heart that it didn't matter how much you kick people, the real people, how much you despise them, if they can stand up and make a pure, just natural noise like that, there's nothing wrong with them, only with everybody else. I've never heard anything like that since. I've never heard it here. Oh, I've heard whispers of it on a Saturday night somewhere. Oh, he's heard it. Billy's heard it. He's heard them singing. Years ago, poor old gubbins. But you won't hear it anywhere now. I don't suppose we'll ever hear it again. There's nobody who can feel like that. I wish to God I could, I wish to God I could feel like that old black bitch with her fat cheeks, and sing. If I'd done one thing as good as that in my whole life, I'd have been all right. Better than all your getting on with the job without making a fuss and all that, or doing something constructive and all that, all your rallies in Trafalgar Square! I wish to God I were that old bag. I'd stand up and shake my great bosom up and down, and lift up my head and make the most beautiful fuss in the world. Dear God, I would. But I'll never do it. I don't give a damn about anything, not even women or draught Bass. Do you think that you're going to do it? Well, do you?

JEAN: I don't know. I just really don't know. I'll probably do exactly the same as you.

ARCHIE: Of course you will. Mind you, you'll make a better job of it. You're more clever, I think you really feel something too, in spite of all that Trafalgar Square stuff. You're what they call a sentimentalist.

You carry all your responses about with you, instead of leaving them at home. While everyone else is sitting on their hands you're the Joe at the back cheering and making his hands hurt. But you'll have to sit on your hands like everyone else. Oh, you think I'm just a tatty old music hall actor who should be told the truth, like Old Billy, that people don't wear sovereign cases and patent leather shoes any more. You know when you're up there you think you love all those people around you out there, but you don't. You don't love them, you're not going to stand up and make a beautiful fuss. If you learn it properly you'll get yourself a technique. You can smile, darn you, smile, and look the friendliest jolliest thing in the world, but you'll be just as dead and smug and used up, and sitting on your hands just like everybody else. You see this face, you see this face, this face can split open with warmth and humanity. It can sing, and tell the worst, unfunniest stories in the world to a great mob of dead, drab jerks and it doesn't matter, it doesn't matter. It doesn't matter because—look at my eyes. I'm dead behind these eyes. I'm dead, just like the whole inert, shoddy lot out there. It doesn't matter because I don't feel a thing, and neither do they. We're just as dead as each other. Tell me, tell me something. I want you to tell me something. What would you say to a man of my age marrying a girl of—oh about your age? Don't be shocked. I told you —I don't feel a thing.

JEAN: You couldn't! You couldn't do a thing like that!

ARCHIE: You've been away from your old Dad a bit too long. We've never seen much of each other, have we? Well, never mind.

JEAN: You're not serious! You couldn't do that to Phoebe—not a divorce.

ARCHIE: Children! (*Laughs.*) Children! They're like the bloody music hall. Don't worry about your old man —he's still a bit worried about young Mick. At least, I suppose he is. I told you, nothing really touches me.

As the man said, I've paid me one and saxpence—I defy yez to entertain me! Let anyone get up there and give a performance, let them get up, I don't care how good it is. Old Archie, dead behind the eyes, is sitting on his hands, he lost his responses on the way. You wouldn't think I was sexy to look at me, would you? You wouldn't think I was sexy to look at me, would you? Well, I 'ave a go, lady. I 'ave a go, don't I? I do. I 'ave a go. That barmaid in the Cambridge. That barmaid who upset poor old Billy in the Cambridge —I had her! When he wasn't looking. . . .

Enter Phoebe.

PHOEBE: I thought you'd got somebody here. They called up from downstairs. There's a policeman at the door for you, Archie.

ARCHIE: It's the income tax man. It's the income tax man. Tell him I've been expecting him. I've been expecting him for twenty years.

PHOEBE: (*to Jean*). I thought he had someone in here. What do you think he wants?

ARCHIE: Just me and my daughter Jean. Me and my daughter Jean—by my first love. Why don't you go back to London? Say, aren't you glad you're normal? I've always been a seven day a week man myself, haven't I, Phoebe? A seven day a week man. I always needed a jump at the end of the day—and at the beginning too usually. Just like a piece of bacon on the slab. Well, it's everybody's problem. Unless you're like Mick and have got no problem. Well, he had a problem, but now he's on his way. Yes, that's a boy without problems. I'm a seven day a week man myself, twice a day. Poor old Phoebe, don't look so scared, love. Either they're doing it, and they're not enjoying it. Or else they're not doing it and they aren't enjoying it. Don't look so scared, love. Archie's drunk again. It's only the income tax man!

PHOEBE: Frank's down there——

FRANK: (*in*). The bastards. *The rotten bastards!* They've killed him! They've killed Mick! Those

bloody wogs—they've murdered him. Oh, the rotten
bastards!

ARCHIE: (*slowly singing a blues*). Oh, lord, I don't care
where they bury my body, no I don't care where they
bury my body, 'cos my soul's going to live with God!

CURTAIN

END OF ACT TWO

CUE 16

INTERMISSION

NUMBER NINE

Blues. Spot on FRANK at piano.

FRANK:

> Bring back his body, and bury it in England.
> Bring back his body, and bury it here.
> Bring back his body, in an aeroplane.
> But don't ever talk to me.
> Those playing fields of Eton
> Have really got us beaten.
> But ain't no use agrievin'
> 'Cos it's Britain we believe in.
> So bring back his body, and bury it here.
> Bring back his body in an aeroplane——
> But just don't ever talk to me.

FADE CUE 17

FOLLOW SPOT

NUMBER TEN

BILLY, PHOEBE, JEAN, FRANK, ARCHIE. BILLY *and*
PHOEBE *are dressed in black. The others wear black
arm bands.*

JEAN: Well, that's that. (*Picks up some newspapers.*)
Can anyone tell me what the whole thing added up
to? (*Pause.*)

ARCHIE: My aunt always used to say the same thing,
"Well, they gave him a good send off." Always said it
without fail. (*To Billy.*) Didn't she?

BILLY: Poor old Rosie.

ARCHIE: I used to wonder what would happen if she
didn't say it.

BILLY: Old Rosie and me used to have some good
times together. Used to go out a lot. Before we were
both married.

JEAN: Well, I suppose it gives somebody a kick. Are
you all right, Phoebe?

PHOEBE: I'm all right, dear. A bit tired.

BILLY: What a place London was then for having a
good time. Best place in the world for a laugh. People
were always ready to laugh, to give you a welcome.
Best audience in the world.
Crosses L.C. Gets chair and sits above table.

ARCHIE: I was in a little village in Donegal once. On
the Irish fit-ups. (*To Billy.*) You remember. The
morning we arrived there, a man came up to me and
said: "Oh, we're great students of the drama here.
Great students of the drama. Our dramatic critics
can lick anyone—anyone!" Turned out he was the
local blacksmith. He said, he said: "If you get past

186

an audience here, you'll get past any audience in the world." It was true too. Think I got a black eye.

BILLY: Some places, they just sit back and stare at you. They just—sit. But, London, that was the place. Old Rosie—she was a beautiful woman. I'm glad she's not here now.

JEAN: (*grabbing at newspapers*). How can you compete against this stuff?

FRANK: You can't.

JEAN: Why didn't somebody get a picture of you stoking your boilers?

ARCHIE: I don't think Mick would have taken it too seriously.

FRANK: Everybody's tired.

JEAN: Everybody's tired all right. Everybody's tired, everybody's standing about, loitering without any intent whatsoever, waiting to be picked up by whatever they may allow to happen to us next.

ARCHIE: Jesus, don't start getting emotional——

JEAN: I don't expect you to.

ARCHIE: That's right.

JEAN: But Frank's different—at least, I hope he is. You don't have to be afraid, Frank. You needn't worry about being emotional, like my talented fiancé. You won't die of it. You may think you can, but you won't.

ARCHIE: Old Mick was a bit like Graham actually. He seemed to know what he wanted, and where he was going.

JEAN: Did he now, that's interesting——

ARCHIE: I remember he was having an affair with a girl called Sylvia. He was about sixteen at the time.

JEAN: What's the matter with you, Archie?

FRANK: Why don't you leave him alone?

ARCHIE: That's right, why don't you leave your old man alone?

JEAN: Oh, you've been left alone all right!

ARCHIE: Shall I tell you—all my life I've been search-

ing for something. I've been searching for a draught
Bass you can drink all the evening without running
off every ten minutes, that you can get drunk on
without feeling sick, and all for fourpence. Now, the
man who could offer me all of that would really get
my vote. He really would. Oh, well, I could always
make a woman better than I could make a point.

JEAN: You know, Archie, you're a bit of a bastard.

PHOEBE: Jean——

JEAN: You really are—you're a bastard on wheels!

ARCHIE: Because I don't care about anything except
draught Bass? Listen, kiddie, you're going to find
out that in the end nobody really gives a damn about
anything except some little animal something. And
for me that little animal something is draught Bass.
Now why can't you stop attacking everyone?

JEAN: I can't.

ARCHIE: What do you think you are—a dose of salts?

JEAN: I owe it to myself.

ARCHIE: Well, I never really believed in all that inner
cleanliness anyway. Did I leave a bottle of beer in
here last night?

PHOEBE: I don't think so, dear.

ARCHIE: If you're not careful, Jean, people will start
putting labels on you pretty soon. And then you'll
just be nobody. You'll be nobody like the rest of us.

PHOEBE: Frank'll get you some. There's some left in
the kitchen. Would you mind, dear?

FRANK: Sure. (*Rises. Crosses L. of chair.*)

JEAN: We can't all spend our time nailing our suit-
cases to the floor, and shin out of the window.

ARCHIE: Scarper the letty.

JEAN: You're like everybody else, but you're worse—
you think you can cover yourself by simply not
bothering. (*Newspapers.*) You think if you don't
bother you can't be humiliated, so you just roar
your life out in four-letter words and just hope that
somehow the perks will turn up.

FRANK: Leave him alone, he's just as upset as you are! So shut up.

JEAN: I'll give you the Archie Rice story. All right. You want the credit titles first?

ARCHIE: I didn't like the clergyman, anyway. I really hated him. He was as chloe as all get out. Did you notice?

JEAN: You don't fool me. You couldn't fool pussy!

ARCHIE: Go on—insult me, I don't mind. One thing I've discovered a long time ago. Most people never know when they're being insulted. And a whole lot of people make a whole lot of money out of that principle. I'm as dim as a bucket really. You know. I'm no better than the rest of them.

JEAN: Oh now, don't start being humble——

ARCHIE: I *am* humble! I am very humble, in fact. I still have a little dried pea of humility rattling around inside me. I don't think *you* have.

JEAN: And that's just about all.

FRANK: What's the matter with her?

ARCHIE: Don't ask me, son. Don't ask me. I've never solved a problem in my life.

JEAN: You haven't got the nous. You've been too busy hating all those feckless moochers out there in the great darkness, haven't you? You've been really smart. (*To Frank.*) I'd like you to know the truth about your father.

FRANK: Listen, Jean, Mick's just been buried. He's buried and nobody wants to start talking about it, or having rows.

JEAN: What do you want, two minutes silence? Not only is your father generous, understanding and sympathetic—he doesn't give a damn about anyone. He's two pennorth of nothing.

ARCHIE: Yes, I should say that sums me up pretty well.

JEAN: You don't need to look at me! I've lost a brother too. Why do people like us sit here, and just lap it all up, why do boys die, or stoke boilers, why do we pick up these things, what are we hoping to get out of it, what's it all in aid of—is it really just for the sake of a gloved hand waving at you from a golden coach?

PHOEBE: I think I'll go and lie down. (*To Jean.*) He's always been good to me.

FRANK: Shall I bring you up an aspirin?

JEAN: Nobody listens to anyone.

PHOEBE: Thank you, dear. If you wouldn't mind. (*To Jean, simply.*) He's always been good to me. Whatever he may have done. Always.

Exit.

FRANK: I'll get you that beer.

BILLY: Always had a decanter on the sideboard at home. I've got the key here.

JEAN: (*to Archie*). You can't do it to her, I won't let you.

BILLY: Yes, here it is.

ARCHIE: He wants to know if I've renewed the ticket. It's all right—I've got another three months on it.

BILLY: Eh? (*To Jean.*) There.

JEAN: What's this?

BILLY: What's the matter—you want your bloody ears syringed?

FRANK: You want some beer, Grandad?

BILLY: Nobody listens to a bloody word you're saying.

FRANK: I said do you want some beer?

BILLY: That's the trouble nowadays. Everybody's too busy answering back and taking liberties. 'Stead of getting on with it and doing as they're told. No, I'm going to bed. I've got to be out early tomorrow. (*To Archie.*) What time did you say?

ARCHIE: About nine.

FRANK: Where are you going?

BILLY: Your father and I have got some business together. Seemed funny all those people taking off their hats to young Mick today.

FRANK: Most of 'em weren't wearing hats anyway.

BILLY: When I was younger, every man—and every

man wore a hat in those days, didn't matter if he
was a lord or a butcher—every man used to take his
hat off when he passed the Cenotaph. Even in the bus.
Nowadays I've watched people just go past it, not
even a look. If you took the flags off of it I expect
they'd sit down and eat their sandwiches on it.

ARCHIE: I was just thinking of young Mick and Sylvia.
She was a nice, attractive little kid. I wonder what
she's doing now. I wonder if she's read about him
in the papers. Being a national hero and getting
killed. I shouldn't think she'd have forgotten him already, would you?

FRANK: I shouldn't think so. Can I have some of your
beer?

ARCHIE: Help yourself. I remember being worried
about Sylvia. I couldn't get it out of young Mick, and
I had an idea she was under-age. It worried me just
a bit. I tried to tackle him about it, but he always
thought I was a bit of a chump, he did, you know. Oh,
I didn't mind. I rather liked it. (*To Jean.*) He didn't
really take me seriously. I hummed and hah'ed, and
finally I said: "Well, look boy, I obviously don't have
to tell you to take precautions." He just grinned like
the clappers, and I suddenly felt like some weird old
clergyman. So I just said to him: "Well, anyway, you
do know what the age of consent is, don't you?" And
he sat there with that great awful grin on his face,
and said: "Sixteen."

JEAN: Where are you taking Billy tomorrow?

ARCHIE: I think I'll have to go back to Brighton, and
become a Beachcomber.

FRANK: (*to Jean*). Got any aspirins on you? There
don't seem to be any.

ARCHIE: Edlins—that was the place. All over Brighton.

JEAN: (*giving Frank aspirins*). Don't you know what
he's trying to do?

ARCHIE: You could get nicely oiled on their draught
cider for a few pence.

FRANK: Why don't you leave them alone?

ARCHIE: Haven't had it for years. How much was it?

JEAN: He thinks he's going to divorce her. He thinks he's going to divorce Phoebe. I've seen her—this girl he wants to marry. He's crazy. That's what he is. What's going to happen to her? (*She nods upstairs.*)

FRANK: What's going to happen to any of us. Listen, Jean, love—darling heart, you are not going to change anybody——

JEAN: Have you seen her? I caught them together yesterday. In the Rockliffe. I've seen her all right. She's a professional virgin.

ARCHIE: I wonder what it's like now. (*To Billy.*) How much did it use to be?

FRANK: I'd better take these (*aspirins*) up to her.

BILLY: What?

ARCHIE: Draught cider, you old gubbins.

BILLY: How the bloody hell should I know? I've never drunk the stuff.

ARCHIE: Yes, it's a bit acid, I suppose.

BILLY: 'Bout a penny, I should say. Penny a pint.

ARCHIE: Be about a bob now, I 'spect. (*Slight pause.*) Might as well drink beer.

JEAN: (*to Archie*). She's pretty, she's spoilt, she's vain, and she's stupid. And her parents are probably stupid. They must be, they must be stupid to produce her— Miss Nothing of 1957.

ARCHIE: That's right.

JEAN: How old is she?

ARCHIE: Twenty.

JEAN: Twenty. They're so stupid, I suppose, they'll even let her marry you?

ARCHIE: You know, I think I've only slept with one passionate woman. What I'd call really passionate. And she was happily married. Her name was Ivy.

JEAN: I suppose you think you'll get them to put up some money for you too?

ARCHIE: That was the idea.

JEAN: You're going to get her to put a ring through your nose, and tell yourself you won't feel it, be-

cause nothing matters to you any more, and nobody
else does either. You think because you can't get
her nobody else can! What about Phoebe?

ARCHIE: Ivy Williams, that's her name. Mrs. Ivy Williams. Mrs. Ivy Wiliams.

BILLY: Well, I'm off. Who're we seeing: Rubens?

ARCHIE: Klein.

BILLY: Charlie Klein. Old Charlie Klein. I was in the
first show he ever put on the road, you know that?

ARCHIE: Twelve thirty.

BILLY: He was younger than Jeannie here. I made him
a member of the National Sporting Club. It was me
who put him up.

ARCHIE: He's a tough bastard.

BILLY: Oh, Charlie should be all right. It was me made
him sign up Eddie Drummer. Good artist, Eddie.
Been earning a thousand a week for twenty-five
years, and just the same. He's a good boy. He's a
sort of in-between. He wasn't one of us real old
timers, and he wasn't one of these new five-minute
wonders with a microphone. They've got no real
personality now. He always had style, Eddie, and
never any real suggestion of offence in anything he
did. We all had our own style, our own songs—and
we were all English. What's more, we spoke English.
It was different. We all knew what the rules were.
We knew what the rules were, and even if we spent
half our time making people laugh at 'em we never
seriously suggested that anyone should break them.
A real pro is a real man, all he needs is an old backcloth behind him and he can hold them on his own
for half an hour. He's like the general run of people,
only he's a lot more like them than they are themselves, if you understand me. Well, Eddie's still up
there all right. He's still up there. (*To Jean.*) I always used to say to him, we all used to say: "Eddie—
always be good to the people on the way up, because
you may meet them on the way down." Old Eddie.
One of the really great ones, I should say he is. I

should say he's probably the last. Yes, I should say he's probably the last. ← ᒐᑯᒪᒪᑕᗯ ᔕᖶᕁ. *Exit.*

JEAN: What are you doing, what are you going to do to him? You're not going to put him back into the business?

ARCHIE: Rubens and Klein twelve-thirty tomorrow morning——

JEAN: You're going to kill that old man just to save that no-good, washed-up tatty show of yours——

ARCHIE: It isn't just to save that no-good, tatty show of mine. It's to save your no-good tatty Dad from going to jail. People may not come to see Archie but they may still remember Billy Rice. It's worth a try anyway.

JEAN: Are you going to destroy that too? He's the only one of us who has any dignity or respect for himself, he's the only one of us who has anything at all, and you're going to murder him, you're going to take him down to—who is it—Rubens and Klein tomorrow morning at twelve-thirty, and you're going to let Mr. Rubens and Mr. Klein sign his death certificate. What are you letting yourself in for now, how on earth did you ever get him to do such a thing? What's happened to him? What's happened to his sense of self preservation?

ARCHIE: He feels he owes it to me.

JEAN: Owes it to you! Owes it to you! Billy doesn't owe you or anyone anything.

ARCHIE: You see, before you got busy lecturing me about inner cleanliness, Billy went and did something. He went and saw my little girl friend's parents, you know, the professional virgin you saw in the Rockliffe. He went and told them I was a married man with three grown-up children. Three acknowledged—anyway, but I don't suppose old Billy needed to mention the rest of them.

JEAN: He scotched it!

ARCHIE: Oh, yes—completely. You see, I hadn't told them about—about Phoebe, and all of you.

JEAN: No, I suppose you wouldn't.

ARCHIE: So you see you weren't wrong, Jeannie, love. Not about Phoebe anyway—old Archie isn't going to get his oats after all.

CUE 18

NUMBER ELEVEN

ARCHIE: Ladies and Gentlemen, Billy Rice will not appear tonight. Billy Rice will not appear again. I wish I could sing a song for him—in his place. A farewell. But, unfortunately, I can't. Nobody can. None of us, any way.

Exit.

Front Gauze. Funeral cortège with ARCHIE, PHOEBE, JEAN, FRANK, GRAHAM and BROTHER BILL. They gather round a coffin C. stage, draping over it a Union Jack, Billy's hat, cane, and gloves. In the background, snatches of old songs, wisps of tunes, the stumble of a banjo. Fade to——

CUE 20

CUE 21

Down L. A lime drenches ARCHIE *and* BROTHER BILL. *Down R. lime on* JEAN *and* GRAHAM DODD. BROTHER BILL *looks like a highly successfully and distinguished lawyer, and he is.* GRAHAM DODD *may well be like him in thirty years, provided he is successful. There are plenty of these around—well dressed, assured, well educated, their emotional and imaginative capacity so limited it is practically negligible. They have an all-defying inability to associate themselves with anyone in circumstances even slightly dissimilar to their own.* GRAHAM DODD *doesn't need much description. If you can't recognize him, it's for one reason only. These two duologues are independent, but run together.*

GRAHAM: Quite honestly, Jean, I don't mean to be rude. I mean, well it is rude to come out and say it, but I can't see what you can possibly have in common with any of them.

JEAN: You can't——

GRAHAM: Well, they're your family and all that, but after all, there does come a point, there does come a point in things——

ARCHIE: He was such a sweet old man. He really was. D'you know who said that? Charlie Klein said old Billy was the nicest old man in the business.

GRAHAM: —you just don't have any more responsibility to people.

ARCHIE: And still a first-class performer, Archie. Still a first-class performer!

GRAHAM: —it's your background and you were brought

up in it, but there are better, more worthwhile things
in life.

ARCHIE: He was one of the great, one of the really
great.

JEAN: I'm sorry, Graham. I'm staying with Phoebe.
I told you I'd really made up my mind before I left.
I can't marry you, and I don't want to any more.
Anyway, I've got to stay here. Now that Billy's dead
Phoebe needs someone with her. Frank's off to Can-
ada in a couple of weeks——

ARCHIE: Jean thinks I killed him.

BROTHER BILL: You didn't kill him, Archie. You don't
kill people that easily. I don't think so.

JEAN: We live differently. You and I don't even draw
breath in the same way.

BROTHER BILL: Look, Archie. This is the last time for
you. It's got to be Canada. You and Frank and
Phoebe can all go out together. Your passages are
all booked. I've got them in my pocket here. There're
yours. You can go out and start a new life, the three
of you.

GRAHAM: Oh, this is just rubbish. You're no different
from me. You were in love with me, you said so.
We enjoyed ourselves together. We could make a
good thing of it. I've got quite a decent career lined
up. We would have everything we want. Come back
with me, Jean.

ARCHIE: You can't get draught Bass in Toronto. I've
tried it.

JEAN: Have you ever got on a railway train here, got
on a train from Birmingham to West Hartlepool? Or
gone from Manchester to Warrington or Widnes. And
you get out, you go down the street, and on one side
maybe is a chemical works, and on the other side is
the railway goods yard. Some kids are playing in the
street, and you walk up to some woman standing on
her doorstep. It isn't a doorstep really because you
can walk straight from the street into her front room.
What can you say to her? What real piece of informa-

tion, what message can you give to her? Do you say: "Madam, d'you know that Jesus died on the Cross for you?"

BROTHER BILL: Those tickets are yours, Archie. Now take them. I'll pay up all your debts, I'll settle everything, I'll see that nothing happens.

JEAN: And then the woman, she looks back at you, and she says: "Oh, yes, I heard all about that."

ARCHIE: What happens if I don't go?

BROTHER BILL: I'm not doing anything for you to stay here, Archie. Not any more. You'll just have to take the consequences, I'm afraid. It's Canada or jail.

ARCHIE: You know, I've always thought I should go to jail. I should think it must be quite interesting. Sure to meet someone I know. D'you know what my landlady in Fulham used to say about you? She used to say: "He looks like a governor's man." Always said it—without fail.

GRAHAM: We're all in it for what we can get out of it. Isn't that what your father was supposed to say?

ARCHIE: You can never get anything at this Labour Exchange anyway. They must have more bums in this place than in any other town in England. Oh, well, thanks anyway, just two more performances. It's a pity though—I should have liked to notch up twenty-one against the income-tax man. I'll never make my twenty-first now. It would have been fun to get the key of the door, somehow.

JEAN: Here we are, we're alone in the universe, there's no God, it just seems that it all began by something as simple as sunlight striking on a piece of rock. And here we are. We've only got ourselves. Somehow, we've just got to make a go of it. *We've only ourselves*.

BROTHER BILL: I'm sorry, Archie, but I've given up trying to understand.

FADE

NUMBER THIRTEEN

Rock-n-Roll. Nude tableau, behind first-act gauze. Britannia. Then; the Archie Rice music, the one and only, interrupting the programme. The stage blacks out. A lime picks out the prompt corner, and ARCHIE *make his entrance. He sings a few bars of "We're all out for good old Number One."*

ARCHIE: We're all out for good old Number One
Number One's the only one for me.
Good old England, you're my cup of tea,
But I don't want no drab equality.
Don't let your feelings roam,
But remember that charity begins at home.
What we've got left back
We'll keep—and blow you, Jack.
Number One's the only one for me.
   —God bless you,
Number One's the only one for me.

I've just come to tell you about the wife. She's gone back to her husband. She has, straight. Don't clap too hard, we're all in a very old building. Yes, very old. Old. What about *that*? What about *her,* eh— Madam with the helmet on? I reckon she's sagging a bit, if you ask me. She needs some beef putting into her—the roast beef of old England. No, nobody's asking me, never mind. Nice couple of fried eggs, anyway. She's a nice girl, though—a nice girl. Going steady with Charlie here—isn't she, Charlie? (*To the conductor.*) She met him in a revolving door, and they've been going around together ever since. I'm doing me nut, you know that, don't you? I'm doing me nut up here. Nudes, that's what they call them,

lady, nudes. Blimey, she's got more clothes on than
I have. It's a lot of madam, that's all it is. A lot of
madam. Oh, I put a line in there. Never mind, it
doesn't matter. I've made a few tumbles in my time.
I have, honest. You wouldn't think I was sexy to
look at me, would you? No, honestly, you wouldn't,
would you, lady. I always reckon you feel stronger
after it? (*Sings.*) "Say, your jelly-roll is fine, but it
don't compare with mine!" There's a bloke at the
side here with a hook, you know that, don't you?
He is, he's standing there. I can see him. Must be
the income-tax man. Life's funny though, isn't it?
It is—life's funny. It's like sucking a sweet with the
wrapper on. Oh, well, we're all in the fertilizer business now, I suppose. Well, I'd rather have a glass of
beer any day—I would. You don't believe me, but I
would. You think I'm gone, don't you? Go on, say it,
you think I'm gone. You think I'm gone, don't you?
Well, I am. What's the matter, you feeling cold up
there? Before I do go, ladies and gentlemen, I should
just like to tell you a little story, a little story. This
story is about a man, just a little, ordinary man, like
you and me, and one day he woke up and found himself in paradise. Well, he looks up, you see, and he
sees a feller standing next to him. It turns out that
this feller is a saint or something. Anyway, he's on
the welcoming committee. And the feller says to him
—the Saint—says to him: "Well," he says, "you're
now in paradise." "Am I?" he says, "You are," says
the Saint. "What's more, you have earned yourself
eternal happiness." "Have I?" he says. "You most
certainly have," says the Saint. "Oh, you're well
away," he says. "Can't you hear the multitudes? Why,
everyone is singing, everyone is joyful. What do you
say, my son?" So the little man took a look around
him at all the multitudes of the earth, spread out
against the universe. So he says to the Saint: "Well,
can I get up where you're standing, and take a proper
look?" So the Saint says: "Of course you can, my

son" and makes way for him. And the little man
stood up where the Saint was and gazed up at the
sight around him. At all the Hosts of Heaven, and
all the rest of it. "All the wonder and the joy of
eternity is round about you," said the Saint. "You
mean, this is all eternity and I'm in paradise?" "That
is so, my son. Well, what have you to say?" So the
little man looks around again for a bit, and the Saint
says: "Well, my son?" "Well," he says, "I've often
wondered what I'd say if this ever happened to me.
I couldn't think somehow." And the Saint smiled at
him kindly and says again: "And what *do* you say,
my son?" "Only one thing I can say," says the little
man. And he said it! Well, the Saint looked as if he
had been struck across the face by some great hand.
The Hosts stopped singing and all the Angels hid
their faces, and for a tiny splash in eternity there was
no sound at all in Paradise. The Saint couldn't speak
for a while, and then he threw his arms round the
little man, and kissed him. And he said: "I love you,
my son. With all my soul, I shall love you always. I
have been waiting to hear that word ever since I
came here." He's there with his little hook, I can
see him. Oh, well, I have a go, don't I? I 'ave a go.
*The cloth goes up, revealing a dark bare stage. The
music starts up softly, and* ARCHIE RICE *stands on the
stage in a little round world of light, and swaggers
gently into his song:*

          Why should I care,
          Why should I let it touch me,
          Why shouldn't I sit down and cry
          To let it pass over me?
He begins to falter a little.
          Why should——
          Why should I let it get me——
          What's the use of despair?
*He stops and stares ahead of him. The music goes
on, then he picks up.*

> If they see that you're blue
> They'll look down on you.

He stares up, then goes on.

> So why oh why should I bother to care?

PHOEBE *appears L. holding a raincoat and hat.*

ARCHIE: Why should I care,
           Why should I let it touch me,
           Why shouldn't I?———

He stops, the music goes on, as he walks over to PHOEBE, *who helps him on with his coat, and gives him his hat. He hesitates, comes back down to the floats.*

You've been a good audience. Very good. A very *good* audience. Let me know where you're working tomorrow night—and I'll come and see *YOU.*

He walks upstage with PHOEBE. *The spotlight is hitting the apron, where* ARCHIE *has been standing. The orchestra goes on playing: "Why should I care"; suddenly, the little world of light snaps out, the stage is bare and dark.* ARCHIE RICE *has gone. There is only the music.*

CURTAIN

THE END

EPITAPH
FOR
GEORGE DILLON

(with Anthony Creighton)

to E.M.C.
with our love

CAST
In Order of Appearance

JOSIE ELLIOT

RUTH GRAY

MRS. ELLIOT

NORAH ELLIOT

PERCY ELLIOT

GEORGE DILLON

GEOFFREY COLWYN-STUART

MR. WEBB

BARNEY EVANS

The action of the play takes place in the home of the Elliot family just outside London.

ACT   I
Spring

ACT   II
Summer

ACT   III
Scene I.   Autumn
Scene II.   Winter

ACT I

The home of the Elliot family, just outside London.
Spring, late afternoon.
The action takes place in the sitting room and hall.
The front door being stage right. In the hall, im-
mediately facing, are the stairs which turn off left.
Flat against the staircase is a hat and coat stand,
shelving hats, coats, magazines, umbrellas, etc., in the
midst of which is a vase of everlasting flowers. Up-
stage of the hall, under the arch formed by the stairs,
is the door leading into the room called the lounge.
Next to this, upstage, is the invisible wall which di-
vides the hall from the sitting-room. The only object
suggesting the wall is a door set upstage. Downstage
of this, set against the "wall" facing into the sitting-
room, is a radiogram, upon which stands a biscuit
barrel and a silver-plated dish containing wax or
real fruit. Nearby an armchair of the "contemporary"
kind faces downstage. Against the upstage wall, right,
is a dining-chair. Centre, an ornate cocktail cabinet
and another dining-chair. On the wall, flanking this,
are two wall lights, in the centre of which is painted a
group of wild ducks, in flight.
Left centre is the door leading to the kitchen, next to
which is the kitchen hatch, which when raised, re-
veals the kitchen beyond. Below the hatch is a tea-
trolley. Above the hatch, on the wall, is a tinted
photograph of a wedding group. In the stage left wall,
french windows which look out on to a small back
garden. Below the french windows, a half-round
occasional table, above hangs a mirror. In front of
the french windows a settee, again of the utility-con-

temporary period. At the head a white-painted wrought-iron floor lamp. Upstage, left centre, a draw-leaf table with dining-chair and arm dining-chair in position. On the cocktail cabinet stands a large china model of an alsatian dog, and a photograph of a soldier in a silver frame, decorated with "Haig" poppies.

At rise of curtain, JOSIE *is on stage alone. She is about twenty, pretty in a hard, frilly way and nobody's fool. At the moment she is not looking her best. The turban she is wearing reveals a couple of curlers above her forehead, her jumper is grubby and her slacks baggy, stained and not very fetching. She is sprawled in the armchair. In a vicious idleness she stares at a highly coloured weekly. Mozart is on the radio, delicate, liquid. She flips through the magazine, is about to put it down when something catches her attention.*

She reads.

JOSIE: Fancy writing up and asking *that!*

(She laughs and goes on with her reading, fondling one of her curlers as she does so. Presently she throws the magazine down.)

Soppy cow!

(She sighs and leans back, thrusts her hands into the top of her slacks, rubbing her stomach and frowning. She gets up and stares at her reflection in the mirror. Pursing her lips experimentally, she watches the effect. She leans forward and tries fluffing up her eyebrows. It doesn't seem very successful and she sighs again.)

Oh, that damn row!

(She goes to the radio, stabs at the knobs, then gives up and switches it off. Her eye catches the magazine again and she goes through it again until she finds what she is looking for. She stares at it sullenly and flings the paper on the floor. At the mirror again

she tries several grimaces, puts out her tongue. A little more speculation, and she goes over to the settee, and sinks down on her knees. She stretches, and, catching sight of the resulting white space between her jumper and slacks, strokes herself dreamily. She slides forward on to her stomach, her hands moving over the arm of the settee, curiosity in her fingers and boredom in her body. She starts to sing, in a studied, offhand way, one of those downward-inflection popular hits.)

"Why don't you Give Me . . . Give Me. . . ." (*Pause.*)
"All that you have to share.
Why don't you Give Me . . . Give Me. . . ."
(*She picks her nose daintily, and turns over on her back.*)
"And tell me you really c-are. . . ."
(*Her hand trails the space beside her, like a hand in rippling water, then stops, as she says deliberately:*)
I wonder—what it *would* be like?
(*She is about to swing her legs above her head, when the front door bell rings.*)
Good-O!
(*She rushes off to the front door, almost reaches it, when she remembers something, and comes back into the dining-room. Her eyes light on her handbag, and she snatches it up, taking it with her, through the hall, straight to the front door. The bell is still ringing, and she calls out:*)
Oh, all right! Wait a minute! Wait a minute!
(*Opens front door.*)
(*We hear a voice saying:*) "Parcel for Mrs. Elliot. Three pounds fifteen and ninepence to pay."
Miss Elliot, if you please. I thought you were never coming. Here you are. You have been a long time. I thought you'd have been here this morning. I haven't even been able to go up the road, waiting for you to come. What? I haven't got it. Well, you'll have to change it.

(*A few minutes of change fumbling before she slams the front door, and goes into the sitting-room with a square cardboard box in her arms, which she starts to open excitedly, kneeling on the floor. Off comes the string and paper, then the lid and a layer of tissue paper. She rises quickly, places the box on the settee, takes a cigarette from her handbag, which she puts in her mouth, kicks off her slippers, and goes to the radiogram, unzipping her slacks at the same time. She raises the lid, switches it on, and takes off her slacks, leaving them on the floor, one leg inside out. She selects a record from the pile beside her, and puts it on. Cigarette in mouth, she waits expectantly until the corncrake growl of a New Orleans trumpet strides off into a piece of fairly traditional jazz. She runs back to her parcel and takes out the contents, in a scurry of paper and impatience, which turn out to be a pair of black, tapering trousers. She puts them on, zipping up the sides with a little difficulty. Hands on hips, she looks down at the result anxiously, then delightedly. She goes nearer to the mirror, to get a better view of herself. She bounces up and down, looking at this angle and that, patting her stomach, feeling the seat until she is finally satisfied. She lights her cigarette, then, putting her hands in her unfamiliar pockets, strikes a more or less elegant attitude and a bored expression, one black undeniably slim leg straight out in front of the other. She inclines her head back, and blows out a cloud of smoke.* JOSIE *may be funny at times, but she is never consciously so. She begins to dance, slowly at first, and surprisingly well, across R., ending up by lying with her back on the floor, and her knees up. The front door opens, and* RUTH *enters hall.* JOSIE *sits up quickly.*)

That you, Mum?

(RUTH *closes the door, but makes no reply.* JOSIE *takes off her new trousers, and starts slipping them*

back in their box. *As she is doing this,* RUTH *enters
from the hall. She is about forty, slim, smartly
dressed, attractive. She carries a small week-end case,
which she puts down when she gets into the sitting-
room.*)

You're in early.

(RUTH *goes to the radiogram, and switches it off.*)

RUTH: Do you mind if we do without New Orleans
just for the moment?

(*She crosses and picks up* JOSIE's *old slacks from
the floor.*)

Are you looking for these?

(*She throws them over, and* JOSIE *manages to catch
them.*)

JOSIE: Thought you were Mum.

RUTH: I don't suppose you'd made any tea?

JOSIE: (*putting on her slacks*). I had some at dinner
time.

(RUTH *goes into the kitchen, and puts the kettle on
to boil.*)

You're in early.

RUTH: (*off*). Why aren't you at work today?

JOSIE: Wasn't feeling very good this morning.

RUTH: (*off*). Oh?

JOSIE: So Mum said I'd better stay indoors.

(*She is staring at the case* RUTH *has left on the floor.*)

Going on your holidays?

RUTH: (*off*). No—coming back. Satisfied?

JOSIE: How can you be coming back, when you haven't
been away? Anyway, I haven't had a day off work
for ages—it won't hurt them.

(*Picking up the case to see if it is empty.*)

New case?

RUTH: (*off*). I picked it up from where I left it last
night—at Leicester Square Left Luggage Office. And
it's full of obscene photographs.

JOSIE: Oh?

RUTH: (*appearing in the doorway*). Josie: give me a

cigarette, will you? I came all the way back in the train without one. (*Back into kitchen.*) There wasn't any post for me, was there?

JOSIE: (*crossing to her handbag R.*). Package came for you—registered.

RUTH: (*off*). No letters?

JOSIE: Just the pools. It's only a small one. Doesn't weigh anything hardly.

RUTH: (*off*). And what's inside it?

JOSIE: (*searching in her handbag*). How should I know?

RUTH: (*off*). Didn't you open it?

JOSIE: What do you mean? Course I didn't open it.

RUTH: (*coming back in*). If you must fry yourself food when you're feeling ill, you might have the decency to clear up afterwards. The gas stove is covered in grease and muck—it's filthy.

(*She takes off her hat, and moves to the occasional table down L., where she sees a small package.*)

Is this it? (*Examines it, and goes on, rather absently.*) You've even left the breakfast things in the sink.

(JOSIE *is holding her packet of cigarettes, watching her curiously.* RUTH *stares at the packet.*)

JOSIE: Typewritten.

RUTH: You've had damn-all to do all day. It's like a slum when your mother comes in.

JOSIE: Aren't you going to open it?

RUTH: (*a quick glance at her*). I said you're a slut.

JOSIE: Oh, did you? I didn't hear.

(*After a momentary hesitation,* RUTH *unwraps the package.* JOSIE *slips her cigarettes back into her handbag, and moves over to the kitchen door. From a small cardboard box,* RUTH *takes out a man's wrist watch.* JOSIE *takes it in, and goes into the kitchen.*)

JOSIE: I'll get a cup of tea.

(*The watch is lying in* RUTH's *hand, as with the other, she takes out a piece of notepaper, and reads it. Then she places the box on the table. She stares at the paper, stroking her temples with her fingers, as if she felt*

a weight in her head. Presently, she calls out to JOSIE
*in the kitchen. The edge has gone out of her voice,
and she sounds tired.*)

RUTH: Josie: be a good girl and get me that cigarette,
will you?

(JOSIE *enters with a cup of tea, which she hands to
her.*)

JOSIE: That man was here again this afternoon, asking
for you.

RUTH: I've asked you twice to let me have one of your
cigarettes. Please! I'll pay you back tonight.

JOSIE: Haven't got one. Sorry.

RUTH: (*turning back to the table*). Oh well, I suppose
I'll have to go upstairs, anyway. There may be some
in the bedroom somewhere.

(*She replaces the watch and note in the little box.*)
Who was here, did you say?

JOSIE: That man. I don't know who he is. The one
who came on Saturday, and again the other day.
That's the third time he's been.

RUTH: I thought you told him I didn't get in till 5:30?

JOSIE: I did. He said he'd come back one evening.

RUTH: (*to arm-chair and sitting*). Well, what time did
he come today?

JOSIE: About four, I suppose.

RUTH: He doesn't sound very bright, whoever he is.
What's he look like?

JOSIE: Not bad. Bit like Frankie Vaughan.

RUTH: Who the hell's Frankie Vaughan. (*Sipping tea.*)
You make a putrid cup of tea, don't you. Doesn't he
say what he wants?

JOSIE: Just that he wants to see you—that's all.

RUTH: Strange way to go about it. Calling at the time
when you've specifically told him I shall be out. You
didn't tell him anything, did you?

JOSIE: Tell him what? That he looked like Frankie
Vaughan?

RUTH: Oh, Josie, for heaven's sake, can't you see I'm
tired? All I want is a cigarette and a bath.

(*The front door opens and* MRS. ELLIOT *comes in. She is a sincere, emotionally restrained little woman in her early fifties, who firmly believes that every cloud has a silver lining. She carries various carrier-bags filled with shopping. At the hall-stand she removes her coat.*)

RUTH: That's your mother. For heaven's sake make a start on that kitchen so that she can get started on the supper without having to clear up your mess first.

JOSIE: (*moving to kitchen*). O.K.

MRS. E.: Are you there, Josie? (*Taking off hat.*)

JOSIE: Hullo, Mum. You're not in any trouble are you, Auntie?

RUTH: In trouble? Do you mean in the general or the popular sense?

JOSIE: What?

MRS. E.: (*coming into sitting-room with bags*). Hullo, dear, hullo Josie. Managed to get a seat on the train today, thank goodness. (*Into kitchen.*)

RUTH: Hullo Kate.

JOSIE: Hullo Mum.

MRS. E.: Oh, Josie, you are a naughty girl, you really are. (*Into sitting-room.*) I was hoping you'd have everything nice and clean and tidy when I came in.

JOSIE: I was just going to do it.

MRS. E.: Just look at it out there. It would be tonight too, when there's so much to do.

RUTH: Here, let me take that from you. (*Taking one of the bags.*)

MRS. E.: Thank you, Ruth.

JOSIE: I'm sorry, Mum. Auntie Ruth was talking to me just as I was going to do it. Everyone seems a bit early tonight. (*Into kitchen.*)

MRS. E.: (*unpacking carrier*). I asked Mr. Beamish to let me off five minutes early. Didn't like it either. I thought I'd just miss the rush. Funny what a difference a few minutes makes. Anyway, I managed to get some shopping up the road before they closed.

Oh dear, what a rush. There we are. You're back early, Ruth dear. Weren't you feeling well? Wonder if George likes parsley sauce.

RUTH: It wasn't anything. Central heating in the office, I expect.

MRS. E.: Well—Josie complained she wasn't too great this morning at breakfast time, so I made her stay at home. I hope you haven't gone and caught something off of her—food poisoning or something.

RUTH: Yes.

MRS. E.: You do look tired, I must say.

RUTH: Oh, I'm better now. Josie gave her *Auntie* a cup of tea.

MRS. E.: You always hate her calling you Auntie, don't you. What can you expect, dear, when that's what you are? Now, I wanted you to do something for me. What was it? Josie, don't bother with those things now. Lay the table for me in here instead, there's a good girl.

RUTH: You seem a bit overloaded.

MRS. E.: Well, I had to get a few extras.

JOSIE: (*in from kitchen*). Where's the fire, Mum?

MRS. E.: Now try and help me a little, Josie. I'm rather cross with you over that kitchen, my girl.

JOSIE: Well, I'm doing it, aren't I?

RUTH: All right you two, I'll help, only don't go on about it, please. (*Into kitchen.*)

JOSIE: Well, she was "going on" a bit herself just now.

MRS. E.: That's enough, Josie. (*Clearing table.*) I had hoped that at least you could have had the table laid.

JOSIE: Yes, Mum, all right.

MRS. E.: I'm in such a muddle, I don't know where I am. I haven't a chance to do a thing. Hope your father comes in on time.

JOSIE: What's all the panic? Don't tell me you've got somebody coming?

MRS. E.: Yes, I have.

JOSIE: Who on earth is it?

(RUTH *comes in with loaded tray, puts it down and she and* MRS. E. *start laying the table.*)

MRS. E.: Young George is coming, that's all.

RUTH: George?

MRS. E.: George Dillon. The young fellow that works at my place. You know. I told you about him.

RUTH: Oh, did you. I don't remember.

JOSIE: Oh, him. (*She yawns loudly and flops into the armchair.*)

MRS. E.: Of course I told you. I've often spoken about him. I've asked him down to tea lots of times. But each time some appointment seems to turn up and he can't come. Well, he's coming now, for certain. He's a very busy chap. Always on the go.

RUTH: Oh, that one. The rather superior young man who's so much younger than the rest of you. Is he still there? I thought you said the job wasn't quite good enough for him.

MRS. E.: I've always felt a bit sorry for him, that's all. He seemed so much on his own all the time. And, one day, I started telling him about our Raymond, and he was most interested. He was in the services as well, you see.

RUTH: Quite a coincidence.

MRS. E.: Yes. He went right through the war.

RUTH: I had the idea we all did.

(*Pause.*)

MRS. E.: No, Ruth, some boys didn't get to see the end of it.

RUTH: I'm sorry, Kate. I've had a bit of a day, I'm afraid. I'm not in the right frame of mind to talk to young men, refined or not. If I can't do anything for you down here, I'll go and run myself a bath, if you don't mind.

MRS. E.: Oh! Were you going to have a bath now?

RUTH: Yes. Why?

MRS. E.: Well, I can't go into a long rigamarole now— I've too much to do before George comes. But you

see—well, you've got to know sometime, I suppose
—I've asked him to stay.

JOSIE: Stay? What, here?

MRS. E.: It won't be for long—just till he finds somewhere else to go.

JOSIE: What's wrong with where he is?

MRS. E.: He's not very happy there. I'll tell you later.
Don't worry me with a lot of questions now, Josie.
There's too much to do.

RUTH: Well, it's your business. It's your house—not
mine. What about Percy?

MRS. E.: Nothing about Percy. It's got nothing to do
with him.

RUTH: You're right, of course. (*Rather dryly.*) It isn't
his house, either.

MRS. E.: There's just one thing—

JOSIE: There won't half be an atmosphere when he
finds out. You know what Dad's like—he hasn't got
over those budgerigars you bought yet.

MRS. E.: He knows what he can do, and it won't take
me long to tell him. Oh, do clear up that paper and
stuff, Josie. The place looks awful. What was I saying?

RUTH: "There's just one thing."

MRS. E.: Oh yes, Ruth. I was going to ask if you would
mind very much moving out of your room for a few
days, and going in with Norah.

RUTH: Why yes, I do mind. Is it really necessary? Does
George What's-his-name have to have my room?

MRS. E.: No, he doesn't have to, but I thought it would
be nicer—being Ray's old room, he'd like it. More
like a man's room. Still—

RUTH: (*quietly*). You know, I do like to have at least
some time to myself. And anyway, Norah sleeps
with her mouth open.

MRS. E.: Oh, very well, Ruth. Josie can go in with her.
You won't mind, will you, Josie?

JOSIE: (*folding up paper*). Oh, all right. All this blessed
fuss! (*Into kitchen.*)

RUTH: I'm sorry, Kate, but you do understand.

MRS. E.: Never mind. I just thought it would be nicer, that's all. It doesn't matter, dear. And there's no fuss, Madame Josie, thank you. God pays debts without money, I always say.

RUTH: You haven't any aspirin, have you? I don't seem to know where any of my things are——

MRS. E.: There are some in the medicine chest, I think. And if you're going up, would you mind getting some of Josie's stuff into Norah's room—as that's going to be the arrangement?

RUTH: Right.

(*She is lost in her own thoughts and does not move.* MRS. E. *is too preoccupied to notice.*)

(*Pause.*)

MRS. E.: Only would you mind doing it now, while Josie and I get straight down here? George'll be here very soon—he's only got to pick up his bag from his digs. Is that your case?

RUTH: (*picking it up, and into hall*). I'll take it up with me. (*Taking off scarf and hanging it up.*) Is there anything else?

MRS. E.: No, thank you very much, Ruth. I must get started now.

(RUTH *goes upstairs.*)

Oh, yes—(*into hall*)—Ruth, dear, would you put a clean towel in the bathroom for George? I expect he'd like a wash when he comes in.

RUTH: (*halfway upstairs*). Yes.

MRS. E.: I'm sorry you're not feeling well, dear.

(RUTH *goes on upstairs.* MRS. E. *returns to sitting-room.*)

MRS. E.: Now, where are we?

(*The table by now is almost laid, and* MRS. E. *completes it.*)

JOSIE: (*in from kitchen*). Will it be the boiled pork, Mum? There isn't much left—least, not after Dad gets his hands on it.

MRS. E.: He can have it all, as far as I'm concerned.

Anyway, it won't worry George, he's a vegetarian.
(*To cocktail cabinet.*)

JOSIE: A what?

MRS. E.: (*triumphantly*). A vegetarian. Now, where's
the sherry got to, I wonder? Oh, yes.
(*She finds the bottle, and puts it on the table.*)

JOSIE: Oh, one of them. He sounds a bit wishy-washy
to me.

MRS. E.: Well, he's not—he's a real gentleman.

JOSIE: That's what I mean. My, we are going posh,
aren't we? Sherry! Anybody'd think it was Christmas.

MRS. E.: (*to kitchen*). That's enough of that, young
lady. Now go and get dressed and make yourself a
bit more presentable, or else George will think I
brought you up in the slums.

JOSIE: (*idly round the room*). George, George, George.
Georgie Porgie puddeny-pie, kissed the girls and
made them cry——

MRS. E.: (*from kitchen*). Now do as I say, dear, please.

JOSIE: All right, Mum. (*She starts to sing.*)
"Why don't you Give Me . . .
Give Me. Give Me . . .
All that you——
All that you
Have to share . . ."

(*Her eyes light on the small package on the table
down L. She moves over to it.*)
(*She extracts the note from the package, and unfolds
it.*)

MRS. E.: (*off*). Draw the curtains before you go, will
you, dear? Thank goodness the days are drawing out
again, though. I'm so sick of the winter.

JOSIE: O.K., Mum.
(*She moves to the french windows L., draws one of
the curtains, and begins reading the letter.*)
(*Reading*). "My dear—You have just left, and I
have found that you have left two pounds for me
on the desk. How thoughtful of you, and, after that
catechism of smug deficiencies you had just recited

to me, how very practical and how like you. I suppose you must have slipped it there while I was swallowed up in the damned misery of our situation.
Make no mistake—for the money, I'm grateful. But
your setting up as a kind of emotional soup kitchen
makes me spit.

(RUTH *is seen to fold her arms to her and shiver.*)

If you had any understanding at all, you would know
what a bitter taste this kind of watery gruel must
have. This is the Brown Windsor of love all right, and
the only fit place for it is the sink. If this is the kind
of thing you and your pals would dole out for the
proletariat and its poor, grubby artists, you had better think again. I'm just going out for some beer.
P.S. Was just going to post this, when I thought I
would return this watch to you. It seems to be the
one thing I have left that you ever gave me. I'd like
to think that my returning it would hurt you, but I
know it won't."

(*Bell rings.*)

(*The lights in the sitting-room blaze on.* MRS. E. *has
switched them on. The door bell goes on ringing
furiously.*)

MRS. E.: My goodness, Josie, can't you please answer
the front door for me? I've got milk on the stove.
(*Into kitchen.*) And I asked you to draw those curtains, didn't I?

JOSIE: O.K. (*Draws curtains.*) All right, all right, I'm
coming.

(*Goes through hall to front door.*)

Oh, it's you. It's only Norah, Mum.

(NORAH *comes in, wearing outdoor clothes. She is
in her middle thirties. She has some of her mother's
restraint but this is due more to having "been let
down twice." There is no bitterness, only a naïve
simplicity in all things and at all times.*)

MRS. E.: That you, Norah?

JOSIE: (*going into sitting-room*). Well, I've just said
so, haven't I?

NORAH: (*following her*). Can't think where I left my
key. It's probably in my other bag. I'll have a look
in a minute. (*Takes off hat and coat.*) Blessed train,
packed as usual. (*Fetches her slippers from under the
settee and changes her shoes.*) I saw Father coming
up the road, but I wasn't going to wait for *him* to let
me in. Not after this morning.

(JOSIE *takes out her "jazz" trousers and holds them
against her waist, dancing and humming quietly.*)

MRS. E.: (*in kitchen*). Had a nice day, dear?

NORAH: Not bad, thanks, Mum. (*To* JOSIE.) You going to the club tonight?

JOSIE: I might. Why?

NORAH: Nothing.

JOSIE: Len's got a new motor-bike. It's a smasher.

NORAH: Fancy.

JOSIE: Mum says he can come to dinner on Sunday.

MRS. E.: (*in from kitchen*). Well, Mum has changed
her mind. He can't.

JOSIE: Oh, Mum! Why?

MRS. E.: I'll tell you why later. For goodness' sake take
that blessed box upstairs. Supper's nearly ready and
there's only George and him to come.

(JOSIE *picks up box and trousers and goes upstairs,
singing her favourite song.*)

NORAH: George who?

MRS. E.: Young George from the office, you know the
one who gave me the necklace.

NORAH: Oh, him.

MRS. E.: Would you like to start your supper, dear? It's
all ready, and I expect you're hungry. (*She goes into
the kitchen.*)

NORAH: You know I'm never hungry, Mum.

MRS. E.: Too many sweets, my girl, that's your trouble.

(NORAH *sits at her usual place at the table.*)

MRS. E.: You know what a state your teeth are in already. (*In with a plate of food which she places in
front of* NORAH.) I'm sure those sweets are half the
trouble. There, see how you like that.

NORAH: Thanks, Mum.

(MRS. E. *goes to the foot of stairs and calls.*)

MRS. E.: Ruth—Ruth, dear! Don't be long, will you? And don't forget that towel. (*She returns to sitting-room.*)

Is it all right, dear?

NORAH: Yes, thanks.

MRS. E.: That's good.

(MRS. E. *goes into kitchen as the front door opens. PERCY, her husband, comes in with a brief-case, mac and umbrella, all of which he deposits at the hat-stand. He is a small, mean little man. Small in every sense of the word, with a small man's aggression. He goes upstairs.*)

NORAH: Mum!

MRS. E.: (*coming in*). Yes, dear? Something wrong?

NORAH: *He's* just come in, I think.

MRS. E.: Oh! (*Going to foot of stairs.*) Percy!—Was that you, Percy? (*She returns to sitting-room.*) I suppose it was him, Norah?

NORAH: Of course it was. I'd know that cat-like tread anywhere. Trust him not to give a civil answer to a civil question.

MRS. E.: The only time your father ever gave a civil answer to a civil question was when he said "I will" at the wedding.

Hope George isn't long, then we can all clear off into the lounge and watch the telly—leave your father to it. Anything on tonight? Not one of them morbid plays, I hope.

NORAH: There's some skating, I think.

MRS. E.: That'll be nice. (*Into kitchen.*) They usually have some nice music with that.

(PERCY *comes downstairs and, after taking an evening paper from his brief-case, goes into the sitting-room and sits at the table in the arm-dining-chair.*)

MRS. E.: (*lifting kitchen hatch*). Will you have boiled pork or boiled eggs?

PERCY: (*reading paper*). Nothing.

MRS. E.: You heard what I said—boiled pork or boiled eggs?

PERCY: And you heard what I said—nothing. Just a cup of tea.

(MRS. E. *slams down hatch.*)

(NORAH *pours out tea for her father and herself.*)

NORAH: Must put some more water in the pot.

PERCY: You'll drown it.

NORAH: And I know something else that needs drowning.

(*Into kitchen with teapot.*)

(MRS. E. *comes in with plate of food, and sets it in front of* PERCY.)

PERCY: I said I didn't want anything.

MRS. E.: You'll no doubt eat it just the same. Josie! Ruth! Come along, now! And another thing: I hope you'll mind your manners, Percy, in future, particularly as I have a young gentleman from the office coming to stay here for a little while. (*To herself.*) It'll be like having Raymond in the house again.

PERCY: Accch! So you've taken to cradle-snatching, have you. Not content with taking another woman's husband, you have to pick up a "young gentleman" as well. Where did all this happen—Dean Street?

MRS. E.: (*with an effort*). Look, Percy, I'm warning you, once and for all, this is *my* house, and I have worked for every penny I bought it with, and everything in it. As far as I'm concerned, you're just the lodger here. Why you've got your knife into Jack Livings, goodness only knows. They're nice, respectable people, and well you know it. I'm sure I don't know what Mrs. Livings would say if she knew about your horrible accusations. Just because Mr. Livings comes in now and again to do a few useful things about the house, that's all it is—things you're too *damn* lazy to do for me.

NORAH: (*mildly*). Mum!

MRS. E.: I'm sorry, Norah, but there it is. There are times when your father goes too far with his insults.

And I'll have you know this too: George is a fine, clean, upright young man. And he's clever too. He's in the theatrical line, he is, and one day he's going to be as famous as that Laurence Olivier, you see, and then perhaps you'll laugh on the other side of your face.

PERCY: Accch! Theatrical line! Don't give me that nonsense. I bet you he hasn't got two ha'pennies for a penny—they never have, these people.

MRS. E.: No—it's true that, at the moment, he hasn't a lot of money to throw around, but he will have, he's that type. He's used to money, you can tell that. He's very cultured.

NORAH: Not like some people we know.

PERCY: How is it he's only a tupenny-ha'penny penpusher then?

MRS. E.: He's not a clerk any longer. There was a little upset at the office today and he walked out. And a good job too, I say. Wasting his time and talent in a place like that. It's not right, and I wouldn't like to see any boy of mine going to waste like that— especially when George has so many plans and ideas to make himself famous. There isn't much he can't turn his hand to in the theatrical line, believe me. Why he doesn't only act in plays, he writes them as well. As a matter of fact, he's bang in the middle of one at the moment. I expect he'll finish it while he's here.

PERCY: That's all very interesting, I'm sure. You've got it all nicely worked out between you, haven't you? But what about me? I'm going to look a proper bloody fool, aren't I? What are the neighbours going to think, I'd like to know?

MRS. E.: No more than they do now, believe me. They know very well what you're like. I haven't forgotten yesterday either—shouting and swearing at the top of your voice. At the front door too. The humiliation of it! I don't mind you swearing at the back door, but the front door—well———

PERCY: Accch! You women—nag, nag, nag.

(JOSIE *comes downstairs and goes into the "lounge." She is now "respectable.")*

MRS. E.: Is that you, Ruth? Josie? Oh, for heaven's sake don't start looking at that thing till we've had supper.

(JOSIE *comes out of lounge into sitting-room.)*

JOSIE: Oh, all right. It's only the newsreel.

(*She gets a chair and sits at the table.*)

(MRS. E. *goes into the kitchen and returns immediately with two plates of food.*)

It's panel-game night, isn't it?

MRS. E.: There you are. (*She places plate in front of* JOSIE.)

And I may as well have mine while I'm about it. And what do you say, Miss Josie? (*Sits at table.*)

JOSIE: Sorry. Thanks, Mum.

MRS. E.: That's better.

(*They are all eating now.*)

(*Pause.*)

JOSIE: Silence in the pig-market, let the old sow speak first.

MRS. E.: Pudding, Percy?

PERCY: No.

JOSIE: Trouble with you, Dad, is you talk too much.

PERCY: Accch!

JOSIE: Can I put a record on, liven things up a bit. Ever so sordid in here, like a mortuary.

PERCY: That blessed racket. If I had my way——

MRS. E.: It's Norah's wireless.

(JOSIE *puts on a record and returns to her seat.*)

JOSIE: The girls are taking a coach up to Salisbury on Sunday. You coming, Mum?

(RUTH *comes slowly down the stairs. Halfway down, there is a knock at the door.*)

MRS. E.: No, I don't think so, dear. I expect Norah will though. She's coach mad.

(RUTH *answers the front door and a man's voice is heard outside. It is* GEORGE DILLON.)

NORAH: That would be lovely.

GEORGE: I'm awfully sorry, but does Mrs. Elliot live here?

RUTH: Yes, she does. Did you want to speak to her?

GEORGE: Well, as a matter of fact she asked me to——

RUTH: Oh, I am sorry. Of course, you must be George. Do come in.

(GEORGE DILLON *enters. He is a little over thirty, boyish, yet still every year his age. He is short, not good-looking, but with an anti-romantic kind of charm. He displays at different times a mercurial, ironic passion, lethargy, offensiveness, blatant sincerity and a mentally picaresque dishonesty—sometimes almost all of these at the same time. A walking confliction in fact. Just at the moment he is rather shy, feeling his way. He is carrying a suitcase and a 'carry-all' bag.*)

GEORGE: Yes, that's right. Thank you.

RUTH: I'm Ruth Gray. Mrs. Elliot's sister.

GEORGE: How do you do?

(*They shake hands.*)

I seem to think we've met somewhere before, haven't we?

RUTH: Yes, I had that feeling too.

MRS. E.: There's someone in the hall. Is that you, Ruth? (*She rises and goes into the hall.*)

RUTH: Mr. Dillon has arrived, Kate.

MR. E.: Oh, good. You found your way all right, then? Glad you remembered it was Targon Wood station you had to get out at—most people think Pelham Junction is nearer, but it isn't really. I didn't hear you ring the bell. I expect you're hungry, aren't you? Would you like a wash before supper? Bring your things up. (*Going upstairs.*) I'll show you where your room is and where you can find the toilet.

(GEORGE *follows her up.*)

GEORGE: That's very nice of you. I couldn't find the bell, so I knocked instead.

MRS. E.: Yes, I thought I didn't hear you ring.

(*They both disappear.* RUTH *stands looking up the stairs for a moment.*)

JOSIE: Must be nearly time for "Classics on Ice." I'm going to get a good seat before that fellow pinches it. (*Rising, she puts chair under table.*) Sounds ever so posh, doesn't he?

NORAH: I thought you were going to the club.

JOSIE: It's a woman's privilege to change her mind. (*Crosses into hall.*) Well, what's he like, Auntie? (RUTH *does not move.*) Auntie, what's he like?

RUTH: I don't know. Of course I don't. Why should I?

JOSIE: Oh, all right. I was only asking. Keep your hair on.

(*Goes into lounge.*)

(RUTH *walks slowly into sitting-room and sits in armchair.* NORAH *collects dirty plates.* PERCY *is still reading.*)

(MRS. E. *comes downstairs into sitting-room.*)

MRS. E.: Well, that's that. Have you finished, Percy? (PERCY *folds newspaper.*)

PERCY: Where's Henry Irving?

MRS. E.: Never you mind. I'd be grateful if you made yourself useful for once and made up the lounge fire. (PERCY *rises and switches off radiogram and goes into lounge.* NORAH *takes things into the kitchen.*) That's right, dear. Can't keep his hands off that wireless, can he? Now, Ruth, what about your supper, dear?

RUTH: (*rising*). Oh, nothing for me, thanks. (*Crosses to small table.*) I think I'll just have some hot milk and go to bed. (*She picks up the small package containing the watch. The note is missing.*) Kate.

MRS. E.: Yes, dear? Why, Ruth, what is it? You look quite pale. If I were you——

RUTH: Has anyone been at this table at all? Have they, Kate?

MRS. E.: My dear, I'm sure I don't know. What a funny thing to ask. Why shouldn't they if they want to?

RUTH: There was a letter of mine here. Quite personal. A private letter. Someone has moved it.

MRS. E.: Now, Ruth, dear, don't go upsetting yourself over a little thing like that. I expect you'll come across it later on. You go upstairs and I'll bring you up some hot milk later on.

(MRS. E. *goes into the kitchen. Then* RUTH *goes into hall, halfway upstairs she stops for a moment, then comes down again, goes to lounge door, opens it and calls. There is the sound of the "Skater's Waltz" from within.*)

RUTH: Josie, come here a minute, will you?

JOSIE: Oh, what do you want, can't you see I'm watching the telly?

RUTH: Come here, please, when I ask you. (*She moves to the foot of the stairs as she waits.*)

JOSIE: (*at lounge door*). What do you want?

RUTH: Shut the door and come here.

(JOSIE *goes to her.*)

JOSIE: Well?

RUTH: Where is it?

JOSIE: Where's what? I don't know what you're talking about.

RUTH: You know damn well what. Give me that letter.

JOSIE: Oh, that. Oh, yes. (*Slowly, reluctantly, she withdraws letter from her jumper.*)

RUTH: Thank you very much. Kindly learn to keep your nose clean in future, will you?

JOSIE: So that's where you've been all these week-ends, with Jock. Does he wear a kilt?

RUTH: Mind your own damned business. (*Gives her a resounding smack across the face.*)

(JOSIE *yells. Enter* MRS. E.)

MRS. E.: Why, whatever's going on?

JOSIE: Going on! It's Auntie Ruth what's been going on. *Carrying* on more like—with a man—and paying him for it what's more.

RUTH: Just you dare read my letters again, and I'll do more than slap your face.

JOSIE: Don't you talk to me like that—you're not my mum.

MRS. E.: If what Ruth says is true, Josie, then I'm very ashamed. I thought I'd brought you up to behave like a lady. Never, never do that again, do you hear? Now kindly leave the room—but first say you're sorry to Auntie Ruth.

JOSIE: (*after some hesitation*). I'm sorry, Auntie Ruth. (*Goes off to lounge singing "If Jock could love me, love me. . . ."*)

RUTH: Slut! slut! slut!

MRS. E.: Ruth—that's no way to talk, and you know it. (RUTH *turns away*.)

MRS. E.: So things didn't work out then?

RUTH: No—I've just walked out on him, for better or for worse.

MRS. E.: But I don't understand. Josie said something about paying him——

RUTH: I don't have to buy my love—or do I? Yes, I gave him the odd pound or two, to keep him alive.

MRS. E.: But surely he could do a job of work?

RUTH: Job of work? He's a writer—the original starving artist in the attic—and I believed he had promise.

MRS. E.: Then why did you leave him?

RUTH: He's been a promising young man for too long. Youthful promise doesn't look too well with receding hair. I've misjudged him—he's the complete flop, and I've spent nearly six years giving all I could to him, giving my love to him—such as it is.

MRS. E.: It's beyond me, dear. It's funny—you're the only one in the family who doesn't have patience or understanding. While you were enjoying yourself at college, we all had to go out to work. I can only say that college gave you a lot of funny ideas.

RUTH: That's right. Funny enough to make me do an inexcusable thing. When he told me he hadn't a penny, not even the price of a packet of cigarettes, I went to his jacket pocket, and inside I found a cheque for eight guineas for some book review or other he'd written. He hadn't even told me about it. Not only did he lie about the money, but he even kept his piffling little success from me. A brainless, cheap little lie. And that did it—the whole works collapsed, the whole flimsy works. (*She walks to the door.*) I suppose that's really why I left him. (*Exits upstairs.*)

MRS. E.: (*crossing to hallway*). George! Supper's ready, dear.

(*Returns to kitchen.*)

(GEORGE *comes down, looking over his shoulder. As* GEORGE *crosses hall,* NORAH *comes out of kitchen into hall. "Skater's Waltz" comes up good and loud.*)

NORAH: Hullo.

GEORGE: Hullo.

NORAH: Your supper's in there. I'm going to watch the skating. (*She goes into lounge.*)

(GEORGE *goes into sitting-room. He coughs slightly.*)

MRS. E.: That's right, dear, make yourself at home. Oh, that blessed telly, it's much too loud, isn't it? (*She crosses to lounge and opens door.*) Do put that telly down a bit, there's good children. We can't hear ourselves think in here. (*She goes back into sitting-room.*)

There, that's better isn't it? You sit there, dear. (*He sits in* PERCY's *place.*) They're all watching the telly, so you can have your supper in peace. And while we're alone, dear—I want you to treat this just as if it were your home, just do whatever you like, won't you?

GEORGE: That's very kind of you, Mrs. Elliot. I just don't know what to say (*he puts out his hand*), I can only say that I won't impose myself on you for one minute longer than I can help. You're so very kind.

MRS. E.: I've never mentioned this before, but I'm helping you all I can because I feel that in some small way I'm helping my son, Raymond. He was killed in the war, you know. That's his picture over there.

GEORGE: Yes, I'm sorry.

MRS. E.: (*very simply*). He was a lovely boy. Clever, like you, artistic, too, but somehow he didn't seem to have that drive, that sort of initiative. Well, he didn't really have much chance to get on. But *you* will, George, I'm sure. With all your talent, you just can't go wrong. You're always planning things—and all the things you've already done too. You've got your acting and your plays and I don't know what, haven't you?

GEORGE: Oh, yes, Mrs. Elliot, don't you worry—the play I'm writing now is just about in the bag. I can finish it in no time here. And I've already got someone interested in it—for the West End, I mean.

MRS. E.: Well, there you are—what did I say? You certainly are one for irons in the fire, aren't you? And to think we shall all come and see your piece, and sit in the posh seats. That will be nice. Well, there we are, dear. And if Ray was here now, I'd be talking to him just as I'm talking to you. What I'm trying to say is that I want you to feel that you are taking his place in the home, and if there's anything you want—anything—please don't hesitate to ask. And don't, please, ever go short of money. Ray used to send me home so much a week when he was in the army, for me to save for him when he came home. I'd like to think it's being put to good use at last by helping you.

GEORGE: Bless you, Mrs. Elliot. (*He coughs slightly.*) You're so very kind and thoughtful. I just don't know how to thank you. I only hope I'll prove worthy of your kindness. I promise I won't let you down in any way, I promise you that.

MRS. E.: (*patting his cheek*). Good. Now we must see about getting you something to eat. Being a vegetarian you must eat lots of strange things. You'll have to tell me about them as we go along. (*Into kitchen.*)

GEORGE: I don't want you to put yourself out.

(*He sits looking around him.*)

MRS. E.: (*lifting hatch*). I've got some nice boiled cod

and parsley sauce. You do eat fish, don't you? (*She sees him staring at the birds on the wall C.*) Yes, Ray painted those. I told you he was artistic, didn't I? (*Hatch down.*)

(GEORGE *rises and walks round the room restlessly, looking at the photographs on the wall, the cocktail cabinet, the general dressings. He then picks up the photograph of* RAYMOND *and looks at it steadily.*)

GEORGE: You stupid looking bastard.

QUICK CURTAIN

ACT II

Summer. There is now a telephone standing on small table in hall. The french windows are open. The settee brought round to face slightly downstage. NORAH, JOSIE, MRS. E., *and* PERCY *are sitting in their customary places at the meal table, eating. After curtain rises, a slight pause.*

MRS. E.: Pudding, Percy?

PERCY: No.

(MRS. E. *rises, taking plates into kitchen. As she does so, the telephone rings and she stops dead.*)

NORAH: (*with awe*). It's ringing!

JOSIE: The phone's ringing!

MRS. E.: Our first call.

PERCY: What a racket—wireless, T.V., and now the blinking telephone.

MRS. E.: Who's it for, I wonder?

NORAH: Answer it and see.

JOSIE: Yes, that's the best way to find out. (*Jumps up and goes into hall.*) I'll go, Mum. (*Lifts receiver.*) Yes, yes it is. Who? Yes. All right, I'll fetch her. (*Into sitting-room.*) It's for you, Mum. Ever such a funny man—he's got a sort of Chinese accent.

MRS. E.: (*giving plates to* JOSIE). Chinese?

JOSIE: Yes.

MRS. E.: But I don't know any Chinamen.

JOSIE: Well, you'd better hurry up and answer it, Mum —he's waiting.

NORAH: Perhaps he's from *Chu Chin Chow on Ice.*

(MRS. E. *goes into hall, and picks up receiver.*)

MRS. E.: Hullo. Yes, it is. (JOSIE *stands in doorway* *listening.*)
Have we what? Well, I don't know. I'll see. (*To* JOSIE.) He wants to know if we've got any laundry that wants doing. (*In phone.*) No, I don't think so, thank you. What are you laughing at? (*She laughs.*) Oh, you are a naughty boy, you really are—you took us all in. (*To* JOSIE.) It's George.

JOSIE: Oh, silly. (*She goes into kitchen.*)

MRS. E.: What's that, dear? Have you? Oh, I am pleased. Yes, oh we will! All right, dear. Good-bye. (*Replaces receiver, goes into sitting-room.*) Says he's got some good news—he's got a job, and something about his play. I didn't quite catch what it was. Fancy young George being the first to ring up—and I had it put in specially for him too. Isn't that nice? Oh, I must sit down a minute—the excitement's too much for me!

(NORAH *pours tea.*)

NORAH: Needs more water. (*Into kitchen.*)

PERCY: *What's* he gone and got?

MRS. E.: You heard, didn't you? A job. What did you think it was?

JOSIE: (*in from kitchen*). Must be something good for him to ring up like that.

MRS. E.: Yes—silly boy. He was only at the station. He'll be home in a minute. I'm so glad. That awful day he left that office, he swore he'd stick it out until he got something really worthwhile.

(NORAH *comes in with teapot.*)

MRS. E.: And it's turned up at last. He always said he wouldn't take anything tatty.

NORAH: What's "tatty"?

MRS. E.: I don't really know, dear—George is always saying it.

JOSIE: Well, now I can really tell the whole of Targon Broadway that we've got a real actor staying with us. That's if he doesn't get too stuck up, and want to go and live in Berkeley Square or something.

MRS. E.: Of course he won't. George has settled down here very well. This is his home now. There's no reason at all why he should have to go.

JOSIE: Well, he'll have to get married sometimes, won't he?

MRS. E.: Well, yes, there is that, of course.

NORAH: How do you know he hasn't got a girl friend already? (*Phone rings.*)

MRS. E.: Well! There it is again—twice in a couple of minutes. (JOSIE *goes to it quickly, lifts receiver.*)

JOSIE: (*on phone*). Hullo. Who? No, I think you must have the wrong number. You're welcome. (*Puts phone down and returns to sitting-room.*) Wrong number.

MRS. E.: Oh.

JOSIE: What were we talking about?

MRS. E.: George. I was just going to say that I think you're a bit gone on him, aren't you. What about poor old Len Cook now, eh!

JOSIE: Well, George will do to fill in while Len does his National Service. I wouldn't mind going to Germany with Len though.

NORAH: You'd have to marry him first, wouldn't you? I mean it wouldn't be very proper just to go and— well—"live" with him——

JOSIE: Oh, I don't know. I don't mind what I do or where I go, so long as my man's got money.

PERCY: The trouble with young girls today is that they spend too much time thinking about love and S-E-X.

JOSIE: S-E-X? Oh, sex. Sex doesn't mean a thing to me. To my way of thinking, love is the most important and beautiful thing in this world and that's got nothing to do with sex.

PERCY: (*producing irrelevances like a bombshell*). Well, I may be a crank and all that, but if I can persuade the council to close the park gates after dark, I shall die a happy man.

NORAH: What on earth's that got to do with sex?

MRS. E.: Well, I don't think we need go on with this

conversation—but Josie is quite right. You keep those beautiful thoughts, dear, and you can be sure you won't come to any harm. Put the kettle on for George, there's a dear. (JOSIE *goes into kitchen.*)
(GEORGE *appears at the french window, waving a bottle of wine.*)

GEORGE: Friends, Romans and countrymen, lend me your ears!

MRS. E.: Oh, George! You did make me jump! (GEORGE *goes up and hugs her.*) And I'm so pleased about your job, dear—we're all dying to hear about it.

JOSIE: Where is it, George, Drury Lane?

GEORGE: Could be, Josie, could be! Come on Norah, cheer up and find the corkscrew for the big Bacchanalia.

MRS. E.: I'll find it. (*Goes to cocktail cabinet.*)

GEORGE: Cast of thousands, ten years in the making. Starring the one and only Mrs. Elliot as Juno!
(*They all laugh with the exception of* PERCY. RUTH *comes in at the front door and stands listening at the foot of the stairs.*)

GEORGE: (*assuming a thick Dublin accent*). And you, Norah, me darlin', you shall play Ariadne.

NORAH: I'm not being a man for you or nobody.

GEORGE: And Josie, let me see, yes, you'll play Semele.

JOSIE: Oh! There's a name to go to bed with!

GEORGE: And that's exactly what you do, my sweet—with me, Jupiter.
(*More general laughter.*)
(RUTH *goes upstairs.*)

PERCY: Accch!

MRS. E.: There you are, Josie, what was I saying only a minute ago? (*Handing* GEORGE *corkscrew.*)

GEORGE: Now let the wine flow on this day of days. And what a day it's been. Do you know, one agent I went to see this morning looked me up and down in this duffel-coat and said: "No, we ain't got no *Biblical* parts today." Must have thought I looked like John the Baptist. Perhaps if I go in a kilt, he'll offer me a gangster part.

Glasses, Mrs. E. Bring out the golden goblets. That's right. For in spite of George continually being told he's too young, too old, too short—in spite of his wig, glass eye, false teeth and wooden leg, George has got himself a job. (*He hands wine to* MRS. ELLIOT.) There we are.

MRS. E.: I mustn't have more than one. I can't go to the meeting tiddly, can I? I don't know what Mr. Colwyn-Stuart would say.

GEORGE: Josie?

JOSIE: I certainly won't say no. (*Takes glass.*)

GEORGE: And what about you, Percy. Will you have a tipple?

PERCY: Well, seeing as how you are in the money.

GEORGE: And Norah! A glass for Norah Mavourneen —me darlin' gal.

NORAH: Not for me, thank you.

GEORGE: No?

NORAH: No, thank you.

MRS. E.: Oh, go on, Norah. It's no use you pretending you're teetotal. You had some on Boxing Day, I remember. Go on, be sociable.

NORAH: I really don't think I could after seeing those great fat men on the telly last night trampling on the grapes half naked. It was horrible.

GEORGE: So Norah isn't going to touch any more wine until they bathe in a respectable manner? Never mind, dear, just one sip won't hurt you. (*Gives her a glass.*)

NORAH: Oh, all right then, just a sip.

MRS. E.: Well, good health, George, and congratulations.

ALL: Good luck, Down the hatch, *etc.*

JOSIE: Well, now tell us what it is.

GEORGE: First of all, there's every chance of my play going on at the Trident Theatre.

MRS. E.: Oh, good.

JOSIE: Where's that, George? In the West End?

GEORGE: Well, no, not exactly. Bayswater. And it means I should get plenty of managers and agents to see it.

MRS. E.: Oh, good.

GEORGE: I saw Ronnie Harris this morning—you know the film man and he said he's got a part for me coming up shortly.

NORAH: What sort of film, George?

GEORGE: Don't really know yet—to do with some Army job or something, so he says.

MRS. E.: That'll be nice.

GEORGE: And finally, I've got a T.V. job coming up in three weeks' time.

JOSIE: George! You going to be on the telly?

GEORGE: Well, yes. But it's not exactly the lead, mind you, but it's something, anyway.

JOSIE: Oh, I'll say it is. Our George on the telly! What are you going to be in, George?

GEORGE: Ever heard of a play called *Hamlet?*

JOSIE: Of course I have.

NORAH: Yes, I saw that a long time ago. That's a very *old* one, isn't it. Very good though. He dies in the end, doesn't he?

GEORGE: He does indeed, Norah, he does.

NORAH: I always like a good laugh really. What I always say is——

NORAH: ⎱ There's enough misery in the world without
GEORGE: ⎰ paying to see it.

GEORGE: I don't think you really like the theatre very much, do you, Norah?

NORAH: Oh, yes I do.

GEORGE: Not really.

NORAH: Yes, but I don't ever go.

GEORGE: Oh, but you should. The theatre is like a shrine, Norah. A cathedral. Do you ever go to church, Norah?

MRS. E.: The only time she goes to church is when she's got a blessed banner stuck in her hand.

NORAH: Oh, Mum. (*Rises and goes into lounge.*)

MRS. E.: And talking of church—I must pop your Saviar in the oven. You'll be able to look after it, won't you? I'm off to the meeting as soon as Mr. Colwyn-Stuart gets here. (*Exit kitchen.*)

GEORGE: Lord, is he coming? I'm in no mood for Mr. Colwyn-pussy-Stuart. Josie, how long will you be?

JOSIE: How long will I be? Oooooh! It's jazz night! I must get changed. (*She runs upstairs.*)

GEORGE: (*sinking exhausted in armchair*). Tired as I am, anything would be better than having to put up with that moron.

PERCY: For once, young man, I agree with you. Thanks for the drink.

GEORGE: (*absently*). Not at all. A pleasure.

PERCY: Now that you're a celebrity, I'm surprised that you want to go jazzing at the Jubilee Hall with Josie.

GEORGE: (*singing*). "Jazzing at the Jubilee with Josie!"

PERCY: And I certainly hope that now you are earning money, you will be able to pay for yourself instead of sponging off other people.

GEORGE: (*looks at him sharply*). What do you mean? (*The front doorbell rings.*)

MRS. E.: (*in from kitchen*). That's him now. Right on the dot as usual. Do I look all right?

(RUTH *comes downstairs.*)

GEORGE: Ravishing.

PERCY: Accch!

MRS. E.: (*into hall*). Answer that, Ruth dear, will you? (*Into sitting-room.*) And if you can't make an effort to make yourself a little more pleasant, you'd better go and watch the telly.

PERCY: (*sitting down*). I'm busy.

(RUTH *opens front door.*)

MRS. E.: All right then. But I don't want any upsets tonight. (GEOFFREY COLWYN-STUART *comes in and follows* RUTH *into sitting-room. He wears an elegant suit, with a beautifully laundered shirt, a carefully chosen green spotted tie, and breast pocket handker-*

chief to match. He is a pale, balding man in his late thirties, all sweetness and light.)

MRS. E.: Oh come in, Mr. Stuart, I'm nearly ready. You know everyone, don't you?

GEOFFREY: Yes. Good evening everyone. Why, Mrs. Elliot, you look blooming tonight.

MRS. E.: Oh not really. I haven't had a minute since I came in.

GEOFFREY: But that's the secret, isn't it? Good evening, Mr. Elliot. How are you?

PERCY: (*half rises, turning to greet* GEOFFREY *but finally doesn't*). How are you?

MRS. E.: You've met George, haven't you?

GEOFFREY: Oh, yes, we've met several times, haven't we?

MRS. E.: Yes. He's been here a long time now.

GEOFFREY: Like one of the family, in fact.

MRS. E.: Well, I won't keep you long. I'll just pop upstairs and put on a spot of powder, then I'm ready. George'll keep you entertained. He keeps *us* entertained, doesn't he?

(PERCY *makes a noise like an aborted whistle, which he keeps up for the next few minutes.* RUTH *sits at the table, drinking tea.*)

MRS. E.: Didn't you want to watch the television, Percy? George has had some good news today, haven't you, George? We've been ever so excited. He's going to be on the telly himself soon. You'll have to come round and see him when he is. I expect he'll tell you all about it. Make Mr. Colwyn-Stuart comfortable. Don't go without me, now! (*Into hall and upstairs.*)

GEOFFREY: It's all right, you needn't hurry. We're early yet. (*Crossing left.*) What a dear she is.

GEORGE: Rather.

GEOFFREY: Mind if I sit here? (*At table.*)

RUTH: Do. There's some tea left, if you'd care for some.

GEOFFREY: No, thank you so much. I've just had dinner.

RUTH: Have you? We've just had supper. (*Removes wine to cocktail cabinet.*)

(PERCY *taps the sides of his armchair pensively.*)

GEOFFREY: And how's the world treating you, Mr. Elliot? I suppose I should say "how are *you* treating the world?" After all, that's what really counts, isn't it?

PERCY: Not too badly, thank you.

GEOFFREY: Your wife's been telling me that you've not been sleeping very well lately. I'm sorry to hear that.

PERCY: (*rubbing his nose*). Oh? She told you that, did she?

GEOFFREY: She mentioned it at our last meeting actually.

PERCY: The last meeting, was it? Actually?

GEOFFREY: How are you feeling now? Any better?

PERCY: Nothing the matter with me. Don't sleep so good sometimes, that's all.

GEOFFREY: Mrs. Elliot says she can't persuade you to go to a doctor about it.

PERCY: Don't believe in them.

GEOFFREY: Well, I think you'll find plenty of people to support you there—including you, eh, George?

GEORGE: Right.

PERCY: I don't believe in a lot of vegetarian rot either. I'm not making *my*self ill. Meatless steaks! (*Grins.*)

RUTH: Yes, I must say, that was rather too much for me. Nut cutlet I can take, but meatless steak's a bit too much of a paradox. Do you think Oscar Wilde could possibly have been a vegetarian?

PERCY: It's just that I have a lot of things on my mind.

GEOFFREY: In your own words, Mr. Elliot. Exactly. The old ravelled sleeve of care, am I right, George?

GEORGE: (*absently*). Eh?

RUTH: Shakespeare, George. Aren't you supposed to stand to attention, or something?

GEOFFREY: The number of people one sees every day, with tired, haggard eyes, dark circles of care underneath them.

GEORGE: I always thought that had another significance.

GEOFFREY: (*smiling*). You're a pretty free sort of chap, aren't you? I hope you don't shock everyone in this respectable household with your Bohemian ways.

GEORGE: By "Bohemian" I suppose you mean crummy. It's rather like calling bad breath "halitosis", don't you think?

RUTH: He's straight out of *Trilby*—didn't you know?

GEORGE: Frankly, I always touch mine up with a brown liner.

GEOFFREY: What?

GEORGE: The rings under my eyes—helps me when I play clergymen's parts. I'm rather good at them.

GEOFFREY: (*refusing to be stung*). You know, you surprise me a little, George. You seem such an intelligent, vital young man, so much in the swim. After all, it's not even considered fashionable to be sceptical nowadays. The really *smart* thing is the spiritual thing.

RUTH: That's true enough.

GEOFFREY: And you too, Ruth. Of course, your interests are political, I know. But shall I tell you something? If I were to invite the Foreign Secretary, say, down here to speak, he wouldn't be able to half fill the Jubilee Hall.

RUTH: Are we supposed to be surprised?

GEOFFREY: On the other hand, if I were to invite someone like Billy Graham—well, take my word for it, you wouldn't be able to get within a mile of the place.

RUTH: With his message of love and all that? Love isn't everything, you know, Mr. Stuart.

GEOFFREY: That's where we disagree, Ruth. I believe that it is.

RUTH: Take justice away from love, and it doesn't mean a thing.

GEOFFREY: Love can change the face of the world.

RUTH: Tell that to the poor black devils in South Africa. Why don't you do something for them?

GEOFFREY: Dear, oh dear—we're going to get involved already if we're not careful. I can see that. Oh, there's nothing I enjoy more than a good old intellectual rough and tumble, and I only wish I could stay and slog it out with the two of you, but there isn't time, unfortunately. The fact is, we've probably got a great deal in common. You know: I have discovered a new way of judging people.

RUTH: You have?

GEOFFREY: I simply ask myself whether their lights are shining.

GEORGE: What about their livers?

GEOFFREY: (*laughing*). Yes. I did phrase it badly didn't I? Perhaps I should have said "lamps". I ask myself whether their lamps are shining. You see, my theory is that inside every one of us is a lamp. When it's alight, the loves and hates, the ambitions, desires and ideas inside it are burning, and that person is really alive. But there are people who go around every day, at work, at home with their families—they seem normal, but their lamps have gone out. They've simply given up. They've given up being alive.

RUTH: And are our lamps alight, do you think, Mr. Stuart?

GEOFFREY: Oh, very definitely. It struck me the moment I came into the room.

GEORGE: Tell me. (*Nodding at* PERCY.) What about Mr. Elliot's lamp?

GEOFFREY: Oh, yes, I think so. I think so. It's burning all right.

GEORGE: You *think* so! You hear that, Percy? You need a new wick.

GEOFFREY: Oh, I hope I didn't sound rude. I think Mr. Elliot is on edge about things a little perhaps, principally because he's tired and can't sleep.

PERCY: All I said was——

GEOFFREY: People are wearing themselves out, worrying about a whole lot of things, unimportant things that don't matter one jot. You, Ruth, you worry about who's going to win the next election.

RUTH: Believe me—I no longer give a *damn*.

GEOFFREY: It's not important. And you, George, you worry about whether you're going to rise to the top of your profession. That's not important.

GEORGE: Thank you. We'll let you know.

GEOFFREY: One day—a few years ago this was—I happened to speak to a very famous clergyman—oh, he's dead now——

PERCY: He's all right then.

GEOFFREY: For years that man was in the habit of addressing as many as six different meetings in one day, often in the same number of towns. So I asked him how it was that he never seemed to get even a little bit tired. And he explained it to me. He said: "Because I believe in every single word that I utter."

GEORGE: Lucky him.

GEOFFREY: You could see his lamp burning at the very back of the hall. He was on fire for what he believed in. And that's the secret. It's no use sitting around moaning. (*Enter* MRS. E. *from hall.*)

MRS. E.: Who's been moaning? I'm all ready. The television's started, Percy. Have you been having a little chat with George?

GEOFFREY: Well, not exactly. I'm afraid I've been rather bad mannered.

MRS. E.: I'm quite sure you haven't. *You're* never bad mannered with anyone.

GEOFFREY: I have been rather monopolizing the conversation. In fact, I've a teeny weeny feeling that George and Ruth think I'm rather an old bore.

MRS. E.: Of course he doesn't. He's a very deep one, George—I know that.

GEOFFREY: What really started us off was—we were talking about tiredness. It's a long time since I heard *you* complaining of tiredness, Mrs. Elliot. Not since those very early days just after—just after the end of the war. I think she's a good advertisement for the system, don't you? No doubt, it sounds a little odd to you, but it's all a question of what *we* call synchronizing yourself with Providence. Of getting into step with the almighty.

MRS. E.: Yes. Well, I think we ought to be getting in step ourselves, Mr. Stuart, don't you?

GEOFFREY: Yes, I suppose we had.

(*She turns to go, and* GEOFFREY *rises.* GEORGE *has hardly been listening, but suddenly he responds, almost as an afterthought to himself.*)

GEORGE: Yes. If only it were as simple as that, Mr. Stuart. But life isn't simple, and, if you've any brains in your head at all, it's frankly a pain in the arse.

MRS. E.: George! Really!

GEORGE: I'm sorry. I apologize. But I've said it now. You see, to me there is something contemptible about a man who can't face it all without drugging himself up to the rings round his eyes with a lot of comforting myths—like all these birdbrains who batten off the National Health. I don't care who it is —you or anyone—you must have a secret doubt somewhere. You know that the only reason you do believe in these things is because they *are* comforting.

GEOFFREY: So you think that religion is just a series of useful untruths?

GEORGE: Yes, I do.

PERCY: Hear! Hear!

MRS. E.: You be quiet!

GEOFFREY: It's all right, Mrs. Elliot. George is like so many young men—he believes that the great thing about the truth is that it must always be unpleasant.

GEORGE: It's just that I believe it's easy to answer the ultimate questions—it saves you bothering with the immediate ones.

MRS. E.: There's such a thing as faith, George.

GEORGE: I believe in evidence. And faith is believing in something for which there *is* no evidence. You don't say: I have faith that two and two are four, do you? Or that the earth is round? And why? Because they're both easily verified.

GEOFFREY: So it all has to be verified for you, does it, George? I think I understand you better than you know.

GEORGE: Oh?

GEOFFREY: You see, I come into contact with a great many artistic people. What *do* you believe in? Yourself?

GEORGE: Right. (*Adding in vocal parenthesis*:) He said, striking attitude of genius.

GEOFFREY: You have faith. You have faith in yourself —in your talent. Am I right?

GEORGE: Well?

GEOFFREY: Your talent, George. You believe in that with all your heart. And your evidence? Where is that, George? Can you show it to me?

(*Pause. They all look at him.*)

RUTH: *Touché*.

(GEORGE *is still for a moment. Then he laughs.*)

GEORGE: What a performance! All this Jesuit subtlety! You're too much for me. Just say that I'm like Christopher Columbus—I haven't discovered America yet. But it's there all right, waiting to be, yes, verified.

GEOFFREY: Yes, I'm quite sure it is. You see, I have faith too. I can see the lamp burning. Well, we really must be off. Come along, Mrs. Elliot. Good night, everybody.

MRS. E.: Yes. Well, I shan't be back late.

(*They both go into hall, and out through the front door.*)

PERCY: (*rising and crossing to doorway*). Lamps! (*Chuckling.*) (*Turns.*) 'E ought to be on the bleeding stage—not you! (*Exit to lounge.*)

RUTH: Are you all right? You look a bit shaken.

GEORGE: I'm all right. I rather stupidly let the conducting of divine lip-service irritate me.

RUTH: So I noticed.

GEORGE: It's just been a pretty awful day, that's all.

RUTH: You surprise me.

GEORGE: Do I?

RUTH: Not really. You aren't very impressed with Geoffrey, I take it?

GEORGE: Right. What the Americans call "strictly for the birds". If there should be any heavenly purpose at all behind Mr. Colwyn-phoney-Stuart, it's that he's God's own gift to the birds. Hope I didn't upset Mrs. Elliot though. She's obviously pretty taken up with the whole racket.

RUTH: It might help if you weren't quite so vicious about it. You sound like a man with a secret doubt yourself.

GEORGE: Why is it you distrust me so much? I had a feeling we were the same kind.

RUTH: Did you? I suppose it's given poor Kate something to think about since Raymond was killed.

GEORGE: Tell me——

RUTH: Yes?

GEORGE: What was he really like?

RUTH: Raymond? Nice enough boy. Hard working, conscientious. Like most decent, ordinary lads of his age. (*Their eyes meet.*) You aren't remotely alike.

GEORGE: I thought you were in the habit of pitching into her yourself, hammer and sickle, over the Colwyn-Stuart.

RUTH: I should have thought that was different.

GEORGE: You mean that you're one of the family, and I'm not?

RUTH: If you like.

GEORGE: Suppose I'd better apologize.

RUTH: I shouldn't worry. I can't imagine what you could do wrong in her eyes. Well—I can imagine it all right, but I can't see you being stupid enough to lose the only good friend you've got.

GEORGE: What makes you think I haven't any good friends?

RUTH: Have you?

GEORGE: I thought you steel-hardened cadres of the far away left had a better defence against the little jokies of right wing deviationists like me. Or is it Wall Street jackal? No—I don't really look much like a jackal. Villiers Street wolf perhaps.

RUTH: Very droll—but not very well timed for some-one who is supposed to be an actor.

GEORGE: Join my fan club, won't you?

RUTH: I'm not in the right frame of mind for shoddy little gags. (*Pause.*) I looked up the Party secretary tonight.

GEORGE: So you've packed it in at last.

RUTH: No doubt you think it's pretty funny.

GEORGE: No. I don't think it's funny.

RUTH: Seventeen years. It's rather like walking out on a lover. All over, finished, kaput. He hardly listened to my explanation—just sat there with a sneer all over his face. He didn't even have the manners to get up and show me out. I think that's what I've hated most of all, all these years—the sheer, damned bad manners of the lot of them.

GEORGE: Farther left you go, the worse the manners seem to get.

RUTH: Well! The house is still fairly ringing with the bloody shovel of *your* opinions.

GEORGE: *I* have a sense of humour. "Bloody shovel of your opinions!" Is that a quotation?

RUTH: Just someone I used to know. Someone rather like you, in fact.

GEORGE: I thought you'd tied me up with someone the moment I met you.

RUTH: Where are you going tonight?

GEORGE: Dancing, I believe. Somewhere Josie knows.

RUTH: Don't sound so apologetic about it. It doesn't suit you. Pass my handbag, will you? (*He does so.*)

RUTH: Looks as though you've a long wait ahead of you, my lad. (*She offers him a cigarette.*)

GEORGE: Have one of mine. (*Fumbles in his pockets.*)

RUTH: You needn't go through the pantomime for me, George. Take one.

GEORGE: No, thank you.

RUTH: Oh, don't look like that, for God's sake! You make me feel as though I'm—setting up as a soup kitchen or something. Please.

(*She throws a cigarette. He catches it, fumbles for a light. She snaps a lighter at him, and he goes over to her. He bends over her for a light.*)

GEORGE: How young you look sometimes.

RUTH: So do you when you're silent, and no longer trying to justify yourself.

GEORGE: What's the time?

RUTH: Seven-fifteen. Where's your watch?

GEORGE: Being repaired.

RUTH: Pawned, I suppose.

GEORGE: Just as you like. I think I'll give Josie a yell.

RUTH: It won't do any good—not for ages yet. I didn't mean to hurt you just now.

GEORGE: Didn't you?

RUTH: Yes. You're quite right. I did mean to hurt you. I wish I hadn't.

GEORGE: What are you doing tonight?

RUTH: I don't know yet. I'm getting rather used to being at home every night. I *did* apologize.

GEORGE: We're neither of us as steel-hardened as we should be, are we? I used to smoke my mother's cigarettes too. Right up until the time she died.

RUTH: When was that?

GEORGE: Couple of years ago. We often used to go out together—she enjoyed that more than anything. She'd pay for the lot: drinks, meals, cinemas—even the bus fares. When the conductor came up the stairs, I would always grope in my pockets. And my mother would bring out her purse, and push my empty, fumbling hands away. "It's all right, dear. I've got change." I used to wonder whether perhaps there might come just *one* day when it might not

have to happen. When I might actually have that
two shillings or half-crown in my pocket. But it
always did. It had become a liturgy. We went
through it the last time we went out together—on
my thirtieth birthday. During the war it was different.
I was well paid then.

RUTH: What did he give you for it?

GEORGE: What?

RUTH: The pawnbroker—for the watch?

GEORGE: Fifteen shillings. I was lucky to get that—it
wasn't a very good one.

RUTH: Here. (*Takes out Jock's watch from handbag,
and holds it out to him.*) Well, take it.

GEORGE: What's this?

RUTH: What does it look like? Try it on.

GEORGE: (*taking it*). Are you giving me this?

RUTH: Yes, but you don't have to make a meal out of
it.

GEORGE: It must have cost a fortune.

RUTH: It did. Try not to pawn it. Or, if you do, tell
me, and I can renew the ticket or something.

GEORGE: I shan't pawn it, I promise you. I think it
must be the nicest present I've had. How do you
fix it?

RUTH: Here—(*she adjusts it for him, he watches her*).

GEORGE: Your—friend?

RUTH: Oh, he doesn't want it any more. He told me.

GEORGE: Can you get the Third Programme on it?

RUTH: There!

GEORGE: Perhaps it'll change my luck.

RUTH: Superstitious too?

GEORGE: Thank you. Very much.
    (*She still has his hand in hers.*)

RUTH: How beautiful your hands are—they're like
marble, so white and clear.

GEORGE: Nonsense.

RUTH: But they are. I've never seen such beautiful
hands.

GEORGE: You make it sound as if I were half dead

already. (*She looks up quickly, disturbed. Quite suddenly, he kisses her. Almost as quickly, he releases her. She soon recovers and moves away.*)

RUTH: Did you notice what I did with my lighter? My cigarette's gone out.

GEORGE: Didn't you put it back in your bag? (*She opens it.*)

RUTH: So I did. What sort of parts do you play? On the stage, I mean.

GEORGE: Good ones.

RUTH: Stupid question deserves a stupid answer. I mean: any particular type.

GEORGE: I suppose so. Reminds me of the actor who was asked at an audition what sort of parts he played, and he replied "Scornful parts". I think I play "scornful" parts—anyone a bit loud-mouthed, around my height, preferably rough and dirty, with a furnace roaring in his belly. The rougher and dirtier the better.

RUTH: A character actor in fact.

GEORGE: I'm sorry I kissed you. So you needn't try to pay me back for it.

RUTH: Don't apologize. I was flattered for a moment. I'm sure there's an explanation somewhere, but I'd rather you didn't try to tell me what it is.

GEORGE: Just as you like.

RUTH: First time I've tasted Brown Windsor.

GEORGE: Tasted what?

RUTH: (*laughing*). The Brown Windsor of love, George. Haven't you come across it.

GEORGE: That—friend of yours sounds rather pretentious to me.

RUTH: It's funny how rhetorical gentle spirits can become.

GEORGE: He's a poet or something?

RUTH: I used to hope so.

(GEORGE *stretches himself.*)

GEORGE: God, I feel tired!

(*He looks all round the room. His eyes rest on*

Raymond's painted birds on the back wall C.)
Blimey! Those birds! (*Goes upstage and walks around and is finally stopped by the sight of the cocktail cabinet.*) I've sat here for weeks now and looked at that. Oh, I've often marvelled at them from afar in a shop window. But I never thought I'd ever see one in someone's house. I thought they just stood there, in a pool of neon, like some sort of monstrous symbol, surrounded by bilious dining-room suites and mattresses and things. It never occurred to me that anyone bought them!

RUTH: Norah's cocktail cabinet? Well, she didn't actually buy it—she won it.

GEORGE: What was her reaction?

RUTH: I think we were all a little over-awed by it. (*GEORGE goes nearer to it.*)

GEORGE: It looks as though it has come out of a jelly-mould like an American car. What do you suppose you *do* with it? You don't keep drinks in it—that's just a front, concealing its true mystery. What do you keep in it—old razor blades? I know, I've got it! (*He sits down and "plays" it vigorously, like a cinema organ, humming a "lullaby-lane" style signature tune. He turns a beaming face to* RUTH.)

And now I'm going to finish up with a short selection of popular symphonies, entitled "Evergreens from the Greats", ending up with Beethoven's Ninth! And don't forget—if you're enjoying yourself, then all join in. If you can't remember the words, let alone understand 'em, well, just whistle the tune. Here we go then!

(*Encouraged by* RUTH's *laughter, he turns back and crashes away on the cocktail cabinet, pulling out the stops and singing:*)

> "I fell in love with ye- ieuw!
> While we were dancing
> The Beethoven Waltz! . . ."

(*A final flourish on the invisible keyboard; he turns and bows obsequiously.* RUTH's *response has exhila-*

rated him, and he stands in front of her, rather
flushed.)

It ought to disappear somehow, but I couldn't find
the combination. (*He watches her with pleasure.*)
That's the first time you've ever laughed.

RUTH: Oh, yes, you can be funny, George. These
flashes of frenzy, the torrents of ideas they can be
quite funny, even exciting at times. If I don't laugh,
it's because I know I shall see fatigue and fear in
your eyes sooner or later.

GEORGE: Oh?

RUTH: You're burning yourself out. And for what?

GEORGE: Go on—but don't think you can kill my con-
fidence. I've had experts doing it for years.

RUTH: I just can't make up my mind about you.

GEORGE: Meaning?

RUTH: Do you really have any integrity?

GEORGE: What's *your* verdict?

RUTH: I'm still not sure. It just seems to me that for
someone who makes a religion out of being brilliant,
you must be very unlucky.

GEORGE: You don't even begin to understand—you're
no different from the rest. Burning myself out! You
bet I'm burning myself out! I've been doing it for
so many years now—and who in hell cares? At this
moment I feel about as empty and as threadbare as
my pockets. You wonder that I should be tired. I
feel played out. (*She applauds.*)

RUTH: Bravo! Not bad at all, George. Bit ragged
maybe, but it'll do. Perhaps you may not be so bad
after all. Tell me about this television job.

GEORGE: That? It's a walk-on—one line which will be
drowned by the rest anyway. And if I know Lime
Grove, it'll be so dark, I shan't be seen at all. All
for twelve guineas. It's a fortune. But what am I
going to do? How can I let them all sit in there—and
probably half the street as well—staring stupidly at
the telly for two and a half hours to watch me make
one thirty-second appearance at the very end? What

a triumph for dear old Percy! And Mr. Colwyn-Stuart and his Hallelujah Chorus!

RUTH: Quite a problem.

GEORGE: As it is, I owe Mrs. Elliot God-knows how much. But I suppose you knew that.

RUTH: It's not exactly a surprise.

GEORGE: She was buying me cigarettes every day up until last week. I did manage to put a stop to that. I told her I was giving it up for my health. To my surprise, she actually believed me.

RUTH: *Are* you any good, George?

GEORGE: (*almost like a child*). That's a moron's question.

RUTH: As you like.

GEORGE: Well, ask yourself. Isn't it? Listen: all I ever got—inside and outside the theatre—is the raves of a microscopic minority, and the open hostility of the rest. I attract hostility. I seem to be on heat for it. Whenever I step out on to those boards—immediately, from the very first moment I show my face—I know I've got to fight almost every one of those people in the auditorium. Right from the stalls to the gallery, to the Vestal Virgins in the boxes! My God, it's a gladiatorial combat! Me against Them! Me and mighty Them! Oh, I may win some of them over. Sometimes it's a half maybe, sometimes a third, sometimes it's not even a quarter. But I *do* beat them down. I beat them down! And even in the hatred of the majority, there's a kind of triumph because I know that, although they'd never admit it, they secretly respect me.

RUTH: What about this film you're going to be in?

GEORGE: It doesn't mean a thing. The old line. You know? Keep in touch—we'll let you know. You *don't* understand, do you?

RUTH: I just don't see much virtue in trying to ignore failure.

GEORGE: There's no such thing as failure—just waiting for success.

RUTH: George—really!

GEORGE: All right, forget it.

RUTH: I know what it is to go on waiting.

GEORGE: And do you think I don't! I spend my life next to a telephone. Every time it rings is like death to me.

RUTH: (*relentless*). What about these plays you write. You do do that as well, don't you?

GEORGE: Oh yes—you think I'm a dabbler. A dilettante who can't afford it.

RUTH: This Trident Theatre—the "three uplifted fingers of Drama, Ballet and Poetry——"

GEORGE: A so-called club theatre, meaning a preciously over-decorated flea-pit, principally famous for its rather tarty bar, and frequented almost exclusively by intense students, incompetent long-hairs, and rather flashy deadbeats generally.

RUTH: I see. I'd like to read some of your work.

GEORGE: Thank you, I'll think about it.

RUTH: Do you charge a fee?

GEORGE: You're not being very funny yourself now.

RUTH: Perhaps your sense of humour has deserted you after all. My politics and your art—they seem to be like Kate's religion, better not discussed. Rationally, at any rate.

GEORGE: I knew you were suspicious of me, that you distrusted me. I didn't realize you detested me this much.

RUTH: George: why don't you go?

GEORGE: Go?

RUTH: Leave this house. Get out of here. If you're what you believe yourself to be, you've no place in a house like this. It's unfair to you. It's stifling. You should be with your own kind. And if you're not what you say you are, you've no right to be here anyway, and you're being unfair to everyone.

GEORGE: Are you serious? I haven't got a penny in the world.

RUTH: You'll manage. You've got to. It's your only

chance of survival. Am I being harsh, George? Perhaps, as you say, we're the same kind.

GEORGE: (*savagely*). That's good! Oh yes! And what about you?

RUTH: (*off her balance*). What about me?

GEORGE: What are *you* doing here? All right, you've had your go at me. But what about yourself?

RUTH: Well?

GEORGE: Oh, don't be so innocent, Ruth. This house! This room! This hideous, God-awful room!

RUTH: Aren't you being just a little insulting?

GEORGE: I'm simply telling you what you very well know. They may be your relations, but have you honestly got one tiny thing in common with any of them? These people——

RUTH: Oh, no! Not "these people"! Please—not that! After all, they don't still keep coals in the bath.

GEORGE: I didn't notice. Have you looked at them? Have you listened to them? They don't merely act and talk like caricatures, they *are* caricatures! That's what's so terrifying. Put any one of them on a stage, and no one would take them seriously for one minute! They think in clichés, they talk in them, they even feel in them—and, brother, that's an achievement! Their existence is one great cliché that they carry about with them like a snail in his little house —and they live in it and die in it!

RUTH: Even if it's true—and I don't say it is—you still sound pretty cheap saying it.

GEORGE: Look at that wedding group. (*Points to it.*) Look at it! It's like a million other grisly groups— all tinted in unbelievable pastels; round-shouldered girls with crinkled-up hair, open mouths, and bad teeth. The bridegroom looks as gormless as he's feeling lecherous, and the bride—the bride's looking as though she's just been thrown out of an orgy at a Druids' reunion! Mr. and Mrs. Elliot at their wedding. It stands there like a comic monument to the macabre farce that has gone on between them in this house ever since that greatest day in a girl's life thirty-five years ago.

RUTH: Oh, a good delivery, George. You're being brilliant, after all. They're very easy people to score off, but, never mind, go on!

GEORGE: There's Josie—at this moment putting all she's got into misapplying half Woolworths on to her empty, characterless little face. Oh, sneer at me for my snobbery, for my bad taste, but, say what you like: I have a mind and feelings that are all fingertips. Josie's mind. She can hardly spell it. And her feelings—what about them? All thumbs, thumbs that are fat and squashy—like bananas, in fact, and rather sickly.

RUTH: You should look an intriguing couple on the dance floor tonight. I'm tempted to come myself.

GEORGE: Why don't you?

RUTH: I should hate to break up this marriage of true minds.

GEORGE: You know damned well why I'm going. People like me depend upon the Josies of this world. The great, gaping mass that you're so fond of. You know? And for tonight, Josie is that mass, all rolled into one. And do you know what? Behind that brooding cloud of mascara, she's got her eye on George, Josie has. Because not only does she suffer from constipation, but night starvation as well. And then, there's Norah. Now what can you say about her? Norah doesn't even exist—she's just a hole in the air!

RUTH: You've a lot to learn yet, George. If there weren't people like the Elliots, people like you couldn't exist. Don't forget that. Don't think it's the other way around, because it's not. They can do without you, take my word for it. But without them, you're lost—nothing.

GEORGE: Don't give me that, Ruth. They drive you mad, and you know it. It's like living in one of those really bad suitable-for-all-the-family comedies they do all the year round in weekly rep. in Wigan. How have you stuck it here? What's the secret? Tell me. Since that mysterious divorce of yours that they all heavy-handedly avoid mentioning—and the week-end trips you don't make any more. How long is it you've been here? How long? Nine years is it? Ten years? Twelve? Oh no, Ruth—*you* can't afford to sneer at me!

RUTH: You've made your point. Don't get carried away with it. Why do I stay? Because I don't earn enough to get me out of it, and somewhere else. I spend too much on clothes, cigarettes——

GEORGE: And—"incidentals"? (*Holding up wristwatch.*)

RUTH: The job I do is so hysterically dull that every time I go into the office, and see myself surrounded by those imitation human beings, I feel so trapped and helpless, that I could yell my lungs out with the loneliness and the boredom of it.

GEORGE: So you do!

RUTH: But, at my age, and with my lack of the right kind of qualifications, there's not much else I can do. Perhaps I haven't the courage to try. At least, I'm safe. And so I go on, from spring, through the summer, to the autumn and another winter, meaningless; just another caricature.

GEORGE: I knew it! I knew it!

RUTH: Thank you for reminding me of it.

GEORGE: The truth is a caricature.

RUTH: Is that meant to be profound?

GEORGE: You hate them, don't you? Shall I tell you why they horrify me?

RUTH: I suppose I give you what is known as the "feed" line now. No—tell me, why do they horrify you.

GEORGE: They've no curiosity. There are no questions for them, and, consequently, no answers. They've no apprehension, no humility——

RUTH: Humility! (*Laughing.*) Good old George!

GEORGE: And, above all, no real laughter. Tell me,

have you ever heard any of them, even once, laugh?
I mean really laugh—not make that choked, edgy
sound that people make all the time. Or, to put it
more unintelligibly: I don't mean that breaking wind
people make somewhere between their eyebrows and
their navels, when they hear about the old lady's most
embarrassing moment. I mean the real thing—the
sound of the very wit of being alive. Laughter's the
nearest we ever get, or should get, to sainthood. It's
the state of grace that saves most of us from contempt.

RUTH: Hooray!

GEORGE: No, it wasn't really spontaneous. Singing and
dancing "Jazzing at the Jubilee with Josie".

RUTH: Why haven't we talked like this before. A few
moments ago you made me feel old. Now, I suddenly
feel younger.

GEORGE: "If you can't give a dollar, give me a lousy
dime . . ."

RUTH: Can't say I've exactly heard *you* falling about
with mirth since you came here.

GEORGE: No, you haven't. I suppose it does sound as
though I'm complaining because everyone doesn't go
around as if they were on parole from "Crime and
Punishment", muttering about God, and laughing
their blooming heads off.

RUTH: Oh, yes, you are a character! I think your little
performance has done me good.

GEORGE: You're a good audience. Even if I do have
to beat you down. That's all I need—an audience.

RUTH: And do you—think you'll find it?

GEORGE: I don't know.
(*He takes a deep breath, and sits down quickly,
suddenly drained. She watches him, fascinated.*)

RUTH: How quickly you change! That's what's so
frightening about you. These agonizing bubbles of
personality, then phut! Nothing. Simply tiredness and
pain.

GEORGE: I've been trailing around all day. I've had a

few drinks, and nothing to eat. It suddenly hit me, that's all.

RUTH: Perhaps you have got talent, George. I don't know. Who can tell? Even the experts can't always recognize it when they see it. You may even be great. But don't make a disease out of it. You're sick with it.

GEORGE: It's a disease some of us long to have.

RUTH: I know that. I met it once before.

GEORGE: Then you must know it's incurable.

RUTH: Galloping—like a consumption.

GEORGE: (*sharply*). What did that mean?

RUTH: Nothing.

GEORGE: But do you know what is worse? Far, far worse?

RUTH: No, Brother Bones, tell me what is worse.

GEORGE: What is worse is having the same symptoms as talent, the pain, the ugly swellings, the lot—but never knowing whether or not the diagnosis is correct. Do you think there may be some kind of euthanasia for that? Could you kill it by burying yourself here—for good?

RUTH: Why do you ask me?

GEORGE: Would the warm, generous, honest-to-goodness animal lying at your side every night, with its honest-to-goodness love—would it make you forget?

RUTH: All you're saying is that it's a hard world to live in if you're a poet—particularly if it should happen that you're not a very good poet.

GEORGE: Unquote.

RUTH: Unquote. Life is hard, George. Anyone who thinks it isn't is either very young or a fool. And you're not either. Perhaps even bad artists have their place in the scheme of things.

GEORGE: Scheme of flaming things! Get us with our intellectual sets on! And we're not even tight. I wish we were spending the evening together, all the same.

RUTH: Why are you so morbidly self-conscious? I thought all actors revelled in exhibitionism.

GEORGE: Don't you believe it. Only insincere old bastards who carried spears with Martin Harvey, and have been choking themselves silly with emotion ever since. "Emotion, laddie—that's the secret!" Shall I tell you a story. Yes, do tell me a story. Well, it happened to me when I was in the R.A.F. during the war.

RUTH: I didn't know you were. You've never mentioned it.

GEORGE: The one thing I never shoot lines about is the R.A.F. Just a gap in my life. That's all. Well, it happened like this: It was one night in particular, when it wasn't my turn to go on ops. Instead, we got a basinful of what we gave the Jerries, smack bang in the middle of the camp. I remember flinging myself down, not so much on to the earth as into it. A wing commander type pitched himself next to me, and, together, we shared his tin-helmet. Fear ran through the whole of my body, the strange fear that my right leg would be blown off, and how terrible it would be. Suddenly, the winco shouted at me above the din: "What's your profession?"

"Actor," I said. The moment I uttered that word, machine-gun fire and bombs all around us, the name of my calling, my whole reason for existence—it sounded so hideously trivial and unimportant, so divorced from living, and the real world, that my fear vanished. All I could feel was shame.

(*He is lost for a moment or two. Then he looks at her quickly, and adds brightly:*)

Gifted people are always dramatizing themselves. It provides its own experience, I suppose.

RUTH: How pompous can you get? You had me under your spell for a moment. Now you've broken it. I'm beginning not to know when you're being real, and when you're not.

GEORGE: Always put the gun in the other man's hand. It's my rule of life.

RUTH: Yes. You're play acting all right. You've done

it all your life, and you'll go on doing it. You can't
tell what's real and what isn't any more, can you,
George? I can't sit here drivelling all night.

(*She turns to go.*)

GEORGE: (*taking her by the arm*). And what if I do?
What does it matter? My motives aren't as simple as
you like to think——

RUTH: ——You're being phoney, George, aren't you?
We're a pair of——

GEORGE: ——What if I am? Or you, for that matter? It's
just as——

RUTH: (*sings*). "It's a Barnum and Bailey world,
                Just as phoney as it can be!"
You've got us both acting it now——

GEORGE: ——just as serious and as complex as any
other attitude. Ruth! Believe me, it isn't any less——

RUTH: ——haven't you, George? Cutting in on each
other's lives——

GEORGE: ——real or sincere. You just never stop standing outside——

RUTH: ——fluffing your emotions——

GEORGE: ——it's a penance——

RUTH: ——that's the word, isn't it? You're fluffing it——

GEORGE: ——the actor's second sense——

RUTH: ——all studied, premeditated——

GEORGE: ——watching, observing, watching me now,
commenting, analysing, giggling——

RUTH: ——timed for effect, deliberate, suspect——

GEORGE: ——just at this moment, don't you want me
more than anything else——

RUTH: ⎱ I've had my lot, George.
GEORGE: ⎰ More than anything?
RUTH: ⎰ We've both had our lots!
GEORGE: ⎱ You're as arrogant as I am!
RUTH: ⎱ You know what, George?
GEORGE: ⎰ That's one of the reasons you're drawn to
me! If only you knew—how much—at this mo-
ment——

RUTH: No, not me. Somebody else—not me!

GEORGE: I mean it, damn you!

RUTH: Strictly for the birds, George! Strictly for the birds!

GEORGE: Ruth!

RUTH: Let me go!

(*He does so.*)

GEORGE: (*simply*). I've botched it. (*Pause.*) Haven't I? (*The descent has been so sudden, and they are both dazed.*)

RUTH: I'm not sure what has happened. Nothing, I suppose. We're just two rather lost people—nothing extraordinary. Anyway, I'm past the stage for casual affairs. (*Turns away.*) You can't go on being Bohemian at forty.

(JOSIE *comes running down the stairs into the sitting-room. She is wearing her "jazz trousers".*)

JOSIE: Ready?

GEORGE: Yes. Yes, I suppose so.

(RUTH *goes quickly out through the french windows.*)

JOSIE: Well, come on then. Had your supper?

GEORGE: No. I don't want anything. Let's have a drink, shall we, before we go?

JOSIE: Oh yes, lovely!

(GEORGE *does not move.*)

Well, what are you standing there for? What are you thinking about?

GEORGE: What am I thinking about? (*To cocktail cabinet for the wine.*) What am I thinking about? (*Pouring drinks.*) Do you realize, Josie, that that is a lover's question? "What are you thinking about?" (*Hands her a drink.*)

JOSIE: Oh, you are daft. You make me laugh when you talk in riddles. Oh, well, cheers!

GEORGE: Cheers. It'll be tonight, Josephine. (*Drinks.*)

JOSIE: Whatever are you talking about? You are in a funny mood, I must say. Let's have some music while we finish our drinks. (*She goes to radiogram.*) We don't want to get there too early, do we?

GEORGE: All the best people arrive late.

JOSIE: (*looking through records*). What shall we have? There's "Mambo Man", "Jambo Mambo", or "Marmalade Mambo".

GEORGE: Oh, let's have something to soothe my rather shabby soul, Josie.

JOSIE: Go on, you haven't got one. What about this then? (*She puts on Mantovani.*)

GEORGE: (*screwing up his face*). Heaven. (*They begin dancing.*) Sheer heaven. (*After a moment.*)

JOSIE: Bit boring isn't it—the music I mean.

GEORGE: The preliminaries always are, Josie, my girl. But they make anticipation all the more exciting. Are you ever excited by anticipation?

JOSIE: No, not really. Only when I see fellows like Len Cook, he's lovely.

GEORGE: That not anticipation, Josie, that's lust, plain lust. Although it never is really plain. Do you know what lust is, Josie?

JOSIE: Of course I do, silly.

GEORGE: Lust, the harshest detergent of them all, the expense of spirit in a waste of shame. Or as Jean Paul Sartre put it—sex.

JOSIE: We were only talking about sex a little while ago. Boring, I think.

GEORGE: Do you? Shall we go?

JOSIE: All right.

(*They move into the hall. At the foot of the stairs,* GEORGE *stops her.*)

GEORGE: Have you ever been kissed, Josie?

JOSIE: Hundreds of times.

GEORGE: Like this?

(*He kisses her fiercely. The lounge door opens and they do not see* PERCY *standing there.*)

(RUTH *comes in through french windows, switches out main lights, leaving just a glow in the sitting-room.* PERCY *remains silhouetted against the light from the lounge as* RUTH *sits in armchair.*)

JOSIE: George—don't, George, there's somebody coming!

GEORGE: I've never tried the etchings line—(*leading her up the stairs*)—let's see if it really works.

JOSIE: But George——

GEORGE: Come and see my etchings. (*They are by now halfway up stairs.*)

JOSIE: What are you——

(GEORGE *smothers her with another kiss.*)

GEORGE: Silly girl.

JOSIE: But George, what will Mum say?

(*They are swallowed up in darkness.* PERCY *moves towards the foot of the stairs and looks up. Then he moves into the sitting-room and looks down at* RUTH *for a moment. She is suddenly aware of him.*)

RUTH: Why, Percy, how long have you been there?

PERCY: Long enough, I think. Quite long enough.

QUICK CURTAIN

ACT III

SCENE ONE

Autumn. One french window is open. GEORGE *is lying on the settee in his shirt sleeves. His jacket is hung on the back of one of the chairs. There are some loose leaves of manuscript scattered by the side of the settee. After a moment,* GEORGE *shivers, gets up, and puts on his jacket.* MRS. E. *comes downstairs into the sitting-room with a breakfast tray.*

MRS. E.: Are you feeling any better, dear? You need not have got up at all, you know. (*She puts tray on table.*) Silly boy—the window open too. (*Crossing to window.*) You'll catch your death. The chrysanths have gone off. Chrysanths always remind me of Father. (*Stands at the window.*) (*Shuts window.*) Oh, dear, the clocks go back tonight. Awful, isn't it. (*Picks up tray.*) You didn't eat much breakfast, dear. (*Into kitchen.*) Your bed's made and your room is done if you want to go up any time. Nearly twelve —(*in from the kitchen*) the others will be back soon. Sure you're all right, dear? Everyone's a bit down in the dumps these days. It must be the winter coming on. Not that I mind it really. It's the awful in-between that gets me down. How's the writing going? All right?

GEORGE: Oh, not too bad, Mrs. Elliot, thanks. Feeling a bit whacked at the moment though.

MRS. E.: Well, you mustn't overdo it, you know. I'll get in some nice cakes for your tea.

GEORGE: Please don't do that, Mrs. Elliot dear, you know I don't eat them.

MRS. E.: All right, dear, just as you like. (*Going to*

him.) I'm ever so sorry about the money, dear. Something will turn up soon I expect—don't worry, dear. Raymond's money didn't go as far as we thought it might, did it? Still, never mind. As long as I've got a shilling or two, I'll see that you're all right. Now I really must go and get some shopping done. I hate Saturdays—the crowds are awful. (*Crosses into hall, and puts on coat.*)

(*The doorbell rings.*)

Oh, that'll be the milkman. Now where's my bag? (*She picks it up from the hallstand, and goes to the front door.*) Oh yes, yes, he does. Won't you come in? (MRS. E. *stands back to admit a tall, official looking man. He carries a brief-case.*)

MAN: Thank you.

(*They go through the hall towards the sitting-room.*)

MRS. E.: I'd better show you the way. He's not feeling so good today. Still, it'll be a nice break for him, having someone to chat to. (*In sitting-room.*) George, dear, someone to see you. Well, I'll leave you to it, if you don't mind. (*Exit through front door.*)

MAN: You are Mr. George Dillon?

GEORGE: That's right.

MAN: I'm from the National Assistance Board.

GEORGE: Oh yes, I wondered when you were coming. Please sit down.

MAN: Thank you.

(*He does so. Then opens brief-case, and extracts papers, file, etc., and fountain pen from jacket. He studies papers for a moment.*)

Hmm. Now, with regard to your claim for assistance —you are Mr. George Dillon?

GEORGE: I thought we'd cleared that up just now.

MAN: (*making notes*). And you are residing at this address, paying rent of thirty shillings a week?

GEORGE: Right.

MAN: What does that entail the use of? A bedroom, and general run of the house, I take it?

GEORGE: Yes.

MAN: May I trouble you for your rent book?

GEORGE: Well, as a matter of fact, I haven't got one. Not right now, that is. I could get you one, if it's really necessary.

MAN: You understand we have to examine your rent book, Mr. Dillon, in order to ascertain the correctness of your statement regarding the thirty shillings which you claim is being paid out by you in the way of rent each week.

GEORGE: Yes, of course.

MAN: So would you please make sure you are in possession of one, the next time I call.

GEORGE: Does that mean that I'll have to wait until then before I get any money?

(PERCY *comes in at the front door.*)

MAN: I'm afraid I can't answer that at the moment, Mr. Dillon. Now, let me see. You are, by profession, an actor?

GEORGE: Yes, I am—by profession.

MAN: Have you any idea when you are likely to be working again?

GEORGE: It's rather difficult to say.

MAN: In the near future, would it be?

GEORGE: That phone might ring at this moment with something for me. Or it may not ring for months. It might not even ring at all.

MAN: You seem to have chosen a very precarious profession, Mr. Dillon.

GEORGE: This money means rather a lot at the moment. I need—something—to show, you see——

MAN: Isn't there something else you could do, in the meantime perhaps?

GEORGE: Do you think I haven't tried? Incidentally, I am rather anxious that no one in the house should know about this——

MAN: Yes, of course.

(PERCY *enters sitting-room, and sits down.*)

MAN: Yes. I see. Well, Mr. Dillon, I can only hand in

my report as I see things, and see what happens. The
board is very hesitant about—paying out money to
strong, healthy men.

GEORGE: Of course. Is there anything else? (*Looking
at* PERCY. *The Assistance Man is not quite sure
what to do.*)

MAN: There's just the little matter of your last job.
When was that?

GEORGE: Oh, about three months ago—television.

PERCY: Accch! You don't call that a job, do you? You
could hardly see it was him. *We* knew it was him all
right—but you had to be sharp to catch him.

MAN: Well, that'll be all I think, Mr. Dillon. (*Rising.*)
You won't forget your rent book, will you?

PERCY: Rent book. Rent book! He hasn't got one!
Shouldn't think he's ever paid any!

GEORGE: He knows that, you idiot. Well, I'll show you
to the door, shall I?

(GEORGE *shows him into the hall. They get to the
foot of the stairs, and the* MAN *turns.*)

MAN: (*officialdom relaxing*). You know, you people
are a funny lot. I don't understand you. Look what
you do to yourselves. And all for what? What do
you get out of it? It beats me. Now take me and
my wife. We don't have any worries. I've got my
job during the day—secure, pension at the end of
it. Mrs. Webb is at home, looking after the kiddies—
she knows there'll be a pay-packet every Friday. And
in the evenings, we sit at home together, or sometimes we'll go out. But we're happy. There's quite a
lot to it, you know. (*Quite kindly.*) What could be
better? I ask you? No, you think it over, son. You
think it over.   '

(*He goes out of the front door.* JOSIE *comes downstairs in her dressing-gown.*)

JOSIE: (*quietly*). Ruth home yet?

GEORGE: No. Not yet.

JOSIE: Know where she is?

GEORGE: She's at the doctor's.

JOSIE: Doctor's? What for?

GEORGE: For me. (*Crossing to sitting-room.*)

JOSIE: For you? Thought you didn't believe in doctors.

GEORGE: (*turns*). I don't. She's picking something up for me.

JOSIE: (*going to him*). I should have thought you could have done that rather well yourself. What's she picking up for you?

GEORGE: What's called a report. You know? Making no progress, but he mustn't try so hard. Unpromising.

JOSIE: Oh, I see. (*Crossing through into kitchen.*) Think I'll have some hot milk.

(GEORGE *goes into the sitting-room after her, and picks up the scattered leaves of his manuscript.*)

PERCY: Well, young man—you're at it again I see.

GEORGE: Yes. I'm afraid I'm not getting very far with it though.

PERCY: I don't mean that. I mean you're busy fleecing money from someone else again.

GEORGE: What the hell are you talking about?

PERCY: Not content with taking the money we bring home, you're even trying to get hold of the money we pay in income tax. You're getting it all ways, aren't you, George?

GEORGE: I certainly am! Look here, Percy, you'd better be careful what you say——

PERCY: And I think you'd better be careful what *you* say. Telling a government official barefaced lies like that! That's a case—(*leaning forward with infinite relish*)—for the assizes, that is!

GEORGE: All right, I admit it. But Mrs. Elliot knows that she'll get back every penny, and more, for looking after me as she has.

PERCY: Accch! I don't believe it. Anyway, you don't think she'll be very pleased when she finds out where it comes from, do you? Assistance Board! To think of us having someone like that at the door. What'll people think of that? I know all about you

my lad. I've checked up on you at my firm—you
owe bills all over the place. Don't be surprised if
you don't have the police after you soon—for debt.
Debt! (*Thrilling with horror.*) Imagine that! Police
coming to my house—to me that's never owed a
farthing to anybody in all his life.

(*Doorbell rings, followed by violent knocking.*)

PERCY: And it wouldn't surprise me if that was them
already. I know a copper's knock when I hear it.
(*Exit quickly into kitchen.* GEORGE *sinks into armchair, exhausted. Doorbell and knocking again. Pause.*
BARNEY EVANS *comes in through the front door. He
is wearing a rather old Crombie overcoat, an expensive but crumpled suit, thick horn-rimmed glasses,
and a rakish brown Homburg hat. He is nearly fifty,
and has never had a doubt about anything in all that
time.*)

BARNEY: Anyone there? Anyone at home? I say?

GEORGE: In here. Come in here.

BARNEY: Where? (*To sitting-room.*) In here? Oh yes.
Good. Sorry to butt in on you like this. The fact
is——

(GEORGE *rises.*) Oh yes, you must be who I am looking for.

GEORGE: Oh? Sit down, will you?

BARNEY: No, no, no—I can't stop a minute. I found
I was passing your door, so I thought I'd just pop
in for a few words. I haven't a London office any
longer—just for a moment, you see. I'm just on
my way to Brighton, as a matter of fact.

GEORGE: For the week-end?

BARNEY: Business and pleasure. (*Thoughtfully.*) Business—mostly. Look, I'll come straight to the point,
Mr.——

GEORGE: Dillon. George Dillon.

BARNEY: (*producing a script from his pocket*). Oh
yes. It's on here. George Dillon. Been in the business
long?

GEORGE: Well—a few——

BARNEY: Thought so. Didn't ever play the Palace, Westport, did you?

GEORGE: No, I didn't.

BARNEY: Face seemed familiar. Well, now—to get down to it——

GEORGE: Is that my script you've got there?

BARNEY: That's right.

GEORGE: How on earth did you get hold of it?

BARNEY: Andy gave it to me.

GEORGE: Andy?

BARNEY: André Tetlock. You know him, don't you?

GEORGE: Oh—the Trident. Is he a friend of yours then?

BARNEY: Andy? I knew him when he was a chorus boy at the old Tivoli. You wouldn't remember that. Why, it was me put him back on his feet after that bit of trouble. You know that, don't you?

GEORGE: Yes?

BARNEY: He hadn't even got a set of underwear—I had to get that for him. Silly fellow! (*Sucks in his breath deprecatingly.*) Still, he's all right now. That was my idea—that bar, you know. Oh, he did it up himself, mind you—Andy's very clever with his hands. But it was my idea. And now that bar's packed every night. Can't get within a mile of the place. He doesn't have to worry whether he puts on a show or not. Get some odd types there, of course, but you know Andy—so everybody's happy. And as long as he can find enough authors willing to back their own plays with hard cash, *he* won't go without his bottle of gin, believe me. (*Produces a packet of cheroots.*) Got a match? I take it you *don't* have any capital of your own?

GEORGE: Right.

BARNEY: Yes, he said you'd told him you hadn't any money to put up yourself.

GEORGE: (*lighting his cheroot for him*). I rang him about it weeks ago. I remember he said he'd liked the play, but he'd passed it on to someone else.

BARNEY: Liked it! That's a good one. Andy doesn't *read* plays—he just puts 'em on. Provided of course he can make something out of it! Now, I've read this play of yours, and I'm interested. Are you willing to listen to a proposition?

GEORGE: Of course.

BARNEY: By the way, I'm Barney Evans. You've heard of me, of course?

(GEORGE *hesitates, but* BARNEY *doesn't wait.*)

Now, Andy's a friend of mine. I've done a lot for him—but he's only in the business in a very small way. Oh, he does himself all right. But it's small stuff. You wouldn't get anywhere much with him—You know that, of course?

GEORGE: Yes.

BARNEY: I'm only interested in the big money. Small stuff's not worth my while. I take it you *are* interested in money?

GEORGE: Is that a rhetorical question?

BARNEY: Eh?

GEORGE: Yes, I am.

BARNEY: That's all right then. I don't want to waste my time. This the first play you've written?

GEORGE: My seventh——

BARNEY: Dialogue's not bad, but these great long speeches—that's a mistake. People want action, excitement. I know—*you* think you're Bernard Shaw. But where's he today? Eh? People won't listen to him. Anyway, politics are out—you ought to know that. Now, take *My Skin is my Enemy!* I've got that on the road at the moment. That and *Slasher Girl!*

GEORGE: *My Skin is my*—— Oh yes, it's about the colour bar problem, isn't it?

BARNEY: Well, yes—but you see it's first-class entertainment! Played to £600 at Llandrindod Wells last week. Got the returns in my pocket now. It's controversial, I grant you, but it's the kind of thing people pay money to see. That's the kind of thing you want to write.

GEORGE: Still, I imagine you've got to be just a bit liberal-minded to back a play like that.

BARNEY: Eh?

GEORGE: I mean—putting on a play about coloured people.

BARNEY: Coloured people? I hate the bastards! You should talk to the author about them. He can't even be civil to them. No—I know young fellows like you. You're interested in ideals still. Idealists. Don't think I don't know. I was an idealist myself once. I could tell you a lot, only I haven't got time now. But, make no mistake—ideals didn't get me where I am.

GEORGE: No?

BARNEY: You spend your time dabbling in politics, and vote in some ragged-arsed bunch of nobodies, who can't hardly pronounce the Queen's English properly, and where are you? Where are you? Nowhere. Crushed down in the mob, indistinguishable from the masses. What's the good of that to a young man with talent?

GEORGE: I should have thought you had a vested interest in the masses.

BARNEY: Most certainly. I admit it. And that's why I believe in education. Education—it always shows, and it always counts. That's why I say let them who've got it run the whole show. We're not going to get anywhere with these foreigners once they see they're no longer dealing with gentlemen. They're always impressed by an English gentleman. Just because they've got no breeding themselves, they know how to recognize it in others when they see it. Oh, yes. I could tell you a lot you don't know. However, I am diverting from what I came about.

(*He sprays his ash over the floor thoughtfully.*)

To get back to this play of yours. I think it's got possibilities, but it needs rewriting. Act One and Two won't be so bad, provided you cut out all the highbrow stuff, give it pace—you know: dirty it up a bit, you see.

GEORGE: I see.

BARNEY: Third Act's construction is weak. I could help you there—and I'd do it for quite a small consideration because I think you've got something. You know that's a very good idea—getting the girl in the family way.

GEORGE: You think so?

BARNEY: Never fails. Get someone in the family way in the Third Act—you're halfway there. I suppose you saw *I Was a Drug Fiend?*

GEORGE: No.

BARNEY: Didn't you really? No wonder you write like you do! I thought everyone had seen that! That was my show too. Why, we were playing to three and four thousand a week on the twice-nightly circuit with that. That's the sort of money you want to play to. Same thing in that: Third Act—girl's in the family way. Course, in that play, her elder sister goes out as a missionary and ends up dying upside down on an ant hill in her birthday suit. I spent six months in the South of France on what I made out of that show. (*Motor-horn toots outside.*) Here, I'll have to be going. As I say, you rewrite it as I tell you, maybe we can do business together and make some money for both of us. I'll read it through again, and drop you a line. In the meantime, I should redraft the whole thing, bearing in mind what I said. Right.

GEORGE: I'll have to think about it. The fact is—I'm not feeling up to much at the moment. I'm completely broke for one thing.

BARNEY: O.K. then. You'll be hearing from me. You take my advice—string along with me. I know this business inside and out. You forget about starving for Art's sake. That won't keep you alive five minutes. You've got to be ruthless. (*Moves into hall.*) Yes, there's no other word for it—absolutely ruthless. (GEORGE *follows him.*)

(BARNEY *picks up his hat from stand and knocks*

over the vase. He looks down at the pieces absent-mindedly.)

BARNEY: Oh, sorry. Now you take Hitler—the greatest man that ever lived! Don't care what anyone says— you can't get away from it. He had the right idea, you've got to be ruthless, and it's the same in this business. Course he may have gone a bit too far sometimes.

GEORGE: Think so?

BARNEY: I do. I do think so, most definitely. Yes, he over-reached himself, no getting away from it. That's where all great men make their mistake—they over-reach themselves.

(*The car horn toots more insistently.*)

Hullo, blimey, she'll start smashing the windows in a minute. (GEORGE *follows him as he hurries to door.*)

Well, you just remember what I said. Tell you what —I'll give you a ring on Monday. I'll be busy all the week-end. (*Opens door.*) By the way, that girl?

GEORGE: What girl?

BARNEY: The girl in your play—what do you call her?

GEORGE: Oh, you mean——

BARNEY: Build her up. Build her right up. She's—she's a prostitute *really*, isn't she?

GEORGE: Well——

BARNEY: Of course she is! I've just had an idea—a new slant. Your title, what is it? (*He doesn't wait for a reply.*) Anyway, it won't bring anybody in. I've just thought of a smashing title. You know what we'll call it? "Telephone Tart", that's it! "Telephone Tart". You string along with me, George, I'll see you're all right.

(*Exit.*)

(JOSIE *looks in from kitchen.*)

JOSIE: (*coming in with a glass of milk*). It's all right, he's gone. (*Sits in armchair.*) Don't know what all the fuss was about.

PERCY: Well, I hadn't shaved, you see. I should hate to let George down in front of his friends—what few he *has* got.

JOSIE: Oh, you are daft, Dad. You don't know what you're talking about half the time.

(GEORGE *comes slowly into sitting-room.*)

JOSIE: Who was it, George? Teddy-bear coat and all!

GEORGE: (*smiling wryly*). I suppose he's what you might call the poor man's Binkie.

JOSIE: What? Whatever's that? What's that, George?

(RUTH *comes in front door into sitting-room.*)

GEORGE: Oh, never mind. It doesn't really matter. Hello, Ruth.

RUTH: (*after a slight pause*). Hullo.

GEORGE: Well, did you go to the doctor's?

RUTH: Yes.

GEORGE: Well—(*laughing*)—don't stand there with the angel of death on your shoulder—what did he say?

RUTH: George—just come in here, will you, for a minute. (GEORGE *follows her into lounge.*)

JOSIE: Well, of all the—I like that, I must say! We're not good enough to know what's going on! (*Rising and going up to radiogram.*) I'm sure I don't want to hear what she's got to say to George. Them and their secrets. (*She puts on Mambo record very loud.*) (JOSIE *then picks up a magazine and glances at it viciously, her foot wagging furiously. After a moment she gets up and goes over to the window and looks out in the same manner.* PERCY *watches her all the time. She catches him doing it.*)

JOSIE: Well, had your eyeful?

(*She walks over-casually towards the lounge door.*) Real heart-to-heart they're having, aren't they?

(*Over to mirror as* RUTH *comes out of the lounge and goes into the sitting-room and says something to* PERCY. MRS. ELLIOT *comes in at the front door, laden as usual. She goes into sitting-room and switches off the radiogram.*)

MRS. E.: Whatever do you want that thing on like that for, Josie? I could hear it halfway down the street. I thought you weren't well?
(*Pause.*)

MRS. E.: Why, what is it? What's the matter with you all? What is it, Ruth?

PERCY: George has got T.B. (*In a voice like sandpaper.*)

MRS. E.: T.B., George. I don't believe it. It isn't true. There must be some mistake——

RUTH: There's no mistake. It's quite true, Kate. The doctor will be coming up soon to let us know what the arrangements are.

MRS. E.: Does this mean that he'll have to go away? (RUTH *nods her head.*)
George—poor old George. (*She moves into hall and up the stairs.*) George dear, where are you? He won't like this at all, will he? George——
(PERCY *comes out of the room to foot of stairs as* MRS. E. *is halfway up.*)

PERCY: (*calling up loudly*). You'll have to burn everything, you know! All his sheets, blankets. Everything will have to be burnt, you know!

JOSIE: Oh, my God. Auntie Ruth! What's going to happen? What about me?

RUTH: You?

JOSIE: Yes, that's what I want to know—what's going to happen to me?

QUICK CURTAIN

ACT III

SCENE TWO

Winter. MRS. ELLIOT *is on stage alone. She is looking up the stairs.* GEORGE'S *hat, coat and suitcase are standing in the hall. She is looking very anxious. She picks up the hat and coat, and hangs them up carefully on the hallstand. Then she goes back to the sitting-room. She goes over to the wedding group picture, and stares up at it. As she is doing this* PERCY *comes in at the front door. He takes off his hat and coat, hangs them up beside* GEORGE'S, *and comes into the sitting-room.*

PERCY: So he's back then?

MRS. E.: Yes.

PERCY: Where is he?

MRS. E.: Upstairs—talking to Josie.

PERCY: Upstairs?

MRS. E.: Yes. She wasn't feeling too good this morning, so I told her to stay in bed. I didn't want to take any chances. I think she was over-excited at the thought of George coming back.

PERCY: Excited, was she?

MRS. E.: Of course she was. She's thought about nothing else for weeks.

PERCY: Well, well! She's in for a bit of a shock, isn't she?

MRS. E.: Listen to me, Percy. I've told you—you're to keep out of this. It's nothing to do with you. The only two people it need concern at the moment are George and myself. Above all, I don't want one word of this to get to Josie's ears. We've no idea what might happen if she was to get a shock like that. And in her present condition. If you so much as

283

open your mouth about it to her—you can pack your bags and go. You understand? Besides, we don't know yet that it's true—not for certain. We've only got your word for it, and we all know what a nasty mind you've got. It would please you to think something rotten of George. You've always been against him. You're jealous of him—that's why.

PERCY: Me? Jealous of him! That wreck!

MRS. E.: He's a gentleman—which is something you'll never be.

PERCY: Oh, he is, is he? Perhaps that's why he can't even earn the price of a cup of tea!

MRS. E.: That's all *you* know.

PERCY: And what does that mean, exactly?

MRS. E.: Never you mind. But there's a lot you don't know about George. George will come out tops in the end—you wait.

PERCY: Seems more like there was a lot *all* of us didn't know about him.

MRS. E.: You don't understand, Percy. And what's more, you never will. You think everyone's like yourself. George is an artist——

PERCY: And what's *that* supposed to mean?

MRS. E.: He's sensitive, proud—he suffers deeply. Raymond was like that—you never liked him, and he was your own son. That boy's gone through a lot—he doesn't have to tell me that. I could tell the first time I ever spoke to him. I knew he was a good fellow, that all he wanted was a chance to bring a little pleasure to other people. I don't think that's so much of a crime, anyway. Oh, he's never said anything to me, but I've known what he's been going through all these months. When he's come back here in the evenings, when he couldn't get a job or any kind of encouragement at all, when people like you were sneering at him, and nobody wanted him. He didn't think I knew when he was feeling sick with disappointment. He didn't think I knew he was trying to pass it off, by making us laugh, and pretending that everything was going to be all right. And I've never been able to tell him because I can't express myself properly—not like he can. He's got a gift for it—that's why he's an artist. That's why he's different from us. But he'll have his own way, in the end, you mark my words. He'll show them all—and you. God always pays debts without money. I've got down on my knees at night, and prayed for that boy. I've prayed that he'll be well, and get on, and be happy—here—with us.

PERCY: With us?

MRS. E.: If that's what he wants. And I believe it is. I know we're not the kind of people George is used to, and probably likes being with—he must have felt it sometimes. Not that he's ever said anything—he's too well brought up for that. He just accepts us for what we are. He's settled in here. And while he's been in that hospital all these weeks, he's known he's got somewhere to come back to. He's known that somebody wants him, anyway, and that's a great deal when you're laying there in bed, and you don't know properly whether you're going to live or die. To know that someone is counting the days until you come home.

PERCY: What's he look like?

MRS. E.: A bit thin. But who wouldn't look thin on that hospital food? I'll soon feed him up.

PERCY: Did you manage to have a word with the doctor?

MRS. E.: No, I didn't.

PERCY: Well, why not?

MRS. E.: Because I wasn't going to ask the doctor a lot of questions behind George's back, that's why. He's back—that's all I care about, that's all I want to know at the moment. Things will work themselves out somehow. George won't let us down.

PERCY: Well, we shall soon see, shan't we? He's a long time up there, don't you think? And what's he going to do about his wife?

MRS. E.: How do I know what he's going to do? Why can't you shut up about it! You've talked about nothing else for days now.

PERCY: You mean to say you didn't tackle him about it?

MRS. E.: I didn't have an opportunity. I couldn't bring it up on the bus, could I? Besides, I couldn't start on him straight away. And as soon as we got back, he wanted to go up and see Josie, naturally.

PERCY: Well, you wait till he comes down. If you're afraid to tackle him about it, I'm not.

MRS. E.: I meant what I said, you know. If you try and cause trouble in this house, you can go.

PERCY: I think it's disgusting. Carrying on in someone else's house—a married man at that! Do you know what? It's my belief that there was something between him and your sister Ruth—and that's why she decided to pack her bags, and go, all of a sudden.

MRS. E.: Oh, don't be so childish, for heaven's sake, Percy. You've got sex on the brain. I must admit you could have knocked me down when Ruth told me she was going to find herself a room somewhere. I mean—it seemed a bit suspicious. She didn't even give a proper explanation. Just said that she felt she had to "get out of it". It seemed a funny thing to say, and especially after all these years. Of course, she always was a dark horse. But, as for her and George—it's ridiculous. Why, she's old enough to be his mother.

PERCY: (*as he goes to lounge*). Oh, you women— you go on and on.

(RUTH *appears at front door—unlocking it, enters, leaving door open.*)

(RUTH *enters sitting-room.*)

RUTH: (*quietly*). Kate. Kate.

(GEORGE *comes downstairs—shuts front door. Then goes towards sitting-room—meets* RUTH *face to face in the doorway.*)

RUTH: Hello George. Are you better?

GEORGE: You're not really going, are you?

RUTH: I was coming to collect my things this morning —but I couldn't.

GEORGE: In fact it's quite a coincidence meeting ycu.

RUTH: No. Not really. I suppose it was silly of me to come when I knew you'd be back. I always seem to let myself in for farewells.

GEORGE: We both ought to be pretty good at them by now. (*Pause.*) Are you really leaving then?

RUTH: Not again, please. There's only a few minutes.

GEORGE: (*very quietly*). What's going to happen to me?

RUTH: George—don't! Try and help a little.
(*Pause.*)

GEORGE: Isn't it hell—loving people?

RUTH: Yes—hell.

GEORGE: Still sounds rather feeble when you say it though. Rather like "shift me—I'm burning". What are you going to do?

RUTH: I don't know. Maybe find some scruffy wretch with a thumb-nail sketch of a talent, and spend my time emptying bits of brown cigarette stubs from his saucer—generally cleaning up.

GEORGE: Did you ever look up your—friend?
(*He lifts up the wristwatch.*)

RUTH: Yes. I did. Soon after you came in here. But he wasn't at the same place any more. His landlord gave me his new address. Number something Eaton Square.

GEORGE: But of course, my dear—everyone lives in Eaton Square.

RUTH: Apparently, she's in publishing. She's just published his book last week. But I mustn't be unfair— she didn't write the reviews as well. They fairly raved. He's on top of the world.

GEORGE: You know I've been waiting for you to tell me that you're old enough to be my mother. Still, mothers don't walk out on their sons—or do they?

RUTH: How's Josie—have you seen her yet?

GEORGE: God! What a farce! What pure, screaming farce!

(*He starts to laugh.*)

RUTH: For heaven's sake!

GEORGE: Sorry. I just thought of something. How to make sure of your Third Act. Never fails! (*Roars with laughter.*) Never fails! (*Subsides almost immediately.*) Don't panic. I'll not get maudlin. I probably would start howling any minute, only I'm afraid of getting the bird from my best audience.

(*He looks away from her, and adds in a strangled voice, barely audible.*)

Don't leave me on my own!

(*But he turns back quickly.*)

You haven't mentioned my—success—once.

RUTH: I didn't know whether you expected me to congratulate you or not.

GEORGE: Second week of tour—I've got the returns here. Look: Empire Theatre, Llandrindod Wells— week's gross takings £647 18s. 4d. Long-hair drama gets a haircut from Mr. Barney Evans!

RUTH: I simply can't bear to go on watching you any longer.

GEORGE: But don't you think it's all very comic? I seem to remember some famous comedian saying once that he'd never seen anything funny that wasn't terrible. So don't think I'll mind if you laugh. I expect it. We should be both good for a titter, anyway. That's why religion is so damned deadly—it's not even good for a giggle. And what's life without a good giggle, eh? That's what I always say! Isn't that what you always say, Ruth?

RUTH: Let go of my hand. You're hurting me.

GEORGE: Well—isn't it? No. Perhaps it isn't. We never really had the same sense of humour, after all.

RUTH: Please don't try to hurt yourself any more by trying to hit back at me. I know how you feel. You're overcome with failure. Eternal bloody failure.

GEORGE: But I'm not a failure, I'm a—success.

RUTH: Are you, George? (*She turns away.*)

GEORGE: Listen! I'll make you laugh yet, before you go. Just a trip on the stage-cloth, and Lear teeters on, his crown round his ears, his grubby tights full of moth-holes. How they all long for those tights to fall down. What a relief it would be! Oh, we should all use stronger elastic. And the less sure we are of our pathetic little divine rights, the stronger the elastic we should use. You've seen the whole, shabby, solemn pretence now. This is where you came in. For God's sake go.

(*She turns to go.*)

GEORGE: No, wait. Shall I recite my epitaph to you? Yes, do recite your epitaph to me. "Here lies the body of George Dillon, aged thirty-four—or thereabouts—who thought, who hoped, he was that mysterious, ridiculous being called an artist. He never allowed himself one day of peace. He worshipped the physical things of this world, and was betrayed by his own body. He loved also the things of the mind, but his own brain was a cripple from the waist down. He achieved nothing he set out to do. He made no one happy, no one look up with excitement when he entered the room. He was always troubled with wind round his heart, but he loved no one successfully. He was a bit of a bore, and frankly, rather useless. But the germs loved him. (*He doesn't see* RUTH *as she goes out and up the stairs.*) Even his sentimental epitaph is probably a pastiche of someone or other, but he doesn't quite know who. And, in the end, it doesn't really matter." (*He turns, but* RUTH *has gone.*)

(*Bell rings,* PERCY *opens door.*)

NORAH: (*coming in*). Only me. Forgot my key again. Is George back yet? (*Into room.*) George! You are back!

GEORGE: Yes, Norah, I'm back again, with a face like the death of kings.

NORAH: (*rushes to him*). Oh, George, you look fine!

Doesn't he, Dad? I thought you'd look awful—but you look fine. (*Kisses him as* MRS. E. *comes in from kitchen.*)

GEORGE: Here—mind my ribs!

NORAH: Oh, we'll soon feed you up, won't we, Mum? (*She takes him into the sitting-room,* PERCY *follows.*)

MRS. E.: We certainly will. We're going to look after him from now on. He can sit in here all day and rest, and—keep himself happy. Can't you, George?

GEORGE: Rather.

MRS. E.: He can lie down on the settee in the afternoons with his books and things, and—oh, I forgot! We got you a little homecoming present, didn't we, Norah?

NORAH: Shall I go up and get it?

MRS. E.: If you like, dear, I don't know whether George feels up to opening presents. He must feel all in after that journey. I expect he'd like a bit of a rest.

GEORGE: I'm all right. I'd like a cup of tea though.

MRS. E.: It's all ready. And I'll get you something to eat in no time.

NORAH: All right, then. I'll go and get it. I'll just pop in and have a look at Josie. Have you seen her, George?

MRS. E.: He's been in there ever since he came in, haven't you, George?

NORAH: (*crossing to and up stairs*). She's been so excited at the thought of you coming back. She's talked about nothing else for days. (*She laughs.*) Isn't love grand! (*Exit.*)

MRS. E.: It's true, George. She's been quite a changed girl since you went away. I'm afraid she did used to be a bit on the lazy side sometimes, but not now—you wouldn't know her. Why, Sunday we spent practically all evening getting your room ready and looking nice. And Norah's been the same. Why, she's even booked seats for a coach ride for all of us down to the seaside.

PERCY: Well? How are you feeling, George?

GEORGE: Sorry, Percy. I haven't had a chance to say hullo yet, have I? (*Offers his hand.*)

PERCY: (*shakes perfunctorily*). How have they been treating you?

GEORGE: Oh, not too bad, thanks. But it's certainly good to be back. You've all given me such a welcome.

PERCY: It's quite a nice place down there, I believe.

GEORGE: It's all right.

PERCY: Nice country.

GEORGE: Oh, lovely.

PERCY: Isn't that near Tunbridge Wells?

GEORGE: Not far.

MRS. E.: I don't suppose he wants to talk much now, Percy. Let him have a rest first. He's tired.

PERCY: They say that's a nice town.

GEORGE: It's pleasant enough.

PERCY: Ever been there, George?

GEORGE: What are you getting at?

PERCY: I think you *know* what I'm getting at.

GEORGE: (*to* MRS. E.). What is it? You're upset about something, aren't you. I could tell something was wrong when you met me at the hospital. And all the way home on the bus.

PERCY: I suppose you didn't happen to be in Tunbridge Wells on June 22nd, 1943, did you?
(*Pause.*)

GEORGE: I see.

MRS. E.: George—it's not true, is it? I was sure he'd made a mistake.

GEORGE: No. He hasn't made a mistake. I *was* married in Tunbridge Wells, and it was in 1943. The middle of June. It poured with rain. How did you find out?

PERCY: Through my firm, as a matter of fact. As you know, it's our job to check on people's credentials, etc., for hire purchase firms and the like. Well, last week, I found myself checking on a certain Ann Scott, on behalf of a building society. She's contemplating buying some big property in Chelsea. Good report—excellent banker's references and all that. Living in large house in upper class district. And it seems her married name is Mrs. George Dillon. Well? What have you got to say?

GEORGE: Well?

MRS. E.: Oh, dear.

GEORGE: What do you want me to say?

MRS. E.: I don't know, George. I'm so upset, I don't know where I am. I suppose it's not your fault, but——

GEORGE: But, my dear, I don't see what there is to be so upset about. This doesn't change anything.

MRS. E.: But—but what about Josie?

GEORGE: Nothing is changed, I tell you. It's simply that neither my wife nor I have ever bothered about a divorce. She's had other things to think about, and I've never had the money. But it's all easily settled. There's nothing to worry about. I promise you.

MRS. E.: You're not just saying this, George? I'd rather——

GEORGE: Of course not. I've come home, haven't I?

MRS. E.: Yes, you have. You've come home, thank heaven.

GEORGE: You see, my wife never was anything. With Josie, it's different. I know exactly where I am.

MRS. E.: She loves you, George. She really does.

GEORGE: Yes. I know.

PERCY: It said on my report that she's an actress, this wife of yours.

(PERCY *feels cheated, and is desperately looking round for something else.*)

GEORGE: Right.

PERCY: She must do pretty well at it then.

GEORGE: She does.

PERCY: Can't say I've ever heard the name.

GEORGE: On the contrary, you know her very well.

PERCY: What do you mean?

GEORGE: I mean that somebody must have slipped up rather badly in your report. They seem to have left out her stage name.

PERCY: Stage name?

GEORGE: We both thought "Ann Scott" a bit commonplace.

PERCY: Who is she then?

GEORGE: Well, you've always told me that she's the only one in your favourite television parlour game who's really any good at all. In fact, you've said so many times.

PERCY: You don't mean—— What? Not *her!*

GEORGE: Her.

PERCY: Well, I'll be . . .

GEORGE: Yes. It's always puzzled me why you should admire her so much. Or anyone else for that matter.

MRS. E.: But George—honestly, I don't know where I am. Now that—well—now that you're a success, how do you know that your wife won't want you back?

GEORGE: Somehow, I don't think that will influence her!

PERCY: What are you talking about? Now that he's a success?

MRS. E.: (*recovered and triumphant*). Well, I don't see why he shouldn't know now, do you, George?

GEORGE: No, I don't see why not.

MRS. E.: George has had his play put on. It's on tour at the moment, and last week it made—tell him how much it made, George.

GEORGE: £647 18s. 4d. (*Flourishing returns.*)

MRS. E.: And he gets five per cent of that every week, so perhaps that will shut you up a bit.

PERCY: (*staring at returns*). Well! Fancy that! Why didn't somebody tell me?

MRS. E.: Why should they? Well, I mustn't stand here wasting time. You must be hungry, George. (*Phone rings.*)

MRS. E.: Do answer that, Percy, will you? Wish Norah would hurry up.

(PERCY *goes to phone.* NORAH *comes downstairs carrying parcel into sitting-room.*)

NORAH: Josie says she won't be long, she's going to get up.

PERCY: What's that? Oh, yes, hang on a minute while I find my pencil. All right—go ahead.

NORAH: Well, George, here we are—I can't wait to see his face when he opens it, Mum.

GEORGE: Well——

MRS. E.: No, wait till Josie comes down. She'll want to be with him when he opens it.

NORAH: Oh, blow that. She's got all the time in the world with him now. If he won't open it, I will.

PERCY: Yes. Yes. I've got that. Who? What? What name? Right. Good-bye.

MRS. E.: All right then. I don't suppose she'll mind. Go on, George, open it.

(GEORGE *starts opening the parcel.*)

PERCY: (*coming in*). That was for you, George. A telegram.

GEORGE: Oh, who from?

PERCY: Somebody called Barney. I've got it written down here.

GEORGE: Read it out, will you? I'm busy at the moment.

PERCY: It says "Playing capacity business. May this be the first of many smash hits together. Welcome home —Barney."

MRS. E.: Well, wasn't that nice of him?

GEORGE: Yes, good old Barney. Now, what have we here? (*Stands back to reveal a portable typewriter.*) Well! Look at that!

MRS. E.: I hope you like it, George.

GEORGE: Like it! I should think I do! I think it must be the nicest present I've had. What can I say? (*He kisses them both.*) Thank you both. Thank you for everything.

MRS. E.: That's all right, George. Believe me, all my prayers have been answered. Mr. Colwyn-Stuart prayed for you too, every week you were away. All I want is for us all to be happy. Come along now, sit down, while I get the supper. Give him a chair, Percy, you look all in, dear.

PERCY: Oh, sorry. Here you are.

NORAH: It'll be nice, having George for a brother-in-law.

GEORGE: Yes, of course it will, Norah. It's about time you got married yourself, isn't it?

MRS. E.: She almost has been——

NORAH: —Twice.

GEORGE: I'm sorry.

MRS. E.: The last one was an American.

NORAH: Yes. The last time I saw him, we were going to get a bus to Richmond. He just simply said suddenly: "Well, so long, honey, it's been nice knowing you" and got on a bus going in the opposite direction. It's swimming on the telly tonight. I think I'll go and watch it, if you'll excuse me.
(*She goes into lounge. Slight pause.*)

MRS. E.: Well, I don't know. What with one thing and another! That's right, George, dear. Just you relax from now on. And you let him alone, Percy. I've always believed in you, George. Always. I knew he'd come out tops.
(MRS. ELLIOT *goes into kitchen.* GEORGE *leans back, tired.* PERCY *turns on radio. Jazz—"If you can't give me a dollar, give me a lousy dime."*)

PERCY: Not too loud for you, George?

GEORGE: No—fine. (*Pause.*)

PERCY: I can't get over it, you know.

GEORGE: What?

PERCY: Your wife, I mean. Big star like that. Surprised she couldn't have helped you on a bit all this time. Still, you're doing all right yourself now, by the look of it. Turned out to be Bernard Shaw, after all, eh? I suppose you'll be writing some more plays when you start feeling better again?

GEORGE: I dare say.

PERCY: I see. Same sort of thing?

(RUTH *comes down slowly with suitcase.*)

GEORGE: Yes. Same sort of thing.

PERCY: Well, that's good, isn't it? What was the name of that theatre again?

GEORGE: The Empire Theatre, Llandrindod Wells.

(*The sound of* JOSIE'S *voice singing comes from upstairs. From the lounge, the telly is playing music.*)

PERCY: Well, I don't think it would do any harm if we all have a little drink on this. (*To cocktail cabinet.*) If we're going to start living in style, we may as well get into the way of using this, eh?

(*He opens the cocktail cabinet, revealing all its hidden glory.* RUTH *exits through front door.*)

PERCY: Now, where are we. (*Staring into cabinet.*)

MRS. E.: That's right. Let's have a little drink.

GEORGE: (*in a flat, empty voice*). Yes, let's have a little drink—to celebrate.

PERCY: Music too, would not be inappropriate.

(*Putting on record.*)

GEORGE: Music too, would not be inappropriate.

(JOSIE *sings, off.*)

PERCY: Well, we can't leave the blushing bride upstairs all on her own, can we? I'll give her a yell, shall I, George?

(*He goes out, calling upstairs,* GEORGE *goes to the door. He looks trapped and looks around the room and the objects in it; he notices the birds on the wall.*)

GEORGE: Those bloody birds!

(*Enter* MRS. ELLIOT. *He stares at her as if for the first time, then his face breaks into a mechanical smile.*)

Come on, Mum, let's dance!

(*They dance together for a few moments.*)

SLOW CURTAIN

DISCOVER
THE DRAMA OF LIFE
IN THE LIFE OF DRAMA

☐	TEN GREAT ONE ACT PLAYS Morris Sweetkind, ed.	2470	•	$1.50
☐	CREATIVE FILM-MAKING Kirk Smallman	2623	•	$2.25
☐	COMP. PLAYS SOPHOCLES	2911	•	$1.95
☐	FOUR GREAT PLAYS BY CHEKHOV Anton Chekhov	6472	•	$1.50
☐	THE CITIZEN KANE BOOK Pauline Kael, Herman J. Mankiewicz, and Orson Welles	7853	•	$2.95
☐	CANDLE IN THE WIND Alexander Solzhenitsyn	8424	•	$1.65
☐	THE NIGHT THOREAU SPENT IN JAIL Jerome Lawrence and Robert E. Lee	10036	•	$1.50
☐	THE PRICE Arthur Miller	10177	•	$1.50
☐	FOUR GREAT PLAYS BY IBSEN Henrik Ibsen	10195	•	$1.50
☐	THE LOVE-GIRL AND THE INNOCENT Alexander Solzhenitsyn	10246	•	$1.50
☐	THE EFFECTS OF GAMMA RAYS ON MAN-IN-THE-MOON MARIGOLDS Paul Zindel	10268	•	$1.50
☐	50 GREAT SCENES FOR STUDENT ACTORS Lewy Olfson, ed.	10331	•	$1.75
☐	THE ORESTEIA Aeschylus/Fagles	10406	•	$2.95
☐	LOOK BACK IN ANGER John Osborne	10758	•	$1.50
☐	THE CRUCIBLE Arthur Miller	11008	•	$1.75

Buy them at your local bookstore or use this handy coupon for ordering:

Bantam Books, Inc., Dept. EDH, 414 East Golf Road, Des Plaines, Ill. 60016

Please send me the books I have checked above. I am enclosing $_____
(please add 50¢ to cover postage and handling). Send check or money order
—no cash or C.O.D.'s please.

Mr/Mrs/Miss_____

Address_____

City_____State/Zip_____

EDH-7/77

Please allow four weeks for delivery. This offer expires 7/78.

Bantam Book Catalog

Here's your up-to-the-minute listing of every book currently available from Bantam.

This easy-to-use catalog is divided into categories and contains over 1400 titles by your favorite authors.

So don't delay—take advantage of this special opportunity to increase your reading pleasure.

Just send us your name and address and 25¢ (to help defray postage and handling costs).